FOOD LOVERS'
GUIDE TO
BROOKLYN

Help Us Keep This Guide Up to Date

We would love to hear from you concerning your experiences with this guide and how you feel it could be improved and kept up to date. Please send your comments and suggestions to:

editorial@GlobePequot.com

Thanks for your input, and happy travels!

FOOD LOVERS' SERIES

FOOD LOVERS'
GUIDE TO
BROOKLYN

The Best Restaurants, Markets & Local Culinary Offerings

2nd Edition

Sherri Eisenberg

Guilford, Connecticut

Editor: Amy Lyons
Project Editor: Lynn Zelem
Layout Artist: Mary Ballachino
Text Design: Sheryl Kober
Illustrations by Jill Butler with additional art by Carleen Moira Powell and MaryAnn Dubé
Maps: Design Maps Inc. © Morris Book Publishing, LLC

ISBN 978-0-7627-8074-7

Printed in the United States of America

10 9 8 7 6 5 4 3 2 1

All the information in this guidebook is subject to change. We recommend that you call ahead to obtain current information before traveling.

To all the food entrepreneurs of Brooklyn,
who inspire me every day

Contents

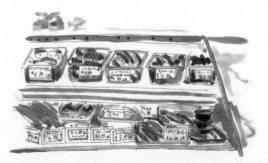

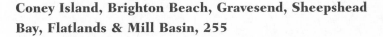

Recipes, 277

Appendices

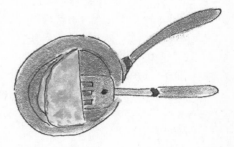

About the Author

Sherri Eisenberg has been a travel and food writer for 15 years and has held positions as an editor at Condé Nast Publications' *Brides, Travel Holiday*, and *Travel + Leisure*. She has also written about travel and food—from New York pizza to Quebec's *foie gras* and Maryland's crabs—for some of the country's other leading publications. Her work has been published in the *Los Angeles Times, Condé Nast Traveler, Budget Travel,* the *Boston Globe,* and the *Baltimore Sun*.

About the Cover

The cover image was shot by Michael Harlan Turkell at Bark Hot Dogs in Park Slope especially for this book. The hot dogs look tasty, right?

From left to right, they are the Pickle Dog (served with house-made bread-and-butter pickles, dill pickles, yellow mustard, and mayo), the Classic Dog (slathered in yellow mustard and ketchup), and the Bark Dog (topped with sweet pepper relish, diced red onion, and mustard).

Acknowledgments

After my husband, my biggest thanks must go to my parents, who were more supportive than I had any right to ask them to be.

I also must thank my research assistants, Alexandra Ilyashov and Amanda Younger, who fact-checked every word of the first edition for me. My sincere appreciation goes to many friends who lent their neighborhood expertise to this book. Danielle and Jeff—you are true pioneers. Dave, Sachiko, Olga, Boris, Peter, Beth, Sam, Neel, Cybele, John, Randi, Scott, Julia, Cindy, Angie, Petar, Leigh, Lawrence, Lauri, Marcus, Becky, Brian, and Casey, I will always be grateful for your willingness to explore. Thanks also to my foodie readers, Erica, Sarah, Lena, and Jen. To all the friends and family members with whom I canceled plans or cajoled into coming to Brooklyn, here's to you!

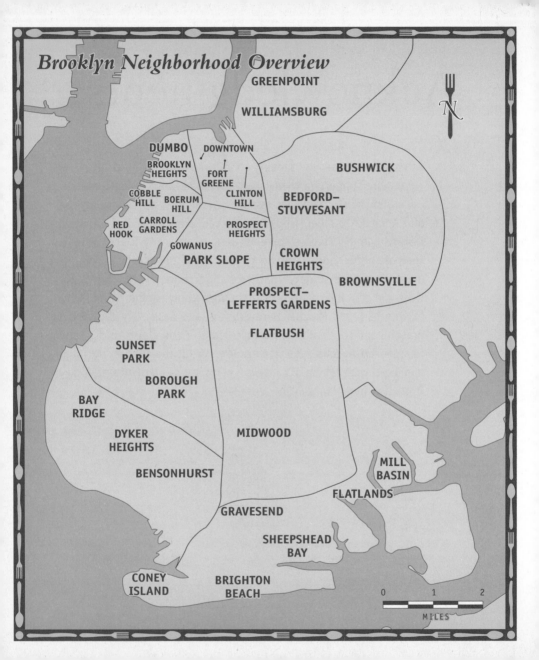

Introduction

Brooklyn has long been a food lover's mecca, and yet the last few years have seen what must be unprecedented growth in the food scene. I could not have predicted when I started writing the first edition that we were truly just at the beginning of a dramatic transformation for Brooklyn, from living in Manhattan's shadow to being a destination in its own right. Today, both domestic and international travelers who are determined to taste the best of New York City make Brooklyn a key part of their trips.

The borough is made up of a series of neighborhoods, each with its own personality and ethnic origins, where the cuisine of an immigrant group's homeland is celebrated at the table each night. You can sample a world of food just by traveling around New York City's most populated borough, from Brighton Beach's impressive Russian cuisine (served at restaurants that had vodka table service long before it was trendy) to the red-sauce places of Bensonhurst, with their murals of Sicily and their unbeatable cannoli. It's these turn-of-the-last-century immigrants, who made their way through nearby Ellis Island, who developed the iconic foods: the thin-crust, coal-oven pizza, the dense and creamy cheesecake, and the snappy-skinned hot dog, all of which are intrinsically connected to Brooklyn.

And now, as Brooklyn has become a haven for the young and creative, you can also immerse yourself in that latest of trends—the handmade artisan food movement. It's an exciting moment for Brooklyn's food scene: In the last few years, a new community focused on locally sourced ingredients has emerged. Throughout the gentrified neighborhoods, where twenty- and thirtysomethings create a new Brooklyn, they've developed a cottage industry of artisan restaurants, food boutiques, and other businesses devoted to the ingestible. According to the *New York Times,* "the borough has become an incubator for a culinary-minded generation whose idea of fun is learning how to make something delicious and finding a way to sell it." Instead of sitting in the shadow of Manhattan's internationally recognized dining scene, as many visitors assume, Brooklyn's food scene is very much its own, separate thing.

This is the ultimate guide to dining in Brooklyn—both the New Brooklyn Cuisine with its hipster enclaves and growing locavore ways and the Old Brooklyn Cuisine with its world-renown classics. There is something for everyone here, from the 14.8 million annual visitors (many of whom are tourists walking across the Brooklyn Bridge for the first time), to the Manhattanites who are curious as to what all the buzz is about, to the Brooklyn natives who know their neighborhood like the palm of their hand, but don't know the adjacent one. All of the iconic—and surprising—food finds of New York's coolest borough are here.

How to Use This Book

Food Lovers' Guide to Brooklyn is separated into neighborhood chapters, and within each you'll find these categories:

Neighborhood Map

The establishements in the book are all included, but some borders—such as Smith Street, which edges Cobble Hill, Carroll Gardens, and Boerum Hill—are contested, so you'll find conflicting info elsewhere.

Foodie Faves

This category is broad enough to include any restaurant we think you should check out and the ones favored by lovers of good food. That could be an old standby, or a new spot that's exciting even to locals.

Landmarks

Many of Brooklyn's older, most beloved eateries have been lost over the years. As a result, the Old Brooklyn—the one where everyone rooted for the Dodgers—is fast disappearing. These are the proud reminders of the past.

Specialty Stores, Markets & Producers

Many types of food shops—from the well-edited locavore grocery store to butchers and bread makers—warrant a visit. We've included what to get and, when necessary, when to go.

Food Events
These mostly annual events include festivals, parades, and fairs—many of which are worth the effort and all of which include plenty of food finds.

Recipes
At the end of the book, you'll find a whole chapter on recipes. Many of these are from the borough's most famous artisan food entrepreneurs.

Restaurant Price Key

The prices and rates listed in this guidebook were confirmed at press time. We recommend, however, that you call establishments to obtain current information before traveling. Dollar signs are only provided for restaurants that provide full meals and some sort of seating (or operate out of a truck). All restaurant prices are based on the following general guidelines for an appetizer, entree, and dessert for one person (using the most common prices) before drinks, tax, and tip:

$	$20 or less
$$	$20 to $40
$$$	$40 to $60
$$$$	$60 or more

An additional note about menus: Many Brooklyn restaurants serve seasonal, farm-to-table cuisine, which means that their menus change frequently. As a result, the example dishes listed may not be available when you visit the restaurant.

Getting Around

I lived in Manhattan for almost 10 years before moving to Brooklyn, and I know how easy it is to be intimidated by the borough. It's big. The streets aren't always numbered. Rumor has it that cabs don't go there. The subway lines splinter off and don't run well on weekends.

To some degree, there is truth to all of these caveats. But to let them deter you from exploring New York City's most food-loving borough would be a mistake. Sure, Manhattan has better special-occasion restaurants. Queens has better Indian and Thai food. Staten Island has better Sri Lankan food. And the Bronx holds its own in the Italian cuisine department. But Brooklyn is the most innovative of all right now, with small food-related businesses popping up all over. There's so much creativity here that no visit to the city—and certainly no life in the city—would be complete without exploring Brooklyn.

So, how do you get around? Certainly, driving is, with a few exceptions, a less intense experience here than in Manhattan, and finding parking is easier and cheaper, too. But in many neighborhoods, the subways are convenient and, at some times of day, faster than driving. So grab a subway map and read the fine print. Then check the MTA's website for weekend schedule changes (mta.info) and bus maps, which are helpful in the rare neighborhood that doesn't have subway coverage.

As for cabs, the old adage that they refuse to go to Brooklyn just hasn't been true for me. Perhaps I have been lucky, but I have never had a cab driver refuse to take me to Brooklyn. Many will say they don't know their way around, and that you'll have to direct them. Plan ahead, and print out driving directions in advance if you don't know the route. (Both mapquest.com and maps.google .com are reliable sources.) In some neighborhoods, particularly the farther afield ones where residents are more likely to own cars and less likely to take taxis, car services are prevalent, and any restaurant can call one for you.

One more tip: Hopstop.com has a New York section that is very helpful. There you can get walking, subway, bus, and driving directions, as well as find out how much a cab or car service will cost.

Keeping Up with Food News

Brooklyn's food scene is growing every day—and there's daily news for the intrepid diner wanting to try the latest. In addition, Brooklyn has not been spared by the recession, and I found that, in the course of researching this book, many restaurants closed, plenty of chefs moved (and popped up in other places), and, as a result, some restaurants got better and others weakened. Fortunately, there are plenty of websites that cover daily developments in Brooklyn. Yes, I read local newspapers, including the *New York Times,* the *New York Daily News,* the *New York Post,* and the *Village Voice.* But the websites below help me to keep abreast of developing food news with impressive immediacy. Many can also be followed on Twitter, as can some of the restaurants and shops in this book, as can I (my handle is SherriNYC). See you there!

BrooklynBased.com: This Brooklyn-centric website has an e-mail newsletter that includes listings of upcoming events. If there's a food happening in Brooklyn, you'll read about it here.

BrooklynHeightsBlog.com: The neighborhood blogs are very useful tools for staying abreast of developments in each neighborhood to a degree that a publication with a larger coverage base never could. Every hood seems to have one these days, including the **CobbleHillBlog.com.** Again, none of these sites focuses solely on food, but they do cover, for example, when a restaurant closes, opens, or gets slammed by the health department, and what's going into shuttered spaces. There's also **OnlytheBlogKnowsBrooklyn .com** and **BrooklynPaper.com**, which both offer borough news.

Brownstoner.com: This site, which sponsors the **Brooklyn Flea** (p. 97) market and begat a generation of small-batch food producers, has a wealth of news about the borough.

Chow.com: I have very mixed feelings about message board sites, like the "Outer Boroughs" section of Chowhound. That said, if a dozen people are writing that a restaurant isn't worth the trip, and nobody is saying otherwise, chances are you've saved yourself some subway fare.

Eater.com: The New York blog was *Eater*'s first, and the passion for the area's food scene shows. The site is updated with news a couple dozen times every day, and while the focus is more on Manhattan than Brooklyn, there's plenty of chef news and opening alerts.

NonaBrooklyn.com: Another Brooklyn-centric site, Nona covers the local and sustainable food scene carefully and diligently. Their "Chalkboard" feature showcases specials and events, and in 2012 they were nominated for a James Beard award for their blog.

Nymag.com: What I really love on *New York* magazine's website is the *Grub Street* blog. These editors stay on top of the city's food news, and they cover Brooklyn carefully. The same company also owns **Menupages.com**, which has thousands of Brooklyn menus, and **Seamlessweb.com**, a site that allows you to order online.

SeriousEats.com: Ed Levine's food-centric website is an interesting amalgam of news, recipes, and reviews. It has an entire New York section, and also includes two food-specific blogs: *A Hamburger Today* and *Slice,* which cover the burgers and pizzas (respectively) of Kings County.

The Best of Brooklyn

This is a very personal list of some of my favorites around Brooklyn. I encourage you to do your own taste tests and see if you agree—I found my comparison eating to be a fun and satisfying way to explore the borough.

Best Appetizer: Blue Ribbon Brooklyn's Beef Marrow and Oxtail Marmalade (Park Slope), 105
Best Banh Mi: Ba Xuyen (Sunset Park), 183
Best Barbecue: Fette Sau (Williamsburg), 149

Best Bread: Georgian Bread's *khachapuri* (Brighton Beach), 271

Best Cannoli: Villabate Alba Pasticceria & Bakery (Bensonhurst), 221

Best Coffee: Stumptown Coffee Roasters (Red Hook), 77

Best Croissant: Bien Cuit (Cobble Hill), 62

Best Dim Sum: East Harbor Seafood Palace (Sunset Park), 184

Best Doughnuts: Peter Pan Donut & Pastry Shop (Greenpoint), 171

Best Hot Dog: Bark Hot Dogs (Park Slope), 104

Best Jerk Chicken: Peppa's Jerk (Flatbush), 241

Best Milk Shake: Brooklyn Bowl's Bourbon Street Shake (Williamsburg), 140

Best Patty: Jamaican Pride Bakery's Beef Patty (Flatbush), 238

Best Pizza: Roberta's (Bushwick), 247

Best Sandwich: Defonte's of Brooklyn's Roast Beef with Fried Eggplant, Mozzarella, and Jus (Red Hook), 66

Best Taco: Ricos Tacos *Al Pastor* (Sunset Park), 189

Most Important Food Landmarks: Grimaldi's Pizza (Dumbo), 20; Junior's Cheesecake (Downtown), 93; Nathan's Famous Frankfurters (Coney Island), 266

Brooklyn Heights & Dumbo

Brooklyn Heights is one of the most beautiful and affluent areas in the Outer Boroughs. Blessed by a stunning waterfront location, at the base of the Brooklyn Bridge, many streets overlook downtown Manhattan and the Statue of Liberty. Originally built as America's first suburb, it remains a commuter area, with many residents working on Wall Street. (After all, you need to have a banker's salary to afford a brownstone here.) But if you do have the money, it's a lovely spot. Most of the neighborhood has landmark status, and the tree-lined cobblestone streets are lit with gas lamps, the flower boxes are carefully maintained, and the varied architectural styles keep the look interesting. Historic churches sit on every other block and, on weekends, this idyllic area comes alive with the sound of bells and churchgoers shuffling off to services.

Despite the affluence here, or perhaps because of it, Brooklyn Heights is an anomaly in Brooklyn—one of the few neighborhoods

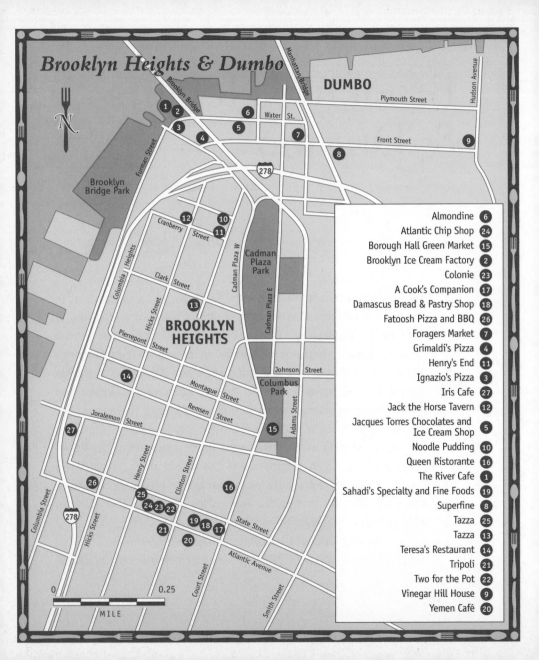

Brooklyn Heights & Dumbo

DUMBO

Plymouth Street

Water St.

Front Street

Hudson Avenue

Manhattan Bridge

Brooklyn Bridge

Furman Street

Brooklyn Bridge Park

278

Cranberry Street

Street

Columbia Heights

Clark Street

Hicks Street

BROOKLYN HEIGHTS

Cadman Plaza W

Cadman Plaza Park

Cadman Plaza E

Pierrepont Street

Johnson Street

Columbus Park

Montague Street

Remsen Street

Adams Street

Joralemon Street

Henry Street

Clinton Street

State Street

Court Street

Atlantic Avenue

Smith Street

Columbia Street

Hicks Street

278

0   0.25

MILE

not known for great food. Blame the long work hours of the hedge fund managers and lawyers who live here. Blame the high cost of rent driving restaurants to other areas. Blame the allegedly pedestrian tastes of the jurors who visit the courthouses. No matter whom you blame, you can't deny that while Brooklyn Heights may be attractive—with fabulous Manhattan views from the overlook called The Promenade—for the food-lover, it is a short stop. There are a few exceptions, many of them centered on the Middle Eastern–influenced Atlantic Avenue. You'll find cars double and triple parked on Atlantic Avenue on Saturday afternoons as visitors buy a pantry's worth of goods—and you'll want to join them.

Dumbo, in contrast to Brooklyn Heights, is relatively new in its current state. The name stands for Down Under the Manhattan Bridge Overpass, and it's located in the shadows of the Brooklyn and Manhattan Bridges, which are omnipresent at the end of most streets. The neighborhood is bordered to the west by swish Brooklyn Heights and to the east by still-gentrifying Vinegar Hill. In the mid-90s, up-and-coming artists began to transform Dumbo from an industrial district of 19th-century warehouses on Belgian block streets into work-live lofts.

Today, an infusion of more formal development has transformed the neighborhood into a stylish enclave of galleries, performance spaces, and high-end apartment buildings. Each fall, the neighborhood artists open up their studios for the annual art tour, and you can wander through the industrial buildings and admire the paintings, sculpture, and photography.

Atlantic Chip Shop, 129 Atlantic Avenue between Clinton Street and Henry Street; (718) 855-7775; Subway: 2, 3, 4, 5, R to Borough Hall; chipshopnyc.com; $. Whether or not you like this place (and its Park Slope sister) has a lot to do with how you feel about British pub grub. The look is pure pub with a white banged-tin ceiling, roughed-up wooden tables, space that's equally divided into bar and restaurant, and a beer list that's as long as the food menu. The menu focuses on gut-busting English basics—fish-and-chips, shepherd's pie, Scotch eggs, Welsh rarebit, and fried Mars bars. More importantly, the friendly bartenders and waiters will remember your pint of choice after a couple of visits. The Park Slope location is at 383 5th Avenue, Brooklyn, NY 11215; 718-832-7701.

Colonie, 127 Atlantic Avenue between Clinton Street and Henry Street; (718) 855-7500; Subway: 2, 3, 4, 5, R to Borough Hall; colonienyc.com; $$$. Like many restaurants based in turn-of-the-century buildings, Colonie certainly fits into the Brooklyn look of the moment: schoolhouse pendant lights, exposed brick walls, mirrors, and plenty of candlelight. Along the side of the bar, you'll find a wall covered in almost two-dozen growing green plants. The menu follows through on the trend of the moment, too, with well-sourced seasonal, local ingredients, such as purple carrots with yogurt, sunchoke soup, fried brussels sprouts with bacon, leeks topped with romesco, or acorn squash agnolotti. When in doubt, order the charcuterie, such as the *salame piccante* with grainy mustard and pickled shallots, duck *rilletes* with pickles, or the rabbit and *foie gras* terrine, and pair it with a seasonal artisan cocktail, like the green apple whiskey sour with house-made rye.

Fatoosh Pizza & BBQ, 330 Hicks Street between Atlantic Avenue and State Street; (718) 243-0500; Subway: 2, 3, 4, 5, R to Borough Hall; $. What Fatoosh misses in atmosphere it makes up for in authenticity. Don't be put off by the laminated tablecloths or fluorescent lighting—you're here for the food, not the surroundings. The pita is the star of the show. Handmade several times a day and always hot and fluffy, the bread alone is worth the trip. Get it wrapped around crisp falafel, tasty hummus, or well-seasoned lamb sausage, or try their own take on a pizza, in which that fabulous pita serves as a crust that's as tasty as the toppings.

Henry's End, 44 Henry Street between Cranberry Street and Middagh Street; (718) 834-1776; Subway: A, C to High Street or 2, 3 to Clark Street; henrysend.com; $$$. This quiet restaurant is best known for its wild game menu, which is served from October through February. That's the time to come for herb-crusted elk chops, reindeer with bourbon–sour cherry sauce, and pheasant ravioli with caramelized onions and pistachios, as well as more unusual offerings such as rattlesnake

salad and pan-seared kangaroo. The rest of the year, the most remarkable dishes have a Cajun influence, such as shrimp with andouille sausage and penne with lobster and cayenne-cream sauce.

Ignazio's Pizza, 4 Water Street between Old Fulton Street and Old Dock Street; (718) 522-2100; Subway: A, C to High Street or F to York Street; ignaziospizza.com; $$. **Grimaldi's** (p. 20) is a hard act to follow, so nobody can accuse Ignazio's—a pizza joint that opened just a block down the road—of not having gumption. It was a clever move. How many tourists plan to go to Grimaldi's and then change their minds when they see the long lines? Probably plenty, and Ignazio's, one must guess, is hoping to become the natural alternative. The dining room is pleasant, with big windows that let in ample light during the day and showcase the city lights after dark. Unfortunately, the sometimes indifferent service is not as impressive as the backdrop. (Hey, that bridge view is hard to beat.) The specialty pies are, at least, worth checking out. Consider the bacon-shrimp special, which comes topped with tender shrimp, crisp chunks of applewood-smoked bacon, roasted red peppers, and garlicky bread crumbs that add shocks of flavor.

Jack the Horse Tavern, 66 Hicks Street between Cranberry Street and Middagh Street; (718) 852-5084; Subway 2, 3 to Clark Street or

A, C to High Street; jackthehorse.com; $$$. Jack the Horse is the friendly, casual neighborhood tavern that every nabe should have. From the exposed brick to the banquettes covered in oversize velvet throw pillows, and the pretty vintage clock collection, the vibe is comfortable. Start with the impressive cocktail list: Drinks are carefully and thoughtfully mixed, shaken, or muddled, with fresh ingredients like just-squeezed citrus juices, mint leaves, and house-made cinnamon syrup. If you stay for dinner, you can start with an artichoke and pancetta cheesecake served with a grape tomato salad, pâté with cornichons and grainy mustard, or fried oysters with lemon confit followed by mussels with frites, crispy soft-shell crabs, or a pork chop with spaetzle and pears. Walk it off with a stroll on the promenade, just a block away.

Noodle Pudding, 38 Henry Street between Cranberry Street and Middagh Street; (718) 625-3737; Subway: A, C to High Street or 2, 3 to Clark Street; $$. Noodle Pudding, a warm and friendly neighborhood hangout, may not be showing the old Italian-American social club types anything they haven't seen. But it's always packed nonetheless, as locals flock to the pasta and meat dishes—such as tagliatelle bolognese, penne arrabbiata, and osso bucco. Because they don't take reservations, waits can be long, but the bar is full of jovial types who welcome newcomers as they down red wine and wait for the cheerful, high-spirited maitre d' to show them to their tables.

River Deli, 32 Joralemon Street between Columbia Place and Furman Street; (718) 254-9200; Subway: 2, 3, 4, 5, R to Borough

Hall; $$. It's just what this area needed: an Italian restaurant to serve as a South Heights hangout. With plenty of original detail, the space feels like an appropriate nod to the past in this historic district, and the simple dishes (plump ravioli, rich tiramisu) are equally comforting.

Superfine, 126 Front Street between Jay Street and Pearl Street; (718) 243-9005; Subway: A, C to High Street or F to York Street; $$. One of the first restaurants to arrive and serve the early artist community, Superfine also serves as a gallery, pool hall, and some-time performance space for local bands. From brunch to dinner, the food draws locals and foodies willing to travel. At brunch, the Southwestern-style treats—huevos rancheros, steak and eggs, and the breakfast burrito—aim to soothe hangovers.

Teresa's Restaurant, 80 Montague Street between Hicks Street and Montague Terrace; (718) 797-3996; Subway: 2, 3, 4, 5, R to Borough Hall; $. On a sunny day, after a visit to the promenade, there is no better Montague Street brunch spot than this sidewalk cafe. And while the diner-size menu offers American staples, it's the Polish fare that's a treat. Meat- or cheese-filled pierogies come boiled or fried, and you can (and should) order yours with onions sautéed in butter and plenty of thick sour cream. The kielbasa is scored and boiled then broiled until crispy. But the blintzes may be the best choice: These thin pancakes are fried and dusted with confectioners' sugar.

Tripoli, 156 Atlantic Avenue between Clinton Street and Henry Street; (718) 596-5800; Subway: 2, 3, 4, 5, R to Borough Hall; tripoli restaurant.com; $$. If you are not familiar with Lebanese food, then consider Tripoli an ideal introduction. This BYOB restaurant is filled with interesting carved wood furniture, winding mahogany staircases, and murals of the owners' hometown. On most nights, the antique-filled rooms are dark and quiet, but just because the restaurant isn't well known doesn't mean there aren't plenty of tasty morsels to be enjoyed. Start with the traditional platter of *maza,* or appetizers, which include dips like hummus and baba ghanoush, crispy fried falafel, cheese, and olives. Or start with a fresh tabouli, a cold Lebanese salad made with parsley mixed with finely diced tomatoes, onions, and cracked wheat. Entrees include a parade of lamb: savory lamb kebabs, house-made lamb sausage filled with pine nuts and wine, and lamb stew flavored with yogurt.

Vinegar Hill House, 72 Hudson Avenue between Front Street and Water Street; (718) 522-1018; Subway: F to York Street; vinegar hillhouse.com; $$$. Drive into quiet Vinegar Hill, at the edge of Dumbo, and you'll stumble upon a small, humble restaurant, with no sign but crowds spilling onto the street. That's how you know you found the place. Inside, the restaurant is warm with vintage wallpaper and reclaimed wood tables that create a suitably homey feel for the menu. Vinegar Hill House serves cheese and charcuterie platters with grainy mustard and rustic house-made crackers, as well as hearty peasant-Italian dishes such as thick pork chops, chicken roasted in a cast-iron skillet, and savory butternut squash ravioli topped with toasted walnuts. For locals, who generally have to drive for dinners, it's a treat to have such a hot restaurant in their midst.

Yemen Cafe, 176 Atlantic Avenue between Clinton Street and Court Street; (718) 834-9533; Subway: 2, 3, 4, 5, R to Borough Hall; $$. You certainly don't come here for the atmosphere. This restaurant, whose modest decor includes cafeteria-style tables and chairs, does one thing, and it does it well: traditional Yemeni-style roasted lamb. The hearty lamb, which is served in a massive portion and falls off the bone at the slightest touch into a steaming heap of tender meat, is roasted and served with roasted vegetables and enormous portions of clay oven–cooked puffy round bread called *rashoosh*. Wash it all down with Yemeni tea.

Landmarks

Grimaldi's Pizza, 1 Front Street between Old Fulton Street and Dock Street; (718) 858-4300; Subway: A, C to High Street or F to York Street; $. This is the most famous of all New York's brick-oven pizza palaces. Is it the best? That will always be open to debate among pizza devotees, but they can agree on this: It sure is popular. Go on a weekend, any time of year, and you will find a line stretching down the block. (They don't take reservations—even for large parties—so there's no getting around the wait.)

Here's why, after almost 100 years, people keep coming back to this legendary restaurant: First, there's the location. It's right under the Brooklyn Bridge, and a great refueling stop after a walk across the bridge from Manhattan. Second, the decor is unpretentious and charming. Picture red-checked tablecloths, Sinatra on the jukebox, and silver trays to hold up the pizzas (which are sold by the pie, never by the slice). Third, and most importantly, the pizza is authentic. The crust is thin and charred from its time in the coal oven; the sauce is sweet and simple, the mozzarella is creamy and mild. The toppings are high quality, especially the pepperoni, which curls up at the sides as it cooks to form little cups. And while this place, like many landmarks, is tossed aside by some locals as a relic resting on its laurels, just as many are devotees. There's no easy answer: You must decide for yourself.

Queen Ristorante, 84 Court Street between Livingston Street and Schermerhorn Street; (718) 596-5955; Subway: 2, 3, 4, 5, R to Borough Hall; queenrestaurant.com; $$$. Located near the courthouse, this 50-year-old, family-run Italian spot serves up nostalgia to lawyers, judges, and neighborhood regulars. As with most of these types of old-school landmarks, the food itself—such as veal scallopini, baked clams, lasagna, and chicken Milanese, all of it cooked by the third generation of the Brooklyn Italian family that originally opened the place—is a throwback to another time. The restaurant makes just about everything in house, including most pasta, the mozzarella, the gelato, and 7 types of bread. (Look for the small cheesy rolls that taste a bit like savory zeppole.) The specials, which may include fresh sardines or a house-made black pasta with mussels and clams, are the way to go.

The River Cafe, 1 Water Street between Old Fulton Street and New Dock Street; (718) 522-5200; Subway: A, C to High Street; rivercafe.com; $$$$. The River Cafe is all about the location. It sits just under the Brooklyn Bridge, and it's the only restaurant right on the water in this part of town. In years past, the restaurant launched the career of many a well-known chef, from Charlie Palmer to David Burke. Today, the candlelight in the dining room may burn a bit brighter than the kitchen's star quality, but the space is as breathtaking as ever. The dining room juts out over the East River, with a water-level view of New York City at night, and the spot-lit entrance feels appropriately grand for special occasions. The food focuses on continental classics (crispy duck, lemon sole). And while it's probably the view that you'll remember (along with your chocolate marquise cake, which is shaped like the Brooklyn Bridge), on the Fourth of July, when fireworks light up the harbor, there's no better reservation in town. Remember: The restaurant requires jackets for men after 5 p.m.

What Exactly Is Brooklyn-style Pizza?

A few years ago, Domino's, the national pizza chain, came out with a limited-time special: Brooklyn-style pizza. And the blogosphere ignited with the time-honored question: "What exactly is Brooklyn-style pizza?"

For most, the pizza itself is the coal-fired Margherita that you find at **Grimaldi's** (p. 20) and **Totonno's** (p. 269)—at its best, a simple thin crust that's crisp at the edges and chewy in the center. It's charred to perfection and topped with a sweet tomato sauce, torn pieces of fresh basil, and slices of fresh buffalo mozzarella that, when baked, polka-dot the pie rather than covering it. Many visitors take one look at it and declare it burnt, but to Brooklynites this is the telltale sign of the coal-burning brick oven.

Old-school Brooklyn pizza is served by the pie, never by the slice, and is always cut into eight wedges. At the places known for their century-old brick ovens, you have to wait in a line—a long line—to get it, unless you go on a weekday during off hours. As a result, it is a special treat. On any given weeknight, time-pressed locals are more likely to hit the neighborhood slice shop, where the pizzas are lined up across the glass counter. There, you point to the type you want, and it's thrown in the big industrial oven behind the counter and reheated. The thin crust is floppier than that on a coal-oven baked pizza, and the mozzarella is of the commercial variety that pools with grease, spreads out across the pie, and strings when you eat it. You'll want to perfect your squat if you are planning to eat it on the street: Fold it in half, and lean back a little so that the grease doesn't drip onto your clothing. Sure, it's messy—but for New Yorkers, it's a taste of home.

And what about those Domino's pizzas? In the end, locals shook their heads. "Domino's," Brooklyn Borough president Marty Markowitz told the *New York Times,* "is about as Brooklyn as Sara Lee Cheesecake is Junior's."

Specialty Stores, Markets & Producers

Almondine, 85 Water Street between Main Street and Old Dock Street; (718) 797-5026; Subway: A, C to High Street or F to York Street; almondinebakery.com; $. Across from the **Jacques Torres** (p. 28) chocolate shop, the Almondine bakery sates Dumbo residents' need for French pastry. Morning croissants come plain or filled with chocolate pieces or almond paste—and some say they're the best in the city. Plus there are delicate madeleines and crusty baguettes, as well as éclairs and custard-filled mille-feuille pastries. They also do an adorable Sunday morning continental breakfast delivery they call "Room Service." What more could a Front Street princess ask for? It's no surprise that their popularity has spurred them into opening a Park Slope location, too.

Borough Hall Green Market, Borough Hall, on Court Street between Montague Street and Remsen Street; Subway: 2, 3, 4, 5, M, R to Borough Hall; cenyc.org/greenmarket. This farmers' market is a collection of stands, largely set up by Hudson Valley and Long Island farms and artisan bakers. Much of the produce is organic and, unlike many Brooklyn markets, it's open year-round on Tues and Sat from 8 a.m. to 6 p.m. and on Thurs during the peak of growing season. The market is small, but after a walk across the bridge on a Saturday morning, there is no better treat than a sun-warmed peach or, on cold days, a warming cup of apple cider. Vendors include Red

Jacket Orchards (apples, stone fruit, berries) from the Finger Lakes, Wilklow Orchards (fruit and jam) from Ulster County in New York, Fishkill Farms (chickens and eggs) from New York's Duchess County, and Phillips Farms from Milford, New Jersey (vegetables and plants). The bakers on any given day could be Not Just Rugelach and Bread Alone, and you can find plenty of cheese: goat cheese from Ardith Mae, sheep cheese from Valley Shepherd Creamery, and water buffalo mozzarella from Bufala di Vermont.

Brooklyn Ice Cream Factory, Fulton Ferry Landing Pier at Old Fulton Street and Water Street; (718) 246-3963; Subway: A, C to High Street or F to York Street. Known for creamy, rich ice cream, this shop has a lovely location in an old boathouse, circa 1922, on the ferry pier. (It may not be a busy depot for travelers actually taking boat rides but it's certainly a major photo op on most tourist itineraries.) The small white clapboard ice-cream shop is the perfect antidote to one of those hot summer days when the heat bounces off the sidewalk and the salty smell of the harbor fills the air. There are no chunks or swirls here: The old-time flavors are simple reminders of local fruit harvests and summers past. The keys to why this ice cream tastes so good are the fresh ingredients and the high milk-fat content—plus the fact that, since they don't use preservatives, no ice cream is more than a few days old. (It's all made here, or in the shop's Williamsburg space, so it doesn't have far to travel.) Order up a cup of creamy coffee, fresh strawberry, or butter pecan, and ask to top it off with the dark chocolate sauce made especially for the shop by **The River Cafe** (p. 22) next door. Take your treat and settle under the red-and-white-striped tent on the pier.

A Cook's Companion, 197 Atlantic Avenue between Clinton Street and Court Street; (718) 852 6901; Subway: 2, 3, 4, 5, R to Borough Hall; acookscompanion .com. No, you don't have to head into Manhattan to stock your Brooklyn kitchen. This small but well-edited kitchen supply shop has everything from the basic (shiny Wusthof knives, Le Creuset pots in candy colors, cast-iron Lodge pans) to the playful (cookie cutters in shapes from the Statue of Liberty to the Brooklyn Bridge). They also sharpen knives and sell dish towels emblazoned with Brooklyn landmarks (Coney Island's Cyclone, the West Indian Day parade in Flatbush), and locally made eau de Brooklyn soap, which smells like pea bergamot. Best of all, they offer signed copies of many local cookbook authors' works.

Damascus Bread & Pastry Shop, 195 Atlantic Avenue between Clinton Street and Court Street; (718) 625-7070; Subway: 2, 3, 4, 5, R to Borough Hall. Brooklyn Heights is blessed with a wonderful Syrian bakery, circa 1930. Damascus bakes pita bread and *lahvosh* wrap, and you can pick up more delicate items as well, including dainty meat- and spinach-filled phyllo-dough pies and a wide selection of nut- and dried fruit–stuffed, honey-soaked pastries in an array of shapes and sizes. (Think pistachio bird's nests and baklava.) It's all fresh and tasty and, better still, open on Sunday when **Sahadi's** (p. 29) is closed.

Foragers Market, 56 Adams Street between Front Street and Water Street; (718) 801-8400; Subway: A, C to High Street or F to York Street; foragersmarket.com. When the Two Trees real estate developers first opened their luxury apartment buildings on Front Street, the early arrivals had a problem: The only grocery store was little more than a glorified bodega. Now, they have Foragers Market, a gourmet shop that sources some of the best locally produced brands as well as fresh produce. Sure, the sandwiches and salads are good, and it's wonderful to be able to buy rotisserie chicken, wild salmon, and organic grass-fed, grain-finished beef here, but what's really special is the attention to detail. Ice-cream cases are filled with local **Van Leeuwen** ice cream (p. 178), and condiments include Brooklyn-based **McClure's** (p. 249) stone-ground mustard. In the summer, produce aisles are filled with local strawberries and radishes. Come fall, Foragers flies in Hatch green chiles from New Mexico, ready to roast and peel. Ask nicely, and they'll order an extra case for you, too.

Iris Cafe, 20 Columbia Place between Joralemon Street and State Street; (718) 722-7395; Subway: 2, 3, 4, 5, R to Borough Hall; iriscafenyc.com; $. This off-the-beaten-path coffeehouse on a quiet residential stretch has become a trendy destination for neighborhood types looking for great food, and it's also well located for those looking to pick up a picnic on their way to Brooklyn Bridge Park. Come at breakfast for **Stumptown** coffee (p. 77) or house-made biscuits with tangy house-made lemon curd, or at lunch for sandwiches. The French Dip, made with jus that's spiked with **Manhattan Special** (p. 167), is a winner, as is the egg salad sandwich. Best of all, with exposed brick walls and tin ceilings, the setting is as charming as the menu.

Jacques Torres Chocolates & Ice Cream Shop, 66 Water Street between Main Street and Old Dock Street; (718) 875-9772; Subway: A, C to High Street, or F to York Street; mrchocolate.com. When Jacques Torres, who first wowed New Yorkers as the pastry chef at Manhattan's Le Cirque in the '90s, opened this shop on a quiet Dumbo side street, many wondered what he was thinking. But it quickly became a destination for Manhattanites on warm-weather weekend bridge walks, who wander over here to fuel up for the hike back like the Swiss do, with sweet cocoa pick-me-ups like chocolate-cookie ice-cream sandwiches and an array of ganache-filled truffles. Too

bad they miss out on Torres's best concoction: a puddinglike hot cocoa that may not be a great summer afternoon treat but certainly hits the spot when the temperature drops. Torres later added on an ice-cream shop. They sell ice-cream sandwiches (in fabulous flavors like strawberry and hazelnut) as well as cones of Torres's chocolate concoctions: white chocolate–raspberry, banana-chocolate, and an impressive ice-cream version of his signature Wicked hot chocolate. Laced with cinnamon, ancho, and chipotle, this flavorful summer treat leaves a pleasant burn long after your cup is empty.

Rickshaw Dumpling Truck, rickshawdumplings.com; $. This Asian food truck spends some time in the neighborhood. On the menu you'll usually find a variety of steamed dumplings, including pork with ginger and chicken with lemongrass and Thai basil, as well as more interesting specials like wild shrimp with wasabi and Peking duck with cabbage. Check their website for current schedules.

Sahadi's Specialty & Fine Foods, 187 Atlantic Avenue between Court Street and Clinton Street; (718) 624-4550; Subway: 2, 3, 4, 5, R to Borough Hall; sahadis.com. There are several spice shops on this stretch of Atlantic Avenue but, for New Yorkers of Middle Eastern descent, the 60-plus-year-old Sahadi's is a mecca for hard-to-find ingredients. Take a number at the nut counter and wait your turn for a chance to order bags of nuts, dried fruit, candy, olives, ground-to-order coffee, and spices. The bulk bins empty out quickly here, so the food is fresh and reasonably priced. They carry 5 kinds of dates at any given time, mostly from California—the best for eating are the jumbo medjools (except from mid-August to mid-September when they sell fresh dates); the pitted dates from Pakistan, called *deglet nour,* are the best for cooking. Also popular are dried apricots from Turkey, which are sweeter than the California variety and less expensive, and almonds, of which they carry 15 different choices. Plus, they roast their own Turkish pistachios, Oregonian filberts, and California and Spanish Marcona almonds in Brooklyn. Another thing to look for: They sell 35 types of olives, which you can get at the same time when your number is (finally!) called.

Next, head to the back of the store and get in line for the prepared food, from crisp falafel to spicy hummus, baked artichokes, stuffed grape leaves, and creamy baba ghanoush, a dip made from roasted, smoky eggplant. Then, peruse the broad selection of olive oils (including 7 different regional oils from Lebanon), cheese, halvah, and honey before getting in line to check out. And be warned: Because they are closed Sunday, on Saturday the cashier line wraps around the store. Frequent shoppers bring friends so they can divide and conquer.

Tazza, 311 Henry Street between State Street and Atlantic Avenue, (718) 243-0487, Subway: 2, 3, 4, 5, R to Borough Hall; 72 Clark Street between Henry Street and Hicks Street, (718) 855-2700, Subway: 2, 3 to Clark Street, or A, C to High Street; tazza bklyn.com; $. While many cities mourn the loss of the small locally owned coffee shops that have given way to Starbucks, Brooklyn Heights is home to both. This small coffee shop has 2 locations.

Brooklyn Bridge Park

When it's completed, the Brooklyn Bridge Park, which lines the waterfront on both sides of the bridge in Dumbo and Brooklyn Heights, will be an 85-acre wonder, with 1.3 miles of waterfront property, paddle boats, volleyball courts, dog runs, fishing piers, playgrounds, an aquatic play area, and a carousel. You can already check out events like movies under the stars in the summertime as well as outdoor fitness classes. On summer weekends, you can also sample the handywork some of Brooooklyn's best food crafters, from **Bark Hot Dogs** (p. 104), which serves hot dogs, hamburgers, and local beer, to **Blue Marble** ice cream (p. 62), Uncle Louie G's Italian Ices, sandwiches by Ditch Plains (from the Manhattan seafood spot by the same name), Calexico *carne asada* tacos, grilled cheese sandwiches and shakes from Milk Truck.

During the week, freelancers and Brooklyn Law School students bring their laptops to work, and mothers of young children gather with their strollers for light lunches or coffee. But the real treats here are the sweets. They make their own scones, but most of the baked goods are sourced from some of Brooklyn's best bakeries; they include peppermint marshmallows, salted caramel brownies, and pink coconut–crusted "snowballs" from **Baked** (p. 60) in Red Hook, and pumpkin spice whoopee pies from **One Girl Cookies** (p. 72) in Boerum Hill.

Two for the Pot, 200 Clinton Street between Atlantic Avenue and State Street; (718) 855-8173; Subway: 2, 3, 4, 5, R to Borough Hall. This quirky tea shop sells more than just tea, though they do have dozens of loose-leaf varieties available in neat little jars as well as strainers, cozies, biscuits, and small British teapots. They have plenty of coffee beans and filters and thermoses, and they supply tea to **The River Cafe** (p. 22). The teas and coffee are nice, as are the canned and jarred English pantry items (salad sauce, HP sauce, spaghetti hoops, and baked beans, for Brits who need their fix of the homeland). Look for the small rotating collection of locally produced items that you may not find anywhere else, including organic grade-A dark amber maple syrup from upstate New York and Cobble Hill Honey, made on Kane Street just a few blocks away by a guy who keeps the hives on the roof of his apartment building.

Food Events

Atlantic Antic, Atlantic Avenue from Hicks Street to 4th Avenue; Subway: 2, 3, 4, 5, R to Borough Hall; atlanticave.org. This annual festival has taken place one Sunday each fall, often in October, for more than 30 years. Over the decades, it has grown from a small neighborhood street festival with funnel cakes and grilled sausages

HERE COME THE FOOD TRUCKS

New York's streets have been filling up with food trucks over the past few years. These restaurants-on-wheels have varied schedules, often visiting Manhattan's Midtown and Financial districts at lunchtime during the week to feed hungry office workers and coming to Brooklyn on some evenings and weekends. Of course, what these trucks serve varies widely. There are juice trucks that mix freshly squeezed concoctions to order (such as the Green Pirate Juice Truck, which serves wheatgrass shots in addition to Creamsicle-inspired mixes of carrot, cantaloupe, and coconut milks. There are dessert trucks, whose menus range from bake sale–style treats (brownies, chocolate chip cookies, oatmeal bars) to fancier restaurant-style desserts like crème brûlée. Of course, there are savory trucks (Cravings, for example, serves Taiwanese-style dumplings and rice dishes; Schnitzel and Things serves German-style cutlet sandwiches) and ice-cream trucks, too. Since their schedules can vary from week to week, you'll want to check out their websites and their Twitter postings for dates and times.

to become a true celebration of Brooklyn cuisine. Today, more than 600 vendors set up shop along a 10-block stretch of Atlantic Avenue, and 10 stages host local bands and entertainers who perform a wide range of acts, from straight up rock 'n' roll to drum circles and belly dancing. Each year, over a million people come to the Antic to see the vintage buses and historic trolleys on display from the nearby New York City Transit Museum (which is located in an abandoned subway station on Livingston Street) and settle in at temporary street-side beer gardens. A few local restaurants try out new dishes—like the Boerum Hill hipster hangout **Building on Bond** (p. 41), which debuted pretzel sandwiches filled with pulled pork that to this day are a menu highlight at the restaurant. Perhaps one of the best finds, though, are stands set up by the local Baptist churches, which serve hearty lunches of fried chicken, mac and cheese, and collard greens that would make any Southern mama proud.

Danish Seamen's Church Christmas Fair, 102 Willow Street between Clark Street and Pierrepont Street; (718) 875-0042; Subway: A, C to High Street or 2, 3 to Clark Street; dankirkeny.org. Every November, this church hosts a smorgasbord in its Willow Street brownstone. It's the type of wholesome event that feels private—a window into a community. The feast includes authentic Danish hot dogs, open-faced pork sandwiches, smoked fish, almond-flavored Danish, and black licorice—plus plenty of Carlsberg beer and glögg (spiced, mulled wine that, to many Danes, symbolizes the holiday season). It's all served up on tables covered in festive red paper tablecloths and served by friendly Danes who are so proud to share their Christmas cheer that it's hard not to get into the spirit.

Dine-in Brooklyn, visitbrooklyn.org. Many cities offer a restaurant week deal, and Brooklyn is no exception. Once a year, for a week in March or April, many of Brooklyn's best restaurants offer 3-course meals for $23 per person. The restaurants include casual spots, like **Atlantic Chip Shop** (p. 14) in Brooklyn Heights, but they also include more expensive places, like **Blue Ribbon** (p. 105) and **Rose Water** (p. 115), both of which are in Park Slope. Also, several restaurants (including **River Cafe,** p. 22) participate in the citywide restaurant weeks at well. It's a great opportunity to eat around but, as always, beware: Sometimes the specials don't add up to a savings; other times, the menus don't show off the restaurants' signature dishes.

Our Lady of Lebanon Lebanese Food Festival, 113 Remsen Street between Henry Street and Clinton Street; (718) 624-7228; Subway: 2, 3, 4, 5, R to Borough Hall; ololc.org. For the past three decades, this Maronite church (a magnet for Lebanese families from all over the city) has shut down Remsen Street between Henry and Clinton and set up tents in the street over the last weekend in May or first weekend in June. They serve up tabouli, stuffed grape leaves, and hummus. The parishioners proudly introduce the neighborhood to grilled specialties, too, like spicy *kefta* kebabs and kibbe meatballs, all in the name of raising money for renovating the historic church.

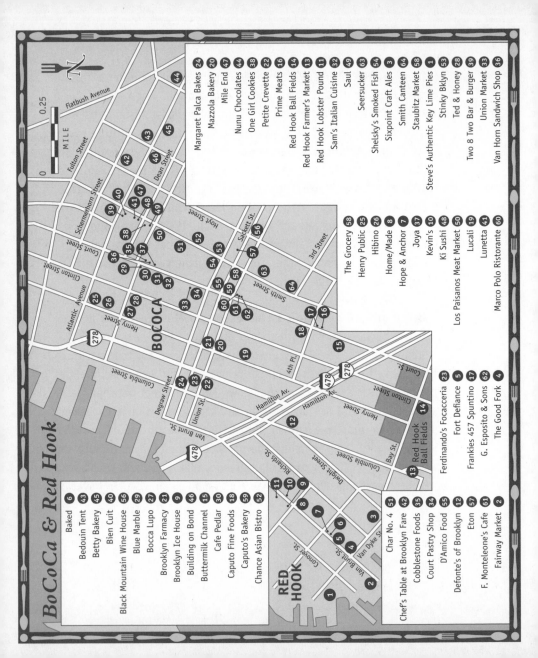

BoCoCa & Red Hook

Baked 6
Bedouin Tent 43
Betty Bakery 45
Bien Cuit 40
Black Mountain Wine House 56
Blue Marble 29
Bocca Lupo 27
Brooklyn Farmacy 21
Brooklyn Ice House 9
Building on Bond 46
Buttermilk Channel 15
Cafe Pedlar 30
Caputo Fine Foods 18
Caputo's Bakery 59
Chance Asian Bistro 52

Char No. 4 51
Chef's Table at Brooklyn Fare 42
Cobblestone Foods 35
Court Pastry Shop 34
D'Amico Food 55
Defonte's of Brooklyn 12
Eton 57
F. Monteleone's Cafe 61
Fairway Market 2

Margaret Palca Bakes 24
Mazzola Bakery 20
Mile End 47
Nunu Chocolates 44
One Girl Cookies 38
Petite Crevette 22
Prime Meats 16
Red Hook Ball Fields 14
Red Hook Farmer's Market 13
Red Hook Lobster Pound 11
Sam's Italian Cuisine 32
Saul 49
Seersucker 63
Shelsky's Smoked Fish 54
Sixpoint Craft Ales 3
Smith Canteen 64
Staubitz Market 58
Steve's Authentic Key Lime Pies 1
Stinky Bklyn 53
Ted & Honey 28
Two 8 Two Bar & Burger 39
Union Market 33
Van Horn Sandwich Shop 36

The Grocery 58
Henry Public 25
Hibino 8
Home/Made 7
Joya 37
Kevin's 10
Ki Sushi 48
Los Paisanos Meat Market 50
Lucali 19
Lunetta 41
Marco Polo Ristorante 60

Ferdinando's Focacceria 23
Fort Defiance 5
Frankies 457 Spuntino 17
G. Esposito & Sons 62
The Good Fork 4

Boerum Hill, Cobble Hill, Carroll Gardens & Red Hook

BoCoCa—the real-estate agent term for Boerum Hill, Cobble Hill, and Carroll Gardens—is as residential as can be. Boerum Hill's fate of late has been tied to the rise of Smith Street's restaurant row. Since the late '90s, restaurants have been popping up along this street, and it has become a destination for both Brooklyn- and Manhattan-based food lovers. Now, some of these restaurants have Michelin stars and Manhattan-worthy prices; others have been killed by the recession. But whether you think Smith Street is over, or just evolving, there's no denying its popularity on Saturday night, when parking fills up and people pour out of restaurants and bars.

Quieter Cobble Hill is known for its brownstone-lined streets shaded by big old trees. Cobble Hill's main shopping street may be Court Street, but the heart of the neighborhood is little Cobble Hill Park, which is often filled with family dogs and baby carriages. Here, wrought-iron picnic tables sit next to carefully tended flower gardens and a playful children's area with swing sets and slides designed to look like cartoonish bugs.

Just to the south, you'll find Carroll Gardens, one of Brooklyn's historically Italian neighborhoods. Here you'll see brownstones decorated with Virgin Mary statues, scalloped awnings, and the front gardens for which the neighborhood is named. Neighbors say hello when they pass, and shop at the Italian bakeries and markets. Carroll Gardens remains a middle-class neighborhood, despite the fact that the price of brownstones skyrocketed in the '90s, and many of the original mom-and-pop shops, from cobblers to funeral homes and bakeries, are still around. The fact that subway service is more limited here than in Cobble Hill, where nearby Brooklyn Heights offers many trains, has curtailed change.

Red Hook was once a major fishing port and the home of the longshoremen who worked it, sailing their boats through Buttermilk Channel (the stretch of water between Governor's Island and the Brooklyn shore). Today there is still plenty of port traffic, and you can watch the container ships sailing past, although much of the industry—from cannonball making to grain factories—is gone. Because the neighborhood is cut off by the Brooklyn-Queens Expressway, gentrification has come very slowly. But the opening of Fairway Brooklyn (the borough's outpost of the city's famed grocery store), the city's first Ikea, and a new cruise ship terminal have helped. The pioneering artists who live there, inhabiting old Dutch shipping warehouses and rehabbing other buildings, have created their own quirky food scene.

Foodie Faves

Bedouin Tent, 405 Atlantic Avenue between Bond Street and Nevins Street; (718) 852-5555; Subway: F, G to Bergen Street or A, C, G to Hoyt-Schermerhorn, or 2, 3, 4, 5 to Nevins Street; $. This unpretentious place looks like a small take-away outfit when you first walk in. But, past the grill and the register, you'll find a small dining room lined with Middle Eastern rugs and glass doors that open up to a small but pleasant backyard. Still, it's the hearty food that steals the spotlight. The house specialties include crisp falafel, pita bread "pitzas" that stretch out over the sides of their plates, a roasted leg of lamb platter that comes with lemon-mint aioli, as well as a house-made *merguez* (lamb sausage) that packs a spicy kick and comes with salad, pita, tahini, and baba ghanoush, all for under $10. It's hard to resist the steaming mint tea, and desserts include the (often complimentary) *basbousa,* a semolina cake made with yogurt and a fragrant touch of honey.

Black Mountain Wine House, 415 Union Street between Hoyt Street and Bond Street; (718) 522-4340; Subway: F, G to Carroll

Street; blackmountainwinehouse.com; $. This lovely wine bar is a pleasant surprise on an otherwise unattractive stretch. Walk up the rather isolated block and it's hard to miss—it's the one that looks like a little wooden cottage, with a wrought-iron fence that hides rough-hewn Adirondack chairs. Food sticks to nibbles that pair well with wine, like a white bean-ricotta-pesto crostini, a cheese tray, a charcuterie plate with pâté and grainy mustard, and a beef stew with polenta. Or check out the cheese list, all of which (including a creamy, shaved French *tête de moine* and a Spanish Idiazábal) are just $4 each and come with spicy chutney, french bread, and thin slices of pear.

Bocca Lupo, 391 Henry Street between Warren Street and Verandah Place; (718) 243-2522; Subway F, G to Bergen Street; $$. This Italian-style wine bar has a casual atmosphere from its twine napkin rings to its menu, which features Venetian tapas, warm pressed panini, and cold finger sandwiches called *tramezzini*. At its best, the warm sausage, mushroom, and broccoli rabe sandwich with gooey Taleggio is comforting, and the cold truffled egg salad sandwich is just what it should be. While late night brings a DJ and more of a barlike atmosphere, there's also a kids' menu—complete with a scoop of chocolate hazelnut pudding you'll want to keep for yourself.

Brooklyn Farmacy, 513 Henry Street between Sackett Street and Union Street; (718) 522-6260; Subway: F, G to Carroll Street; brooklynfarmacy.blogspot.com; $. Adults and children alike cheered when this old-fashioned ice-cream shop moved into the neighborhood. With a stool-lined counter and proper soda "jerks," it's a pleasure to order a sundae topped with fresh fruit or a malted in this nostalgic space. Better still, come on a Saturday morning when they carry **Peter Pan** (p. 171) doughnuts from Greenpoint.

Brooklyn Ice House, 318 Van Brunt Street between Pioneer Street and Visitation Place; (718) 222-1865; B61 bus to Van Brunt Street at Verona Street.; $ No wine bar or fancy cocktail lounge is this. Instead, the Ice House owners kept the rough edges of the former Pioneer BBQ dive intact: Picture wood-paneled walls, TVs, and red vinyl booths as well as arcade games like Big Buck Hunter, and a large backyard full of umbrella-topped tables. The beer list is from around the world, including a large Belgian section you wouldn't expect in such an unpretentious space. They also kept the smoker, and (in addition to bar food like nachos) you can munch on pulled pork or brisket sandwiches on pillowy buns.

Building on Bond, 112 Bond Street between Pacific Street and Atlantic Avenue; (347) 853-8687; Subway: F, G to Bergen Street, or A, C, G to Hoyt-Schermerhorn, or 2, 3 to Hoyt; buildingonbond.com; $$. This restaurant first burst onto the scene at the **Atlantic Antic** (p. 32), where the chef wowed the crowd with pretzel sandwiches filled with braised pork, apple-jicama slaw, and red pepper aioli, as well as a stylish booth that looked a bit like a hip take on a plywood clubhouse. Now, their restaurant's design reflects their cool Antic stand. Picture salvaged fixtures like cabinets designed to hold architecture plans, rustic wood tables, and a time card holder (filled with time cards, of course), as well as pipes fashioned into beer taps. The menu includes their pretzel sandwich, a roasted turkey sandwich on cranberry-walnut bread with apricot-rhubarb spread, as well as new American comfort food like Reuben empanadas and bourbon-soaked chicken wings. And if conventional wisdom says that whenever bacon can be added to mac and cheese, it's clearly the right decision, Building on Bond does not challenge that thought. During the day, the restaurant has free Wi-Fi to cater to the working-from-home crowd, and at night they turn it off, dim the lights, and serve cocktails, including some made with their house-infused vodkas.

Buttermilk Channel, 524 Court Street between Nelson Street and Huntington Street; (718) 852-8490; Subway: F, G to Smith-9th Street; buttermilkchannelnyc.com; $$. This new Southern-influenced hot spot may be named after the channel of water that flows off the East River between Brooklyn and Governor's Island, but there's enough buttermilk used in the menu that it's an apt name. Start with house-made buttermilk-laden ricotta with ramps followed by buttermilk-marinated fried chicken and buttermilk whipped potatoes. The non-buttermilk dishes—maple-roasted almonds, duck

Getting In on a CSA

The concept of the CSA has been around for a while, but in recent years it has certainly grown in popularity in Brooklyn as the farm-to-table movement has exploded. Now it seems just about every neighborhood has one. So what is a CSA? The name stands for Community Supported Agriculture, and it's a club of sorts, a community of neighbors who band together to support local farms and orchards. When you join a CSA, you sign up to buy a "share" of a farm's produce. Each week you are delivered farm-fresh, often organic, fruits and vegetables—a portion of the crop, from the beginning of growing season to the end, which on the East Coast is June through December. Once a week, you go to an appointed spot (in Cobble Hill, that's at the corner of Clinton and Kane), and pick up your box of fruits and vegetables, which costs approximately $20 per week for approximately 6 pounds of fresh produce.

In most CSAs, the crop changes weekly, but you don't get to choose what you want, and the amount of food you get depends on the yield. One week, you may get lavender, strawberries, snap peas, cilantro, lettuce, and radishes; another you may find sweet potatoes, lettuce, cranberry beans, mustard greens, leeks, and red peppers. Some CSAs require members to volunteer to help unload trucks. Many also offer flower shares, free-range egg shares, and canning shares, which is a large quantity of tomatoes for putting up. If you're interested in joining your local organization, be sure to sign up while it's still cold outside—they fill up early (justfood.org/csa).

meat loaf, and bacon-wrapped trout—are pretty good, too. The bread basket consists of warm popovers drizzled with so much honey you'll want to eat them with a fork. They serve only New York State beer, and much of the wine list is from New York, too. One word of advice: Whether you come for Sunday's sweet brunch treats, which include pecan-pie french toast, apple cider doughnuts, and buttermilk pancakes served with warm maple syrup, or for a week-night dinner, be sure to come early.

Chance Asian Bistro & Bar, 223 Smith Street between Butler Street and Baltic Street; (718) 242-1515; Subway: F, G to Bergen Street, or A, C, G to Hoyt-Schermerhorn or 2, 3 to Hoyt; chance cuisine.com; $$. Brooklynites from this part of town often throw up their hands when asked about good Chinese food and send people back to Manhattan's Chinatown, which is, after all, just a few subway stops away. But Chance could hold its own in C-town, and it has a sexy lounge-style decor to boot. Start with dim sum–style appetizers, like steamed dumplings stuffed with corn and shrimp or pan-fried dumplings filled with savory meatball-like ground beef. Follow that with a perfect Peking duck (a miracle of crisp, glossy skin and still-juicy meat, served with shaved scallions, plum sauce,

 and pancakes) or the house special, chicken in a spicy orange sauce served with dried chili peppers and steamed broccoli. It's a tweak on a take-out classic, elevated to the next level.

Char No. 4, 196 Smith Street between Warren Street and Baltic Street; (718) 643-2106; Subway: F, G to Bergen Street, or A, C, G to Hoyt-Schermerhorn, or 2, 3 to Hoyt; charno4.com; $$. It's hard to say what the bigger draw is here—the 150 types of American whiskey behind the bar (not to mention all the foreign varietals), or the house-smoked meats on the menu of Southern dishes. Start with smoked-then-fried pork nuggets, the house-cured lamb pastrami, or the house-smoked bacon, and follow that with a BLT or house-smoked beef sausage links served with mustard potato salad. Not a smoked meat fan? They also have shrimp and grits, and crispy Canadian-style cheddar cheese curds with pimiento sauce. All together, it's a feast of rich and porky goodness that's worth the cholesterol.

Chef's Table at Brooklyn Fare, 200 Schermerhorn Street between Hoyt Street and Bond Street; (718) 243-0050; Subway: F, G to Bergen Street or A, C, G to Hoyt-Schermerhorn or 2, 3 to Hoyt; brooklynfare.com; $$$$. This is the little 18-seat restaurant that could, a hot spot attached to a grocery store that quickly went from an unknown gem to an international superstar after it won three Michelin stars, beating out every other restaurant in the borough for the honors. Reservations feel nearly impossible to land, so you'll have to be patient and persistent if you want to check it off your culinary to-do list. Dishes include luxe ingredients like truffles and Wagyu, and the prix-fixe, 20-course dinner here is said to be as epic as the process of getting a res. Truth? I am not that patient, and this is the only restaurant in the book that I haven't dined at.

Eton, 359 Sackett Street between Hoyt Street and Smith Street; (718) 222-2999; Subway: F, G to Carroll Street; $. This tiny shop looks a bit like a Chinese take-out place and sells just 4 things— handmade dumplings, noodles, bubble tea, and Hawaiian shaved ice. Since the dumplings are made to order, then pan-seared and steamed, it usually takes awhile to get yours, so be sure to call ahead to order. (You never know when a Little League team is going to show up right before you.) The dumplings come in 3 varieties: vegetable, chicken and mushroom, and pork and beef. They're served with a variety of dipping sauces, like black vinegar and Sriracha topped with chili oil, but don't miss the house-made salted plum sauce. While you wait, take some time picking out your perfect shaved ice combination. Chan fell in love with the stuff on his honeymoon in Hawaii and modeled his icy treats after the ones at Matsumoto on Oahu's North Shore. It comes in basics like cherry and lemon as well as Asian flavors including green tea and lychee. You can get your ice topped with mochi, azuki beans, or sweetened condensed milk. Fortunately, it seems hard to go wrong here. See recipe for Eton's **Pork & Beef Dumplings** on p. 283.

Ferdinando's Focacceria, 151 Union Street between Hicks Street and Columbia Street; (718) 855-1545; Subway: F, G to Carroll Street; $$. This quirky little 100-year-old Italian place makes otherwise hard-to-find Sicilian dishes like *panelle* (chickpea pancakes) and *vastedda* topped with fresh, creamy ricotta cheese. They also have tasty *arancini,* the rice balls that are filled with peas, tomato sauce, and ground beef that are common in Carroll Gardens but not always as tasty as these. Unfortunately, the place is a bit out of the way—in the Columbia Waterfront district, on the far side of the BQE from the subway—and keeps limited hours.

Fort Defiance, 365 Van Brunt Street between Dikeman Street and Coffey Street; (347) 453-6672; B61 bus to Van Brunt Street at Wolcott Street; fortdefiancebrooklyn.com; $$. The pastries here may come from **Colson Patisserie** (p. 122) and **Trois Pommes** (p. 132) in Park Slope, but the muffuletta is all theirs. This New Orleans–style sandwich is only served at lunch, and it's a true feast. Picture sopressata, mortadella, capocollo, provolone, and olive salad piled high on fresh focaccia-style bread that they have commissioned especially  from **Royal Crown Paneantico** (p. 220) bakery. Order yours with a chocolate egg cream, made with a sophisticated on-tap seltzer system that filters the water, chills it three times, then carbonates it. The seltzer is so powerful that, once it is poured into the drink, no additional stirring is required to create that classic foamy head.

Frankies 457 Spuntino, 457 Court Street between 4th Place and Luquer Street; (718) 403-0033; Subway: F, G to Smith-9th Street; frankiesspuntino.com; $$. This small neighborhood hangout was opened by a couple of local chefs named Frankie in 2004. Since then, they have expanded into Manhattan and have grown the Carroll Gardens location to include a garden and a backyard special events space—and they also bottle and distribute their own Sicilian olive oil. All of that is almost enough to distract from how charming their little restaurant, with its exposed brick walls and banged-tin ceiling, is and how good their simple, homespun Italian menu can be: Order escarole soup, house-made gnocchi or linguine, and antipasto platters laden with **Faicco's** (p. 214) capocollo and aged provolone. Or come at lunch and get a sandwich filled with tender meatballs or broccoli rabe and Faicco's sausage layered on Grandaisy's rosemary bread.

The Good Fork, 391 Van Brunt Street between Coffey Street and Van Dyke Street; (718) 643-6636; B61 bus to Van Brunt Street at Van Dyke Street; goodfork.com; $$$. This eclectic restaurant serves up the only fine dining experience in otherwise casual Red Hook. Even here, while the food is artfully prepared and the wine is carefully poured, you don't have to dress up too much. But the menu is pricier and fancier than anything else in the neighborhood. Dishes span the globe, with fish-and-chips sitting next to house-made papardelle with lamb ragout, but the best choices have an Asian influence. Start with handmade pork-and-chive dumplings or mussels steamed in kaffir- and lemongrass-scented coconut milk, followed by Korean steak-and-eggs with kimchee. And be sure to request a table in the lovely, overgrown garden—as raw and elegant as the restaurant itself.

The Grocery, 288 Smith Street between Sackett Street and Union Street; 718-596-3335; Subway: F, G to Carroll Street; thegrocery restaurant.com; $$$. Request a table in the low-key, unpretentious garden (yes, you're willing to wait) and dine on upscale takes on grilled food, a modern-day, sophisticated take on a backyard cookout. Appetizers are seasonal, but may include grilled asparagus topped with charred onions and house-smoked bacon; entrees include grilled trout, pork loin, and lamb chops. Dessert is equally homey, from the crisp apple tart to the homemade coconut or sour cream–lemongrass sorbet. This was once the best meal on Smith Street, and prices are high—perhaps too high for the casual service and the occasional misstep, such as a risotto that never quite came together. But the staff is warm, and meals often include several *amuse-bouche,* which might be crispy little potato croquettes and miniature silver jiggers of leek-and-potato soup, as well as tiny silver plates of hibiscus sorbet.

Henry Public, 329 Henry Street between Atlantic Avenue and Pacific Street; (718) 852-8630; Subway: F, G to Bergen Street or 2, 3, 4, 5, R to Borough Hall; henrypublic.com; $$. This Prohibition-style speakeasy serves wonderful cocktails, which is the main reason to go, but the food is worth a look, too, though choices are limited. Choose the "hamburger sandwich," made with grass-fed beef and served with juniper-scented pickles—topped with bacon and cheese, if you choose to add them—or a sandwich filled with milk-braised turkey leg meat. The dessert menu is simple, too: They offer *ebelskivers,* which are Danish filled pancakes, and they serve them with a rum-spiked caramel sauce that packs a punch—they're the perfect pairing for an after-dinner cocktail.

Hibino, 333 Henry Street between Atlantic Avenue and Pacific Street; (718) 260-8052; Subway: F, G to Bergen Street or 2, 3, 4, 5, R to Borough Hall; hibino-brooklyn.com; $$. It was a Japanese friend who insisted that this sleeper was worth a second look, and she was right. Hibino makes its own tofu daily and uses it in 5 preparations, from a deep-fried chunk served in dashi broth to a Kyoto-style spring roll wrapped in tofu skin. But it's the *obanzai* (tapas-style appetizers) specials that keep my friend going back. Start with a plate of tempura-fried asparagus, fried crisp and topped with matcha green tea salt, or a potato-curry croquette that's been coated in panko and served with savory *tonkatsu* sauce. Their new takes on, for example, a chirashi bowl will either please you (the rice is covered with shredded tamago-style cooked egg and topped with green peas, sea urchin, and salmon roe!) or disappoint (such tiny pieces of sashimi!). For dessert, consider the green tea mochi when they are available. They come laced with wasabi, adding an interesting bite to an otherwise sweet ending.

Home/Made, 293 Van Brunt Street between King Street and Pioneer Street; (347) 223-4135; B61 bus to Van Brunt Street at Verona Street; homemadebklyn.com; $. This tiny, feminine, white restaurant looks a bit like a flower shop, with white linen couches and benches; vases, bottles, and candelabra in the window; and lilies on all the mismatched tables—but it smells like warm melted gruyère. That gooey cheesiness is not what my house smells like, but I would be happy to call this place home. Breakfast dishes include truffled eggs with Parmesan cheese and a wild mushroom and fontina scramble, both made with locally raised Red Hook eggs. At dinnertime, the place still has the welcoming smell of toasted cheese, with a menu that features fondue (choose from a gruyère-emmentaler combo or the more unusual Gorgonzola with dried fruit), a ham-and-cheese tart, and a rich truffled grilled cheese, plus the added bonus of a lovely cassis Lambic on tap. Tip: In summer the best table in the house is the lone one in the backyard. Snag it, and order up some berry-infused lemonade or the citrus-infused ice tea.

Hope & Anchor, 347 Van Brunt Street between Wolcott Street and Dikeman Street; (718) 237-0276; B61 bus to Van Brunt Street at Wolcott Street; $. This retro diner was one of the first in the area, and it gained a loyal following with young artist types who were happy to have a hangout of their own. Breakfast is standard egg-and-bacon fare, the lunch menu includes plenty of burgers, and dinner features hearty faves like chicken potpie, mac and cheese topped with house-made bread crumbs, and meat loaf with mashed potatoes. Pick a dessert, including apple pie, from the spinning glass case. Just remember: They're most famous for their drag queen karaoke nights.

Joya, 215 Court Street between Wyckoff Street and Warren Street; (718) 222-3484; Subway F, G to Bergen Street or 2, 3, 4, 5, R to Borough Hall; $. Beloved as much for its low prices and lovely back-yard garden as for the food itself, Joya really makes you work for it. This no-reservation restaurant often has killer waits, and while they say they have delivery, it takes so long to get them on the phone that you might as well go there. Also, once inside, the steam and clang of the open kitchen fills the room as much as the DJ's loud music, making it impossible to hear your dining companions over the din. All of that aside, Joya is not authentic Thai food in the strictest sense. Few dishes here are redolent of chilies, lemongrass, or galangal. So what's all the fuss? Joya is all about freshness and a light hand. Each dish tastes bright, with crisp green vegetables and just-done seafood that's still tender. Many of the entrees, from shrimp in basil sauce to chicken with broccoli in oyster sauce, taste like stir-fry done right. Top yours off with their Thai ice tea cocktail—a sweet mix of Thai tea, sweetened condensed milk, and vodka.

Kevin's, 277A Van Brunt Street between Visitation Place and Pioneer Street; (718) 596-8335; B61 bus to Van Brunt Street at Verona Street; mooreparties.com; $$. On weekend mornings, this 25-seat diner fills up with a mix of hipsters sporting hangovers and mussed hairdos left over from the night before, young parents with their up-at-dawn offspring, and fanny-pack-toting middle-aged couples fresh off a cruise ship. The fluffy buttermilk pancakes

Flea Markets Go Online

Sure, it sounds circular to go online and shop for locally made treats, but you can learn a lot about local food artisans that way. Web-based **Etsy.com** launched in 2005 and quickly became the leading marketplace for handmade and homemade goods—an online flea market, if you will. Soon after, bakers and jam makers joined in with the knitters and necklace beaders.

Brooklynites, many of whom look for handcrafted items, have become big fans. Today, you can find beadwork and screen-printed T-shirts from around the borough listed on Etsy, but you can also find some of the city's handmade foods there. What's offered changes from week to week and spikes around the holidays. But on a regular basis you can find local legends such as Whimsy and Spice, who sell their entire lines—from marshmallows to brownies and fudge—on the site. Another website to check out is the more recent phenomenon, **Foodzie .com.** It may be smaller, but they only carry homemade food. Here, the majority of the New York State offerings are out of Brooklyn, from **Margaret Palca Bakes**'s (p. 69) rugalach from Carroll Gardens to Peeled Snacks's dried fruit from Park Slope and Nanny's Cucina marinara sauce from Bushwick.

have a tangy zip and ooze sweet blueberries from every pore. Eggs Benedict is done the Maryland way, with a crab cake instead of Canadian bacon. And coffee, served in massive headache-banishing french presses, is strong, dark, and made from rich **Stumptown** (p.

77) beans; it's an eye-opener that you won't soon forget. At dinner, the menu contains several lobster dishes using crustaceans from the neighboring **Red Hook Lobster Pound** (p. 73).

Ki Sushi, 122 Smith Street between Dean Street and Pacific Street; (718) 935-0575; Subway: F, G to Bergen Street or A, C, G to Hoyt-Schermerhorn or 2, 3 to Hoyt; ki-sushi.com; $$. Fans say, "Sit at the sushi bar, and go for the *omakase*" at this sleeper Japanese restaurant, which some neighborhood regulars call the best in Brooklyn. Whether or not you think it's the best in Brooklyn, the *omakase* (which starts at just $33 per person) is a steal. Letting the chef select the freshest catch of the day for you may mean you get picks that have been air shipped from Tokyo's Tsukiji Market. Or go your own way and start with edamame, rock shrimp tempura, or crispy pork gyoza, followed by fresh sushi sashimi or creative *maki* rolls such as lobster-tuna rolls topped with a dollop of caviar or tuna-avocado rolls wrapped in smooth slices of peach that mimic the texture of sashimi. Yes, it's canned peach, but you have to give them points for creativity.

Lucali, 575 Henry Street between Carroll Street and First Place; (718) 858-4086; Subway: F, G to Carroll Street; $$. This tiny, cash-only, BYOB newcomer has taken the pizza world by storm. When the owner bought the place, he did so to save what was originally his childhood-favorite soda fountain and candy shop from becoming yet another bank or drugstore. Then, he lovingly restored the building and taught himself to make pizza. And, boy, did he learn fast: In 2009 Lucali won *GQ* magazine's second-best pizza in the country award, and the highest ranking in New York. Unfortunately, it can be hard to get a table, with waits stretching up to 2 hours on weekends. (Celebs like Beyonce and Jay-Z are rumored to practically shut down the place when they get cravings.) Most locals call ahead to get put on the list, and you should too, but you still won't get elbow room or escape the massive oven's smoke. The menu, too, is small—wood-fired, brick-oven pizza, with a limited number of toppings (fresh basil, pepperoni, olives, mushrooms) and calzones. But the pizza itself is spectacular. It's thin with a charred and chewy crust and an olive-oil scent. You'll dream of it, even if you won't get a table again anytime soon.

Lunetta, 116 Smith Street between Pacific Street and Dean Street; (718) 488-6269; Subway: F, G to Bergen Street or A, C, G to Hoyt-Schermerhorn or 2, 3 to Hoyt; lunetta-ny.com. While there are plenty of Manhattan restaurants that have opened Brooklyn offshoots, this is the rare restaurant that made its fortune here and opened a Manhattan location later. Unfortunately, despite its popularity, the Manhattan outpost closed. Perhaps that's because Lunetta is a classically Brooklyn take on upscale Italian fare, with casual service and casual diners ordering somewhat fancier food made of carefully chosen ingredients. Appetizers include bruschetta topped with house-made ricotta and honey or house-cured mackerel with farro, and entrees are highlighted by pastas topped with, say, Berkshire pork ragout or rapini and house-made sausage. These dishes are rich and satisfying, and they keep the locals coming back for more.

Marco Polo Ristorante & Enoteca, 345 Court Street between Union Street and President Street; (718) 852-5015; Subway: F, G to Carroll Street; marcopoloristorante.com; $$$. This red-sauce Italian spot feels like Old Brooklyn—the walls are adorned with murals of Italy, the music tends toward Sinatra classics, and there's valet parking for diners driving in from Bay Ridge, Staten Island, or New Jersey. The menu is equally Italian-American traditional: Start with the house-made mozzarella served with roasted peppers and basil, roasted artichokes stuffed with bread crumbs, oysters Rockefeller, or a bowl of pasta fagioli soup, followed by the house-made lobster ravioli or veal Marsala, and finish the meal with a proper espresso. There are no surprises here, but that's not what you came for, right?

Mile End, 97A Hoyt Street between Atlantic Avenue and Pacific Street; (718) 852-7510; Subway: F, G to Bergen Street or 2, 3 to Hoyt or A, C, G to Hoyt-Schermerhorn; mileendbrooklyn.com; $$. Montreal-style smoked meat arrives in Brooklyn at this small sandwich shop and lunch counter. In addition to sandwiches and platters of smoked meat (which is a cross between corned beef and brisket) you can also order *poutine*—a Québécois treat of french fries smothered in rich gravy and cheese curds—and Canadian-style bagels (which are smaller and crunchier than the New York variety) brought in from Montreal.

Petite Crevette, 144 Union Street between Hicks Street and Columbia Street; Enter on Hicks Street between President Street and Union Street; (718) 855-2632; Subway: F, G to Carroll Street; $$. This BYOB, no-reservations, cash-only seafood restaurant gets as many rave reviews for its prices as for its French-influenced menu of simply prepared fish. The catch is displayed on ice in the glass case at the front of the restaurant, so you can see it on your way in (though, fortunately, there is no "pick your fish" gimmick here). Continue to the back room, a former garden shop, and dine among flea-market finds like porcelain pitchers, a stone fountain, an old sewing table, and a turn-of-the-last-century stove that now serves as an end table, all pulled together with a garland made of feathers that winds its way around the room. The menu is simpler: Appetizers include an heirloom tomato salad made of some of the prettiest red stunners you've seen. Best of all, the whole grilled fish, which can include porgy or snapper, is done with  a light touch, as are the pan-seared soft-shell crabs. Or, for a more casual meal, order a tuna burger, which is flame broiled and served with wasabi mayo and perfectly crispy frites.

Prime Meats, 465 Court Street between 4th Place and Luquer Street; (718) 254-0327; Subway: F, G to Smith-9th Street; frankspm .com; $$$. This restaurant, owned by the team behind **Frankies 457 Spuntino** (p. 47), looks as New Brooklyn as can be: Think exposed brick walls, a mirror behind the bar, antique brass light fixtures, and an ornately hammered banged-tin ceiling—the bartender even wears a vest. They serve breakfast and lunch, but at night the spot transforms into a candlelit lounge serving Prohibition-era  cocktails like Sazeracs and bar nibbles like pâté with strong grainy mustard or weisswurst sausages with house-made soft pretzels. Stay for dinner, and you can order up the rich choucroute garni platter of pork belly and knockwurst atop pleasantly mild sauerkraut, or the juicy grass-fed Creekstone Farms Black Angus burger, served on a house-made bun with house-made malolactic fermented dill pickles. The service is friendly and casual (sometimes a little too casual, like when drinks come out after you've finished your appetizers), but the food is worth the wait.

Sam's Italian Cuisine, 238 Court Street between Baltic Street and Kane Street; (718) 596-3458; Subway: F, G to Bergen Street or 2, 3, 4, 5, R to Borough Hall; $. Yes, the sign says steaks and chops, but it's Sam's pizza that has garnered a following. The restaurant has been here since the 1930s, and the old school decor is a bit fusty (picture red-checked plastic tablecloths, red vinyl booths, and wood paneling). The father and son who own it are clearly neighborhood characters, as are the slow and gruff grandfatherly waiters. But the pizza is thin, crispy, and worth seeking out. Top yours with ricotta, anchovies, pepperoni, or bright green olives, and remember—the sign in the window says no slices, and they mean it.

Saul, 140 Smith Street between Bergen Street and Dean Street; (718) 935-9844; Subway: F, G to Bergen Street or A, C, G to Hoyt-Schermerhorn or 2, 3 to Hoyt; saulrestaurant.com; $$$. It's little surprise how seafood heavy this menu is, considering that this chef-owned restaurant's proprietor trained with Eric Ripert. The setting is casual, with exposed brick walls and a small space that easily fills with noise. That said, the service is polished, and the dishes themselves are surprisingly precious—appetizers include small portions of seared mackerel and raw *hamachi,* and entrees feature a small square of line-caught cod topped with a poached egg, as well as roasted sweetbreads.

Seersucker, 329 Smith Street between Carroll Street amd President Street; (718) 422-0444; Subway: F, G to Carroll Street; seersuckerbrooklyn.com; $$$. Brooklyn has fallen in love with Southern food, and Seersucker is one of the best. The menu is predictable—in the best possible way. Look for shrimp and grits, chicken and dumplings, ham with biscuits, crispy fried chicken that fills the plate, and pimento cheese. Fortunately, this popular spot finally takes reservations on OpenTable.com.

Two 8 Two Burger Bar, 282 Atlantic Avenue between Smith Street and Boerum Place; (718) 596-2282; Subway: F, G to Bergen

Street or A, C, G to Hoyt-Schermerhorn or 2, 3 to Hoyt; two8two burger.com; $. This burger and fry shop is a welcome addition to the neighborhood, with great onion rings and crisp fries. The menu doesn't stray too far from the basics, but they're exactly what you would want them to be, and the burgers themselves are made from meat from **Los Paisanos** (p. 68), the fabulous butcher around the corner on Smith Street. They open at noon, but the lovely outdoor space is a great place to be on a summer night

Van Horn Sandwich Shop, 231 Court Street between Baltic Street and Warren Street; (718) 596-9707; Subway: F, G to Bergen Street; vanhornbrooklyn.com; $. Brooklyn is mad for Van Horn. Order up one of their tasty sandiwches, such as the the fried chicken, cornmeal-crusted catfish, North Carolina–style pulled pork, or pimento cheese, with a side of hush puppies or mac and cheese. The cute, polished space also has an adorable backyard that's a lovely place to sip a cocktail in the summer.

Specialty Stores, Markets & Producers

Baked, 359 Van Brunt Street between Wolcott Street and Dikeman Street; (718) 222-0345; B61 bus to Van Brunt Street at Wolcott Street; bakednyc.com; $. This bakery and coffee shop's design theme is a modern nod to a wilderness lodge (wood-paneled walls,

raw-wood benches, wrought-iron stag heads, cupcakes topped with coconut "snow" and plastic reindeer)—possibly a witty nod to the idea that Red Hook, which is still developing, is Brooklyn's Western frontier. Aside from the neighborhood spirit and sense of humor, they're best known for their malted chocolate cupcakes (decorated with malted milk balls) and their seasonal marshmallows (think cinnamon in fall, peppermint in winter). They also make whoopee pies (strawberry in summer and pumpkin in fall), house-made granola, and salted caramel brownies, which contain a mix of Valrhona and Callebaut chocolates. They do everything by hand, and for the brownies they don't even use mixers. According to the owners, that's why they're dense and fudgy rather than cakey. See recipe for Baked's **Sweet & Salty Cake** on p. 300.

Betty Bakery, 448 Atlantic Avenue between Bond Street and Nevins Street; (718) 246-2402; Subway: F, G to Bergen Street or A, C, G to Hoyt-Schermerhorn or 2, 3 to Hoyt; bettybakery.com. Ellen Baumwoll and Cheryl Kleinman have been baking some of the city's best wedding cakes for years, but the store itself is new. Lined up on the counter of the '50s-inspired bake shop, you'll find apple pie, rustic fruit tarts, scones, lemon squares, delicate petits fours, and butter cookies, but the signature here will always be the chocolate cake, which includes Valrhona and red velvet. Both owners still have their very well-respected wedding cake businesses—Bijou Doux and Cheryl Kleinman Cakes, respectively—and the window display is often filled with striped, polka-dotted, and star-covered white cakes with pretty pastel decorations.

Bien Cuit, 120 Smith Street between Dean Street and Pacific Street; (718) 852-0200; Subway: F, G to Bergen Street; biencuit .com; $. From breads to pastry, Bien Cuit fufills the carb-starved needs of the neighborhood. It bakes up loaves of *pain de campagne* that remind me of the semester I spent in Paris like no other bakery in New York does. Come at breakfast for twice-baked, brandy-spiked almond croissants that set the standard, or at lunch for baguette sandwiches on their spectacular bread. Yes, the fillings are interesting (their BLT uses lamb bacon, the croque monsieur is spiked with pink peppercorns, and their meatball sub is a mix of venison meatballs, Taleggio cheese, and lingonberry jam), but it's the bread that will bring you back again and again.

Blue Marble, 196 Court Street between Wyckoff Street and Congress Street; (718) 858-0408; Subway: F, G to Bergen Street or 2, 3, 4, 5, R, to Borough Hall; bluemarbleicecream.com. This is what every neighborhood needs—an old-fashioned ice-cream shop that makes all their own ice creams and sorbets in seasonal flavors from the freshest, organic ingredients. The decor is farmhouse inspired (with whitewashed bead board, salvaged fencing, and plenty of porcelain chickens), and they have benches out front and a patio out back. Choose from strawberry or blackberry ice cream in summer, maple or pumpkin in fall, and peppermint around the holidays. It's all creamy and not-too-sweet, as are the limited-edition flavors, like the sought-after banana-chocolate-fluff that has neighborhood fans checking the board each day on their way home from work. Order yours in a milk shake, a sundae, or topped with interesting syrups like balsamic, maple, or caramel sauce made by neighboring **Nunu Chocolates** (p. 70). Blue Marble also has a Prospect Heights shop (186 Underhill Avenue; 718-399-6926).

Cafe Pedlar, 210 Court Street between Wyckoff Street and Warren Street; (718) 855-7129; Subway F, G to Bergen Street or 2, 3, 4, 5, R, to Borough Hall; cafepedlar.com; $. The reason to come here is simple: It's not the small cafe space, with its handful of tables and banged-tin ceiling. It's not the desserts and pastries, like olive oil cake and biscotti. It's the **Stumptown** (p. 77) coffee. Created in Seattle, Duane Sorenson's beans are the true best of the West Coast, and now the rich, not-at-all-acidic brew is available at a few select outposts in New York, including this, Cobble Hill's most serious coffeehouse. One sip of a latte, espresso, or ice coffee, and you'll be a convert too— there just aren't any baristas in these parts that can compete. And that explains the long lines, both in the mornings and on weekends. It also explains why, after opening this one, they also opened one in Manhattan.

Caputo Fine Foods, 460 Court Street between 3rd Place and 4th Place; (718) 855-8852; Subway: F, G to Carroll Street. A great source for all things Italian, Caputo serves house-made fresh mozzarella

in a variety of sizes, and their own fresh and dried pasta in every shape you can imagine. Add that to the wide array of olives, olive oils, and imported Italian foodstuffs, and you'll find everything you need to create an Italian dinner at home. Or come at lunchtime for the cured meats, sliced cheeses, and the impressive Italian sandwiches they make with them.

Caputo's Bakery, 329 Court Street between Union Street and Sackett Street; (718) 875-6871; Subway: F, G to Carroll Street. From the moment you walk in and see the giant ovens just past the cash register, you'll be devoted. Their Italian breads, which come seeded or plain, are fresh and often warm from the oven. They also make a dense and chewy ciabatta, olive loaf, and onion focaccia, all of which have their own fan clubs. Your favorite will probably be whichever is fresh from the oven when you arrive.

Cobblestone Foods, 199 Court Street between Wyckoff Street and Bergen Street; (718) 222-1661; Subway: F, G to Bergen Street or 2, 3, 4, 5, R, to Borough Hall; cobblestonecatering.com. This tiny shop carries a wide variety of prepared foods from around the city, as well as cooked foods they make themselves, an impressively stocked cheese counter, and a rotisserie full of chicken. They carry **Gorilla Coffee** (p. 125), which is roasted in Park Slope, as well as ice cream and yogurt from Ronnybrook Farms and cheese from 3-Corner Field Farms in the Hudson Valley.

Court Pastry Shop, 298 Court Street between Douglass Street and Degraw Street; (718) 875-4820; Subway: F, G to Bergen Street. Walk into this Italian pastry shop, and you'll feel like you're stepping into the past. The smell of anise is strong in the air, and the sound of Old Brooklyn accents calling out to each other from the kitchen are a reminder that the Old World mingles with the new here. The highlights change with the seasons (Sicilian cookies at Christmas, *sfingi* for St. Joseph's day in March), but they also sell all of the Italian classics: ricotta-filled cannoli, licorice-scented anisette toast, butter cookies in a rainbow of colors, and *sfogliatelle,* a cream puff of sorts filled with ricotta cream and candied orange peel. They have a cult following for the lobster tails that are available only on weekends, and for their near-mythical apple turnovers.

On hot summer days, though, the most popular order changes from the warm and baked to the cold and refreshing. The line often winds down the sidewalk as adults and children alike wait for water ice. The pistachio is shockingly green, but the lemon is properly tart, and the custard is rich enough to keep you coming back for more.

D'Amico Food, 309 Court Street between Degraw Street and Sackett Street; (718) 875-5403; Subway: F, G to Bergen Street; damicofoods.com. Sure, they make sandwiches here and sell an assortment of Italian imported cookies and candies. But there's no denying what's special here—the coffee. The smell, and sometimes the smoke, of the beans swirling around the roaster in the front of the store hits your nose the minute you walk in the door. At this 60-plus-year-old shop, you can ask what they've just finished roasting that day, or choose from a large variety of regular and decaf, light and dark roasts, beans by the pound, and flavored coffees like cinnamon, vanilla, hazelnut, and, at the holidays, eggnog. Or select one of the blends from the Brownstone Collection, which have been named after Brooklyn neighborhoods.

Defonte's of Brooklyn, 379 Columbia Street between Coles Street and Luquer Street; (718) 625-8052; B61 bus to Van Brunt Street at Commerce Street; defontesofbrooklyn.com; $. Unless you're a construction worker, you may feel out of place when you first walk into this small take-out sandwich shop near the BQE. Shrug it off, because these sandwiches are worth the hike. Come at breakfast for egg-and-potato sandwiches, or at lunch for a meatball sub, or a roast beef sandwich topped with fresh mozzarella, lightly fried eggplant, and a spoonful of oregano-flecked jus. Defonte's would be the perfect Super Bowl or game-night treat, if only they were open on Sunday or in the evening. Insider note: There was an episode of NBC's hit show *30 Rock* that featured the Teamsters catering lunch for the crew from a secret sandwich shop. Yep, this is the place.

F. Monteleone's Cafe, 355 Court Street between President Street and Union Street; (718) 852-5600; Subway: F, G to Carroll Street.

This Carroll Gardens Italian pastry shop is an institution, and it serves a wide array of Italian sweets—gelato, breads, wedding and First Holy Communion cakes, and pastries. But while the Sicilian-style cheesecake by the pound is memorable and the lard bread competes with the best in the neighborhood, it's the dozens of varieties of Italian cookies that stand out. The delicate chocolate lace cookies are light and crispy and drizzled with chocolate, the tender *ricciarelli,* a Sienese almond cookie, are soft and fragrant with marzipan, and the butter cookies with their colored sprinkles are equally rich and decadent.

Fairway Market, 500 Van Brunt Street between Reed Street and Erie Basin; (718) 694-6868; B61 bus to the end of the line; fairway market.com; $. It sounds a little odd to send someone to a grocery store for lunch, but this is no ordinary grocery store. Fairway is beloved by New Yorkers across the city, known for its excellent produce and large inventory as much as for the grannies and moms wielding carts and strollers as weapons. It's crowded, but if you make your way through the Brooklyn location, and out the back door, you'll find a lovely waterfront terrace with a spectacular view of the Statue of Liberty. Grab a cup of coffee, a pastry, or a sandwich (the lobster rolls have a cult following for their bargain price) and take in the view and the salty air. Whether or not you decide to troll the aisles for local favorites, like Red Jacket Orchards Fuji apple juice, Ronnybrook creamline milk, Sarabeth's berry-packed preserves, and Old Chatham Hudson Valley sheep's milk yogurt, it's still worth visiting.

G. Esposito & Sons Pork Store, 357 Court Street between Union Street and President Street; (718) 875-6863; Subway: F, G to Carroll Street. This butcher shop, circa 1922, has a giant plastic pink pig by the door, and there's no denying that pork is what they do best. From sausages to the house-made sopressata and salami, they sell pork and, well, things that go well with pork, like their own aged provolone and fresh and smoked mozzarella. They also have a wide variety of peppers, pasta, and pasta sauces as well as fat, juicy green olives stuffed with garlic. Looking for something a little more obscure, like fresh lard for biscuits or the perfect pie dough? Yeah, they have that, too.

Los Paisanos Meat Market, 162 Smith Street between Bergen Street and Wyckoff Street; (718) 855-2641; Subway: F, G to Bergen Street or A, C, G to Hoyt-Schermerhorn or 2, 3 to Hoyt; lospaisanos meatmarket.com. Los Paisanos is really two great shops in one: a butcher shop with a dedicated following and a fabulous sandwich shop. The meat selection includes a wide variety of free-range, organic, and locally grown choices. In the window, you'll see aged porterhouse steaks and marinated pork shoulders. They also carry the popular Niman Ranch bacon and Berkshire pork sausage, as well as exotic meats like frog legs, venison chops, and ground ostrich—and their own house-made duck sausages. On your way out, order an Italian cold-cut sandwich, topped with prosciutto, mortadella, capocollo, or sopressata, served on a seeded baguette.

Margaret Palca Bakes, 191 Columbia Street between Degraw Street and Sackett Street; (718) 802-9771; Subway: F, G to Carroll Street; margaretpalcabakes.com. This tiny bakery is best known for its rugalach, which come in chocolate, apricot, and raspberry flavors. But there's way more to the place than just rugalach: They also sell granola, several types of brownies, plenty of cookies, and, at Christmastime, elaborate gingerbread houses covered in gumdrops. The shop does breakfast and lunch, too, but it seems most people are here for the baked goods. If you can't get to this store in the Columbia Waterfront district, you can also buy these treats at shops throughout the five boroughs.

Mazzola Bakery, 192 Union Street between Henry Street and Clinton Street; (718) 643-1719; Subway: F, G to Carroll Street. Mazzola is best known for baking the best of the neighborhood's famed lard bread, an Italian bread made with lard and filled with salami, provolone, and lots of black pepper. (It makes a spectacular egg sandwich and a memorable hostess gift at dinner parties.) Of course, they also make great seeded and plain Italian bread, as well as Tuscan and olive loaves. Many neighborhood residents talk fondly of smelling the bread baking from the open side door when they return home late at night, since the bakery opens early in the morning and bakes overnight. Convince the baker to sell you a hot loaf, and you'll agree that there's no better midnight snack.

Red Hook Ball Fields

What first started out as a few grills by the soccer fields has turned into a summerlong food festival. Each Saturday and Sunday from May through October, a dozen or so trucks line the ball field, serving mostly Central and South American treats. The silver *huarache* truck always has a long line for these super-size wraps, which come on warm corn tortillas filled with, say, spicy pork, lettuce, tomato, cilantro, sour cream, and crumbly *queso fresco*. Take yours to the truck's salsa bar where you can choose from a rainbow of hot sauces—red, green, orange, and an almost-brown one filled with large peppers and chunks of onions. Next door, Victor and Ana's Blended Wonders offers creamy horchata, a sweet rice-milk drink, as well as strawberry milk shakes, sliced fruit (papaya, mango), and *elote,* which is grilled corn on the cob dipped in mayo then topped with cheese and chili powder. The *agua fresca* truck serves watermelon, tamarind, and *jamaica* (made with dried hibiscus blossoms) drinks that beat the humidity.

Sure, there are also Guatemalan tamales, an Ecuadorian ceviche truck that has empanadas, and a Guatemalan truck serving up chile

Nunu Chocolates, 529 Atlantic Avenue between 3rd Avenue and 4th Avenue; (917) 776-7102; Subway: G to Fulton or C to Lafayette or 2, 3, 4, 5, N, Q, R, B, D to Atlantic-Pacific; nunuchocolates .com. It's hard to resist this tiny chocolate shop's hand-dipped salt caramels, which are enrobed in chocolate and topped with chunky crystals of fleur de sel. They're expensive, sure (a box of four is

rellenos, but no matter how hot it is, there's always a long line at El Olomega, a Salvadorian truck that's famous for warm *papusas*. These grilled-to-order corn cakes can be stuffed with milky white cheese and a dozen other fillings, including black beans, spinach, loroco flowers, pork, chicken, beef, or any combination thereof, all topped with pickled red onions and *crema*. They also sell interesting sides, such as homemade chicharrónes (fried pork skin that puffs up in oil.) After a wait in the always-long lines, you'll feel victorious as you take your treats to the picnic tables. Just consider yourself warned: The hot sauces are hot, no matter which cart you choose from, and some will flame a fire too big for any *agua fresca* to quench. Also, this is definitely a place in which you want to follow the wisdom of the crowds. As one friend said, "Once I was hungry and went to a different *papusa* stand that didn't have a line. I learned my lesson—good things come to those who wait."

Red Hook Ball Fields, Louis J. Valentino Park at Clinton Street and Bay Street; B61 bus to Van Brunt and Van Dyke; redhookfoodvendors .com; $.

$7), but they are truly decadent. The shop also sells more playful items, like the soft caramel lollipops that are molded in the shape of a star and drenched in chocolate. Also, check out the organic raspberry–filled chocolates and ones filled with espresso brandy made from local Crop

to Cup Coffee. All of their rich chocolate treats are dark chocolate and made with Evans Farms cream from upstate New York. You can sometimes find Nunu Chocolates at the **Brooklyn Flea market** (p. 97), where the chocolate-covered cocoa nibs are a hit. (And, also at the Flea, Kumquat Cupcakery sells cupcakes festooned with the nibs.) Nunu added a bar in the Atlantic Avenue space, too, and the shop serves flights of beer and wine paired with their chocolates. See recipe for Nunu's **Espresso-Brandy Truffles** on p. 304.

One Girl Cookies, 68 Dean Street between Boerum Place and Smith Street; (212) 675-4996; Subway: F, G to Bergen Street or 2, 3, 4, 5, R to Borough Hall; onegirlcookies.com. This little bake shop made an instant splash with its pretty decor and sweet little baked goods. Now, their caramel-chocolate-shortbread bars and whoopee pies, in chocolate or pumpkin with cream cheese filling, are sold all over town. They make marshmallows, macaroons, and meringues, as well as custom cakes in sweet flavors like almond with dulce de leche filling and banana cake with coconut buttercream frosting. See recipe for One Girl Cookies' **Fresh Apricot Cake** on p. 306.

Red Hook Farmers' Market at Added Value Farm, 590 Columbia Street between Sigourney Street and Halleck Street; B61 bus to Van Brunt and Van Dyke; added-value.org. You have to time this weekly Saturday morning market at the Red Hook Community Farm just right: It's only open from 9 a.m. to 3 p.m., and only from July through Nov. Get lucky, and you'll be able to buy arugula, cucumbers, and collards grown just a few feet away, and eggs still warm from the chickens in the hen house, right there in the back of the field. They also sell pasture-raised poultry and lamb, locally caught fish, and locally baked breads and pastries. Plus, they have dairy products from Ronnybrook Farm and Red Jacket Orchards apples and peaches. The farm, run by volunteers and a local youth group, is designed to teach community children a sense of responsibility. Several times a year, the program offers farm tours and demos, and puts out a call for help with the harvesting. You can also sign up for CSA shares.

Red Hook Lobster Pound, 284 Van Brunt Street between Verona Street and Visitation Place; (646) 326-7650; B61 bus to Van Brunt Street at Verona Street; redhooklobsterpound.com. This seafood shop sells live, whole Maine lobster, right from the boat. Every Thursday, the owner drives up to Maine to meet the fishing boat and pick up his 1,000 pounds of lobster. Order ahead on holidays as they take reservations and sometimes the whole catch sells out. It's easy to see why: These beauties clamor around large clear tanks of water that are as big as hot tubs. The shop also sells cooked Jonah crab claws from Maine, freshly prepared lobster rolls, steamed lobsters, as well as crackers, picks, and bibs. Best of all, every order comes with instructions on how to dismantle your lobster so that the uninitiated aren't left in the cold. They also sell their popular lobster rolls at the **Brooklyn Flea market** (p. 97).

Red Hook Winery, (347) 689-2432; redhookwinery.com. A winery? In industrial Red Hook, you say? Yes. The grapes yield from vineyards on Long Island's North Fork, and they are crushed, aged, and barreled at a former cannonball factory and a former bordello in Red Hook, all under the loving watch of winemaker Christopher Nicolson, as well as many of his well-known sommelier friends. They sell in Brooklyn wine shops (including Brooklyn Wine Exchange), and their bottles include a smooth Sauvignon Blanc and an oaky Chardonnay and Riesling blend, both of which range in price from $25 to $60 per bottle. (That's comparable to other wines made from North Shore grapes.) But, for local oenophiles, many of whom are thrilled at the idea of uncorking a bottle of Brooklyn-made wine, the celebration of this new experiment began before they even took their first sip.

Shelsky's Smoked Fish, 251 Smith Street between Douglass Street and Degraw Street; (718) 855-8817; Subway: F, G to Carroll Street; shelskys.com. Step into their cheerful, brightly lit store on a Saturday morning, and you may wonder why this area has gone so long without an appetizing store in a city with so much love for Nova, scallion and horseradish cream cheeses, and bialys. While they don't smoke their own fish, Shelsky's sources their products from all of the best local places. Smoked fish comes from **Acme** (p. 159) in Greenpoint and The Smoke House in Mamaroneck; bagels and bialys come from Kossar's on the Lower East Side of Manhattan and, on weekends, Davidivitch in Queens. (Their pickles come from

Guss's on the Lower East Side, too.) However, they make their own pickled herring, gravlax, and Mexican achiote salmon; they also bake their own rugalach and babka. Some nice extra touches: They fry their latkes in schmaltz, and they add duck fat to their house-made chopped liver.

Sixpoint Craft Ales, 40 Van Dyke Street between Dwight Street and Richards Street; B61 bus to Van Brunt Street and Van Dyke Street; sixpointcraftales.com. You can sample pints of their Sweet Action Cream Ale, Brownstone, Righteous Ale, Apollo Wheat Beer, and Otis Oatmeal Cream Stout, all at the in-house bar. (Unfortunately, their popular Hop Obama Ale was retired the day he was elected.) They also make a limited edition coffee porter, in partnership with Park Slope's **Gorilla Coffee** (p. 125)—cheekily called Gorilla Warfare—a spicy pale ale for Manhattan pizza joint, Lil' Frankie's, and a Vienna Pale Ale for Williamsburg barbecue spot, **Fette Sau** (p. 149). And, fortunately, for those who don't want to trek out to Red Hook, many Brooklyn bars serve their brews on tap, including Barcade in Williamsburg and Pacific Standard in Boerum Hill.

Smith Canteen, 343 Smith Street between Carroll Street and 1st Place; (718) 422-0444; Subway: F, G to Carroll Street; smithcanteen .com; $. This offshoot of **Seersucker** (p. 59) is their casual, take-out sandwich and coffee shop. But just because the style is low-key doesn't mean that the food isn't artfully prepared. Come for the chicory coffee and the baked goods (picture scones, muffins, and cinnamon buns) in the morning or the sandwiches and salads at lunchtime.

Staubitz Market, 222 Court Street between Warren Street and Baltic Street; (718) 624-0014; Subway: F, G to Bergen Street or 2, 3, 4, 5, R to Borough Hall; staubitz.com. This third-generation German butcher has been in this location since 1911, and is often considered the best in the borough. The place has a nostalgic feel with an original screen door, a banged-tin ceiling, and stained glass. Don't let the simple storefront fool you though: Quality doesn't come cheap. The prime aged beef, their specialty, is a masterpiece. It's well-marbled and well-colored, and comes dry-aged or grass-fed and grain-finished. It also comes with a steep price tag, as do the other custom-cut meats like organic free-range chicken, goose, and rabbit. Staubitz can special order wild game like boar and ostrich, and at Thanksgiving the orders flood in for the wild turkeys that they source from Long Island.

Steve's Authentic Key Lime Pies, 204 Van Dyke Street between Conover Street and Ferris Street; (718) 858-5333; B61 bus to Van Brunt Street and Van Dyke Street; stevesauthentic.com. These tart pies, made with a buttery graham-cracker crust and freshly squeezed key limes, are as quirky as Red Hook itself. But if you luck into a pie, either at their pier-front bakery, **Peter Luger** (p.

158), or a Brooklyn food festival, you'll agree that these creamy treats—topped with a sweet, not-too-tart filling made with lime juice, sweetened condensed milk, and butter and finished off with whipped cream swirls—are worth the effort of tracking them down. The bakery also serves frozen key lime truffles, frozen key lime pie on a stick (they call it a Swingle), and limeade that's sure to make you pucker right up.

Stinky Bklyn, 215 Smith Street between Baltic Street and Butler Street; (718) 522-7425; Subway: F, G to Carroll Street; stinkybklyn .com. Cheese lovers rejoiced when this shop opened a couple years ago, and they celebrated once again when it moved to a larger space. And they weren't disappointed: Step through the door to the alluring smell of, well, cheese. In addition to selling American, French, Spanish, and Italian cheeses, they also carry cured meats like prosciutto, a smattering of jarred foods (pickles, mustard, vinegar), and some local baked goods. Check their website for cheese classes as well as information on their annual cheese-eating contest, which is affectionately dubbed **Stinkfest** (p. 80).

Stumptown Coffee Roasters, stumptowncoffee.com. When Duane Sorenson, a Pacific Northwest roaster with outlets in Portland and Seattle, opened a branch of his coffee bean operation in Red Hook in fall 2008, he took the city by storm. He travels around the world, selecting beans and partnering with small farms. Then he ships his finds back to the States and roasts them to his own specifications in cast-iron German Probat machines, and also trains shops how to best brew the perfect cup. You can't come watch the roasting and cooling yet, but since the Seattle and Portland offices are open to the public, we can all hope that it's just a matter of time until this one is, too. Fortunately, you can taste his coffee and buy his beans around the borough, including at **Cafe Pedlar** (p. 63), **Marlow & Sons** (p. 152), **Frankies 457 Spuntino** (p. 47), and at the **Brooklyn Flea** market (p. 97) where, sometimes, Sorenson himself can be found manning the pots.

Ted & Honey, 264 Clinton Street between Warren Street and Verandah Place; (718) 852-2212; Subway F, G to Bergen Street or 2, 3, 4, 5, R to Borough Hall; tedandhoney.com; $. This brother-and-sister team, who named their shop after their childhood nick-names, quickly found a following in the neighborhood. Located next to Cobble Hill Park, the breakfast-and-lunch spot serves egg sandwiches, lemon-blueberry scones, a sweet pastry they call a "pop tart," and roasted apple-topped oatmeal with raisins that are the perfect morning takeaway. The coffee comes from nearby **D'Amico** (p. 65) on Court Street, and the long list of sandwiches (filled with roasted vegetables, house-made aioli, and locally sourced ingredients like Dines Farms turkey and Rick's Pick's pickles) make great picnic food for an afternoon in the park.

Union Market, 288 Court Street between Degraw Street and Douglass Street; (718) 230-5152; Subway: F, G to Bergen Street or 2, 3, 4, 5, R to Borough Hall; unionmarket.com. When this Park Slope chainlet of upscale grocery stores opened a much-needed outpost in Cobble Hill, neighbors cheered. Now, **Ladybird Bakery**'s (p. 128) Chocolate Blackout Cake and **Steve's Authentic Key Lime Pies** (p. 76) are right at their fingertips, as are fine produce, rotisserie chickens, a lovely selection of cheeses, and condiments from around the world.

Food Events

Bastille Day on Smith Street, Smith Street between Pacific Street and Dean Street; (718) 923-0918; Subway: F, G to Bergen Street or A, C, G to Hoyt-Schermerhorn; bartabacny.com. Every Bastille Day, when France celebrates its version of Independence Day (the day the people stormed Paris's Bastille and began the French Revolution), Brooklyn holds the largest celebration in the US on the Sunday closest to July 14. Sponsored by local restaurants Bar Tabac and Robin des Bois, the event closes down Smith Street between Pacific and Bergen. They cover it with sand in order to turn it into an enormous *pétanque* court, for this country's biggest tournament. (There were 80 teams one year.) Several bands play French gypsy music, there is a fake guillotine set up, and of course there is plenty of French food and drink. Bar Tabac and Robin des Bois serve Pastis cocktails, grilled *merguez* sausage and chicken (you can smell the grill smoke from blocks away), and pâté with cornichons and spicy French mustard. Bars are set up with beer on tap, and crowds fill the streets in various states of inebriation from drinking all afternoon. It's a party, albeit a packed and sometimes frustrating one—have a drink and join the crowds in the revelry, or you're best off moving on.

Greek Festival, 64 Schermerhorn Street between Boerum Place and Court Street; (718) 624-0595; Subway: 2, 3, 4, 5, R to Borough Hall; stcon stantineandhelen.org. Once a year, usually during the second weekend in June, the downtown Greek Orthodox cathedral closes off a block and sets up a mini agora, with stands doing face painting, pony rides, games for children, and plenty of food. Some years, they roast whole pigs and lambs right in the middle of the street. Regardless, you will always find stuffed grape leaves, pastitsio, savory spanakopita, meatballs, and plenty of honey-drenched Greek desserts, from baklava to honey balls. On Saturday and Sunday night there is also Greek music and folk dancing, all fueled by Greek wine.

StinkFest, stinkybklyn.com. Yes, the crowd really does go wild at this annual cheese-eating contest when the Brooklyn Borough president gives out the award (a golden belt emblazoned with wheels of cheese) to the winner of the competition who eats the most cheese in 2 minutes. (Currently, the 2-year record-holder Will "The Champ" Millender's best show was in 2008, when he consumed 14.9 ounces.) The competition takes place during the annual Smith

COOKING THE BOOKS

After the first edition of this book came out in 2010, the food scene in Brooklyn (and the attention it received) continued to grow. Since then, a variety of the borough's top artisans and chefs have come out with their own cookbooks. Here are a few of the best:

Baked Explorations: Classic American Desserts Reinvented by Matt Lewis and Renato Pollafito (10/2011)

The Frankies Spuntino Kitchen Companion & Cooking Manual by Frank Falcinelli, Frank Castronovo, and Peter Meehan (6/2010)

Jam On: The Craft of Canning Fruit by Laena McCarthy (8/2012)

One Girl Cookies: Recipes for Cakes, Cupcakes, Whoopie Pies, and Cookies from Brooklyn's Beloved Bakery by Dawn Casale (1/2012)

People's Pops: 55 Recipes for Ice Pops, Shave Ice, and Boozy Pops from Brooklyn's Coolest Pop Shop by Nathali Jordi (6/2012)

Tart and Sweet: 101 Canning and Pickling Recipes for the Modern Kitchen by Kelly Geary (3/2011)

Street Fun Day Fair in June, during which the street is shut down and restaurants set up tables to sell tastes of their menus. There's also plenty of the normal street fair stuff (bad jewelry, political cause tables, piles of socks for sale, and inflated children's rides) in addition to less interesting carnival-style food like funnel cake and Italian sausages.

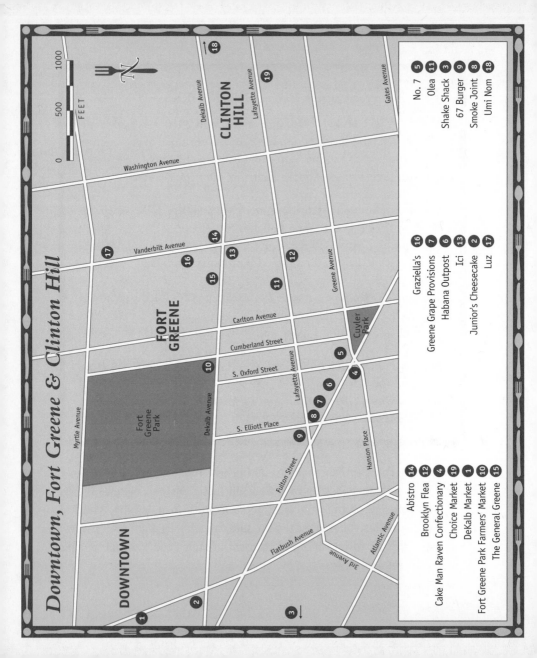

Downtown, Fort Greene & Clinton Hill

DOWNTOWN

FORT GREENE

CLINTON HILL

Fort Greene Park

Cuyler Park

FEET
0   500   1000

N

Washington Avenue
Vanderbilt Avenue
Myrtle Avenue
Dekalb Avenue
Lafayette Avenue
Gates Avenue
Greene Avenue
Carlton Avenue
Cumberland Street
S. Oxford Street
S. Elliott Place
Fulton Street
Hanson Place
Flatbush Avenue
3rd Avenue
Atlantic Avenue

Abistro **14**
Brooklyn Flea **12**
Cake Man Raven Confectionary **4**
Choice Market **19**
DeKalb Market **1**
Fort Greene Park Farmers' Market **10**
The General Greene **15**

Graziella's **16**
Greene Grape Provisions **7**
Habana Outpost **6**
Ici **13**
Junior's Cheesecake **2**
Luz **17**

No. 7 **5**
Olea **11**
Shake Shack **3**
67 Burger **9**
Smoke Joint **8**
Umi Nom **18**

Downtown, Fort Greene & Clinton Hill

Graceful Fort Greene is blessed with the 30-acre Fort Greene Park, a series of grass-covered hills that was once championed by Walt Whitman and is now a big draw. The park, like Prospect Park to the south and Central Park in Manhattan, was designed by Frederick Law Olmsted. Up until the late '80s, when resident Spike Lee set up shop here and launched several decades of gentrification and development, the neighborhood was a victim of urban blight. Now the bustling historic district boasts racial and economic diversity and cultural magnets such as BAM (the Brooklyn Academy of Music) and Steiner Studios (a massive film and TV production studio built alongside the riverfront Brooklyn Navy Yard). All of these factors have resulted in an increasingly creative restaurant scene.

Clinton Hill, just past its borders, is still gentrifying, slowly and a bit painfully. Interesting restaurants and food businesses serve the area's pioneers, who settle in Clinton Hill thanks to low real-estate prices, even as crime rates remain high. The Pratt Institute, an art school, also continues to draw creative types into its fold.

Downtown Brooklyn has long been the legal and business heart of Brooklyn, and as of late has received some serious attention for a few high-profile restaurant newcomers, as well as a series of hotel and high-rise apartment building developments that have changed the landscape in the last couple years.

Foodie Faves

Abistro, 250 Dekalb Avenue between Vanderbilt Avenue and Clinton Avenue; (347) 384-2972; Subway: G to Fulton or C to Lafayette or B, Q, R to Dekalb; $$$. If you've never had Senegalese food, and you've always wanted to try it, well, this isn't the place. Dishes here are a Senegalese-French fusion that's much more its own thing than it is the cuisine of either of those places. The crispy calamari appetizer is mixed with fried jalapeños and comes with a sweet mango sauce that's spiked with chipotle, and the roasted brook trout is topped with an onion-pepper relish that's rich with capers. Steak frites and moules frites are the most traditionally French choice on the menu, but the Senegalese fried chicken is the most memorable dish. It's pan fried and sits atop a sweet pineapple-rice cake, savory sautéed collard greens that are cooked slowly until they're soft and sweet, and a creamy dijonnaise sauce that's drizzled with chili oil. It's not from anywhere in particular, but you'll agree with just one bite that it belongs in your stomach.

The General Greene, 229 Dekalb Avenue between Clermont Avenue and Adelphi Street; (718) 222-1510; Subway: C to Lafayette Avenue or G to Clinton-Washington or 2, 3, 4, 5, N, Q, R, B, D to Atlantic-Pacific; thegeneralgreene.com; $$. This casual neighborhood bistro serves up some lovely cocktails, so even if your main event is dinner, plan to come a little early. Order a drink, such as the minty vodka-spiced "green lemonade," and then check out the bar food menu. The offerings here, such as the old-fashioned deviled eggs without any froufrou garnishes like caviar or Spanish paprika, will make you want to linger on your barstool. When you do make your way to a table, you'll find that the menu is made up of comfort food classics with a moden twist. The fried chicken is appropriately crisp, and the burger garners rave reviews, too. But, whatever rib-sticking fare you order, do save room for dessert, as the owner has a pastry-chef background. The restaurant has a small grocery shop in the rear, where you can buy locally produced ingredients (such as Evans Farmhouse butter) and harder-to-find items (including Benton's bacon). Also, they've built an ice-cream cart that, when parked out front in the warm-weather months, is worth considering—especially the salted-caramel pretzel flavor filled with big chunks of pretzels.

Graziella's, 232 Vanderbilt Avenue between Dekalb Avenue and Willoughby Avenue; (718) 789-5663; Subway: C to Lafayette Avenue or G to Clinton-Washington or 2, 3, 4, 5, N, Q, R, B, D to Atlantic-Pacific; graziellasmenu.com; $$. This Italian hideaway serves up simple but tasty thin-crust pizzas, hot from the wood-burning oven in the back of the dining room. Take a seat among the Pratt students and other creative types who are changing the face of the neighborhood, and the smell of pizza will win you over. Appetizers stick to the Sicilian classics (garlicky baked clams, crispy chickpea fritters called *panelle*, rice balls filled with meat and cheese). The pizza itself is simple, so go for flavorful toppings, like sausage and mushroom, anchovies and olives, or prosciutto and baby arugula. The brick-walled dining room is pleasant enough (when there aren't Pratt students playing drinking games or kids running around), but if you come on a warm evening, ask for a table on the roof deck.

Habana Outpost, 757 Fulton Street between S. Portland Avenue and S. Oxford Street; (718) 858-9500; Subway: C to Lafayette Avenue or G to Fulton Street or 2, 3, 4, 5, N, Q, R, B, D to Atlantic-Pacific; habanaoutpost.com; $$. How you feel about this seasonal restaurant has a lot to do with how you feel about a place that's a mix of bar scene . . . and children. Walk into the festive tiled room and order a **Sixpoint** (p. 75) beer or one of several frozen drinks sloshing about in slushy machines, as well as some food. Then bring your receipt out to the yard, hand the ticket to the guy in the truck, and take a seat at a picnic table to wait for your name to be called. Sitting in the yard under one of many umbrella-topped picnic tables, watching the twentysomethings eye each other and the toddlers run around the kiddie play area, you may wonder just how good the food could be. And then they call your name. Yes, it's loud and a little embarrassing, but they are holding a tray of food with your name on it. And it looks good. Great, actually. You sit down with your *media noche,* your Mexican grilled corn on the cob, and (if you're smart) a darn tasty frozen mojito. You dig in. The corn is warm and grilled and topped with chili powder and tons of fall-all-over-your-shirt crumbly cheese. (Yes, it's held on by mayo, but mayo-phobes should just get over it—if I didn't tell you, you wouldn't know that mayo was the glue.) It's all, well, surprisingly wonderful. Note: They close from Nov through Apr each year.

Ici, 246 Dekalb Avenue between Vanderbilt Avenue and Clermont Avenue; (718) 789-2778; Subway: C to Lafayette Avenue or G to Clinton-Washington or 2, 3, 4, 5, N, Q, R, B, D to Atlantic-Pacific; icirestaurant.com; $$$. At first, this little French place seems simple. The backyard, strung with twinkling white fairy lights and filled with little white cafe tables, is often quiet, with most of the noise coming from the bar a few doors down. Inside, the small dining room has a fireplace, whitewashed brick walls, and bars on the windows, a relic from a time when that would have been a requirement in these parts. And the menu of seasonal dishes, many of which are made with local ingredients, seems familiar. But the surprise is that the food actually delivers where some of these shrines to locavore eating do not. Start with a rich thimble-size ramekin of chicken liver mousse, served with cornichons and toasted baguette, or, better still, the stone-ground grits (made with Anson Mills, arguably the best grits in the South) topped with a poached egg (from Tello's Green Farm in New York's Duchess County) and a truffle-infused aioli. The don't-miss entrees, which change with the season, could include a decadent duck confit over swiss chard and leeks from **Red Hook Farmers' Market at Added Value Farm** (p. 72) or a crisp pan-seared chicken breast from Violet Hill over Added Value turnips. Desserts are tarted-up versions of classics, like a lemon bar topped with pomegranate seeds and mint. End your meal with a pot of tea, sourced from serendip-iTea in Manhasset on Long Island. The fair-traded and organic lavender-chamomile one, called "Zzz," will send you into dreamland with a smile.

Luz, 177 Vanderbilt Avenue between Myrtle Avenue and Willoughby Avenue; (718) 246-4000; Subway: G to Clinton-Washington or B, Q, R to Dekalb; luzrestaurant.com; $$$. This Latin restaurant feels a bit more Miami than Brooklyn. The dining room pulses with merengue and salsa music, and the look is modern, with gray walls emblazoned with red stripes, vases filled with palm fronds, and dim, funky lighting that hangs beneath a skylight. The most popular order seems to be pitchers of cocktails, usually watermelon mojitos or white sangria, which may explain the volume level and the feeling that, even on a Monday night, this place is a party. Despite that, the food isn't an afterthought. In lieu of a bread basket, you'll get crisp plantains to dip in a spicy sauce. Follow that up with a fancy take on that Central American street food, the *arepa* (they come sprinkled with creamy white cheese and drizzled with a cilantro pesto), and then the Peruvian-style roasted chicken. The meat is juicy and moist, and the chicken has such a crisp skin you'd think it was fried.

No. 7, 7 Greene Avenue between S. Oxford Street and Cumberland Street; (718) 522-6370; Subway: C to Lafayette or G to Fulton Street or 2, 3, 4, 5, N, Q, R, B, D to Atlantic-Pacific; no7restaurant.com; $$$. Hidden behind a subway entrance, this New American restaurant turns out some pretty impressive dishes. It's a short menu—just 5 apps, 5 entrees, and 3 desserts—and they change often. Some of the descriptions don't do a very thorough job explaining the dishes, but what the kitchen turns out is creative and surprising: Order the soft-boiled fried egg, and you'll get an egg that's crispy on the outside and lush in the middle, topped with caviar and served with marinated artichokes and an endive salad. Or choose the enigmatic fried broccoli. Yes, the broccoli is tempura fried and served with a small salad of dill, grapefruit, and bitter greens, as the menu says, but first it's dipped in a batter seasoned with balsamic and sesame oil. The roast chicken, when it is offered, is the clear star of the entrees, and nothing about the menu introduces its brilliance. It is served as a roll of white and dark meat wrapped in crispy brown, salted skin and sliced into lovely wedges, then plated with fried capers, Israeli couscous, and plump little tomatoes. Dessert holds surprises too, like chocolate pudding topped with chocolate crumbles and "root beer" whipped cream. The space is as pleasant as the food. The room itself feels truly Old New York—think subway-tiled walls, schoolhouse lights, and a long marble bar. Once just a local darling, this restaurant has spun off a sandwich shop by the same owners in Manhattan's hip Ace Hotel.

Olea, 171 Lafayette Avenue between Adelphi Street and Clermont Avenue; (718) 643-7003; Subway: C to Lafayette Avenue or G to Fulton Street or 2, 3, 4, 5, N, Q, R, B, D to Atlantic-Pacific; oleabrooklyn.com; $$$. On Friday nights, this charming little Mediterranean spot turns into a Spanish paella house complete with flamenco guitar player and sangria. Start with tapas, like goat cheese or salt cod croquettes, as well as piquillo peppers stuffed with tuna and bright anchovies marinated in light white vinegar. Then share a platter of paella. This Friday night special is served on an enormous porcelain pan filled with rice, chicken, chorizo, shrimp, clams, and mussels. Finish the meal with crème brûlée, and the trip across the Atlantic is complete. On warm evenings, the tables spill out onto the sidewalk, and, like many popular Brooklyn nightspots, the service and the kitchen can be slow, so dinner stretches into the night—just the way the Spaniards like it.

Shake Shack, 409 Fulton Street between Willoughby Street and Adams Street; (718) 307-7590; Subway: 2, 3, 4, 5, R to Borough Hall or A, C, F, N to Jay Street or A, C, G to Hoyt-Schermerhorn or B, D, N, Q, R to Dekalb Avenue; shakeshack.com; $. One of Manhattan's best indulgences has opened a location in downtown Brooklyn, breathing fresh air into Fulton Mall. The menu is the same as at all of Danny Meyer's heavenly burger locations, with burgers made from their proprietary blend and frozen custard in rotating flavors that include red velvet and salted caramel as well as seasonal treats such as egg nog, figgy pudding, gingerbread, and candy cane.

67 Burger, 67 Lafayette Avenue between Fort Greene Place and S. Elliott Place; (718) 797-7150; Subway: C to Lafayette Avenue or G to Fulton Street or 2, 3, 4, 5, N, Q, R, B, D to Atlantic-Pacific; 67burger.com; $. Every neighborhood should have a casual burger spot like this one. The burgers are tasty and come in interesting combinations, like the Southwest burger, which is topped with Pepper Jack, roasted red peppers, and chipotle mayonnaise, and the signature burger, which is decked out with bacon and a dollop of creamy blue cheese. The sides, such as the crisp, hot sweet-potato fries arrive fresh from the fryer way before your burger, and the milk shakes (which come in classic flavors like strawberry and Oreo, as well as the more unusual beer variety) are thick and creamy. Prices may seem high for a fast-food-style joint—instead of table service, you order your burgers and then go to a table with a numbered sign; the staff delivers your food as it's ready. The burgers themselves are certainly worth the price.

Smoke Joint, 87 S. Elliott Place between Fulton Street and Lafayette Avenue; (718) 797-1011; Subway: C to Lafayette Avenue or G to Fulton Street or 2, 3, 4, 5, N, Q, R, B, D to Atlantic-Pacific;  thesmokejoint.com; $$. This Fort Greene barbecue place may not be a veritable trip to Kansas City or Texas Hill Country, but for barbecue-starved Brooklynites, it will do just fine. The owners call their amalgamation of styles "real New York 'cue"—a mix of different regions' favorites, from North Carolina–style pulled pork sandwiches, with pickles, slaw, and plenty of vinegar, to smoky Texas hot link sausages and their own house specialty, smoked short ribs. The food isn't perfect (sometimes the meat is too dry, sometimes it just isn't flavorful enough), but they do have a breakout hit: the hot dog. It's a skinny, crisp-fried all-beef Black Angus masterpiece that you can top with chopped pork, beef, or chicken, making barbecue sauce a more appropriate condiment than mustard or relish.

Umi Nom, 433 Dekalb Avenue between Classon Avenue and Taaffe Place; (718) 789-8806; Subway: G to Classon Avenue; uminom.com; $$. This Pan-Asian restaurant's Filipino dishes really stand out in a borough with very little food from this country. Start with a cool fruit drink—perhaps *buko* (a young coconut water that's flecked with chunks of coconut), or a *kalamansi* juice (made from sweet Asian limes)—and a plate of spring rolls. Then, consider the *bahay kubo,* a garlicky mixture of fried rice, chicken, and sweet pork sausage. At brunch there's a similar garlic rice dish topped with the sausage and the addition of fried eggs, as well as their take on the *banh mi*, made with rich pork belly and without any of the usual mystery meats. See recipe for Umi Nom's **Garlic Fried Rice** on p. 295.

Landmarks

Junior's Cheesecake, 386 Flatbush Avenue Extension between Dekalb Avenue and Willoughby Street; (718) 852-5257; Subway: B, Q, R to Dekalb or 2, 3, 4, 5 to Nevins; juniorscheesecake.com; $$. A lot has changed in downtown Brooklyn since the 1950s, but it's still all about the cheesecake at this famous spot that put New York cheesecake on the map. Located on Flatbush, on the border of Fort Greene and Brooklyn's downtown governmental seat, Junior's is as much a driving destination as it is a walking one. ("You have ruined me for all other cheesecakes," bemoaned my cousin after we

DEKALB MARKET

Sure, there are plenty of flea and food markets in Brooklyn now, but Dekalb is unique. Located on Flatbush Avenue, the market is made up of salvaged shipping containers that serve as mini shops. During the warm-weather months, the market is open 7 days a week, and is home to food and craft vendors and boutiques, all lined up around a tented eating space filled with picnic tables. There's Joe Coffee, Dub Pies, Maharlika Filipino cuisine, and plenty of other notable food stands, but you could also come just for Robicelli's cupcakes, a local favorite in a crowded category. One day you might find a pear–olive oil cupcake topped with blue-cheese buttercream and candied walnuts, another it could be a Harry Potter–inspired Butterbeer cupcake, an entirely

 butterscotch dessert topped with gold dust. Or, perhaps you will luck into a day when they are serving Car Bomb cupcakes, a Guinness cupcake with frosting infused with Jameson Irish Whiskey ganache and Bailey's Irish Cream buttercream, and the Elvis, a banana cupcake with peanut butter buttercream that's topped with plenty of crumbled candied Berkshire bacon. The result? It's smoky and strong and not for the faint of heart. **Dekalb Market,** 322 Flatbush Avenue Extension between Willoughby Street and Fleet Stret; Subway: B, Q, R to Dekalb or 2, 3, 4, 5 to Nevins; dekalbmarket.com.

brought him here.) Get the traditional cheesecake or splurge, both with your wallet and your waistline, on one of their cheesecakes layered into regular cakes, like devil's food. Each slice is more than a pound of decadence—the devil's food, for example, is a tall chocolate layer cake—sliced in half with a cheesecake baked into the middle. They do a similar thing with carrot cake—and it is undeniably sublime. Of course, the place has a restaurant too, but you'll want to save your calories for cheesecake.

Specialty Stores, Markets & Producers

Cake Man Raven Confectionary, 708 Fulton Street between S. Portland Avenue and S. Oxford Street; (718) 797-2598; Subway: C to Lafayette Avenue or G to Fulton Street or 2, 3, 4, 5, N, Q, R, B, D to Atlantic-Pacific; cakemanraven.com. This cake shop is a little odd. The sign says it's open until 10 p.m. 7 days a week, but often the gate is closed way before that. Get inside, and a video loop of the red velvet cake episode of Food Network's *Throwdown with Bobby Flay* plays on a ceiling-mounted TV. (The Cake Man lost, but no matter.) The glass counter case holds one thing: dozens of little plastic containers of bright red velvet cake. And when I say bright, I mean neon, gotta-wear-shades bright. That cake will remind you what old-fashioned, Southern red velvet is supposed to taste like. Buttermilk and vinegar provide a lot of tang, and food coloring adds the shocking hue. But the cream cheese frosting is smooth and sweet, and the whole thing goes down easily enough that it may leave you wondering when you'll be getting your next slice.

Choice Market, 318 Lafayette Avenue between Grand Avenue and St. James Place; (718) 230-5234; Subway: G, C to Clinton-Washington; $. This little Clinton Hill shop fills at breakfast time, when diners spill out onto street-front benches. Strollers line up quickly, and the counter staff seems to remember some of the regulars' names, including toddlers who get a regular fix of spongy soft madeleine cookies. Most adults come in the morning for the bacon, egg, and cheddar sandwiches, which are pressed on slices of fresh bread or a croissant until the cheese oozes out the side. At lunchtime, the sandwich of choice is a BLT on seven-grain bread that's slathered with a healthy spread of house-made rosemary mayo. The front glass counters are filled with pastries, loaf cakes, muffins, and brownies, and the clear glass jars are full of cookies in classic flavors like chocolate chip and chocolate-chocolate. Hint: They also sell their baked goods at the **Brooklyn Flea market** (p. 97) on many Saturdays and have a small but well-curated grocery store around the corner called Choice Greene.

Fort Greene Park Farmers' Market, Washington Park between Dekalb Avenue and Myrtle Avenue; grownyc.org/fortgreenemarket.

BROWNSTONER'S WILDLY POPULAR BROOKLYN FLEA

Sure, you can buy rehabbed antiques and records, but many go to this moving market (get the schedule at brownstoner.com/brooklynflea) just for the food. This phenomenon is the brainchild of Jonathan Butler, who owns the Brooklyn website Brownstoner.com, and Eric Denby, who used to work in Marty Markowitz's office. It's an outdoor, community-supported flea market that has found enormous support from Brooklyn hipsters, families, and, of course, local celebs. (Yes, that is Marisa Tomei behind you—she lives near here. And, yes, you should tell your husband to stop drooling, it's just not cool.) It started as a salvage yard swap, but the food stalls became popular fast. "It was overwhelming how much people cared about the food," says Denby.

Arrive around lunchtime? Grab a hot dog from AsiaDog, with fun toppings like curry-apple-kimchee, *banh mi*–style condiments, or pork belly. Or choose a wood-fired pepperoni pizza from Pizza Moto, a cult favorite at the Flea for the built-by-hand mobile brick oven. Interesting tidbit: The oven was originally built to make pizzas for the wedding of Rachel and Betsy, the owners of Salvatore Bklyn. Check out the cannoli and ricotta-tomato sandwiches from Salvatore Bklyn, and Argentine empanadas from **Baked** (p. 60), made by a mother-in-law/son-in-law team who bake up tender pastry filled with raisins and beef.

Kumquat Cupcakery bakes tiny, perfect cupcakes (cupcakelettes?) in flavors like red velvet with a light cream-cheese buttercream, coffee-caramel-bourbon, maple-bacon-pecan, peanut butter-banana-honey, and chocolate cupcakes with chocolate frosting flecked with cocoa nibs from **Nunu Chocolates** (p. 70), another Flea stand. Ready for more sweets? Whimsy & Spice serves marshmallows (in caramel and maple flavors), butterscotch bars, and passionfruit limeade.

THE BURGER INVASION

Perhaps Brooklyn was underserved in the burger category in the past, despite some impressive standouts, such as **Dram Shop** (p. 108) in Park Slope and **Dumont Burger** (p. 147) in Williamsburg. But in the last few years, there's been an explosion of burger spots in the borough. The most exciting is **Shake Shack** (p. 91), on an otherwise unexciting stretch of Fulton Mall, but there's also **Two 8 Two Burger Bar** (p. 59) in Cobble Hill and Williamsburger in Williamsburg as well as a half-dozen others.

It's a great tribute to the positive changes in the neighborhood that this park, once associated with crack addicts and the homeless, now hosts children running among the chestnut trees and people playing Frisbee in summer and sledding in winter. Year-round you can find dogs out on their walks and this little farmers' market. Open Sat from 8 a.m. to 5 p.m., this farm market is smaller than some of the others, but a welcome sight for those who don't want to walk over to Grand Army Plaza. With just a dozen stalls, they manage to cover the basics—fruit, vegetables, herbs, dairy, fish, baked goods, and flowers—and with lighter crowds, you can often go later in the afternoon without getting stuck with what feels like leftovers. The variety is impressive—it can include, on some days, such a range of produce that you can choose from a dozen different types of tomatoes and, say, 4 different-colored carrots. (The sweet, low-acid "pineapple" tomatoes are worth the trip alone.) You'll find

Conuco Farm's greens from Nazareth, PA, Connecticut's Cato Corner's farmstead raw cow's milk cheese, Pura Vida's fish, and J. Glebocki Farm's potatoes and tomatoes. In the fall you can also get pumpkins and gourds that locals use to decorate their brownstone stoops, as well as DiPaola Turkey for Thanksgiving, warm cranberry-apple cider from Red Jacket Orchards, and apple pies from Wilklow Orchards and Meredith Bakery.

Greene Grape Provisions, 753 Fulton Street between S. Portland Avenue and S. Elliott Place; (718) 233-2700; Subway: C to Lafayette Avenue or G to Fulton Street or 2, 3, 4, 5, N, Q, R, B, D to Atlantic-Pacific; greenegrape.com. The Greene Grape folks have several Fort Greene outposts, all in a short stretch of Fulton, including this grocery, the original wine shop, and the smaller Greene Grape Annex across the street, which is home to coffee from Williamsburg's Blue Bottle. Locals in the know buy key groceries here, from sustainably fished seafood to grass-fed beef and organic, local produce. Of course, you'll also find many of Brooklyn's best products here,  including **McClure**'s (p. 249) Bloody Mary mix, Sour Puss pickles, Liddabit Sweets, and The Stand jams. A fabulous house-warming present for Brooklyn neighbors: Their "Built in Brooklyn" basket of goodies from around the borough.

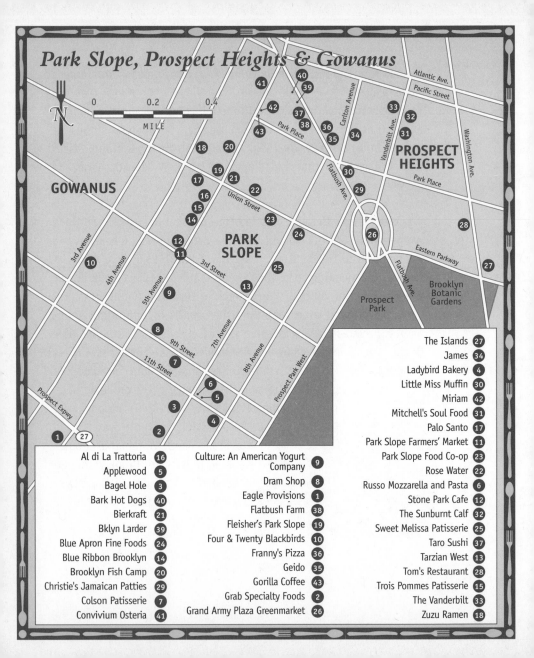

Park Slope, Prospect Heights & Gowanus

0   0.2   0.4

MILE

N

GOWANUS

PROSPECT HEIGHTS

PARK SLOPE

Prospect Park

Brooklyn Botanic Gardens

Atlantic Ave.
Pacific Street
Carlton Avenue
Vanderbilt Ave.
Washington Ave.
Park Place
Flatbush Ave.
Park Place
Union Street
3rd Avenue
4th Avenue
5th Avenue
3rd Street
7th Avenue
8th Avenue
9th Street
11th Street
Prospect Expwy
Prospect Park West
Eastern Parkway
Flatbush Ave.

Park Slope, Prospect Heights & Gowanus

Park Slope's original asset may be its location—right on the edge of gorgeous Prospect Park, the borough's biggest green space and home to not only picnic-perfect lawns and jogging trails but also a large weekend green market and several summer concert series. Locals like to brag that when Frederick Law Olmsted designed Manhattan's Central Park, he was just warming up for Prospect Park. Today, the "Slope" is the preeminent destination for young families in Brooklyn. Weekends bring stoop sales (an urban take on the garage sale) in front of the neighborhood's many brownstones. Fleets of strollers march down the sidewalks, a phenomenon that has caused conflict in the local businesses as these prams cram into small spaces. (As a result, many shops have NO STROLLERS signs.) There are also plenty of crunchy young singles and couples, too, all of whom seem to grocery shop at the co-op as well as at the green market. They brunch in the Slope on weekends and dine out here during the week. As well they should: This vibrant neighborhood is home to a well-rounded restaurant scene with as much to offer as any in Manhattan.

As for Prospect Heights, it may play second fiddle to Park Slope as a residential area, but it is very much the cultural heart of Brooklyn. Here, you'll find the Brooklyn Museum of Art—the second-largest museum in New York City—and the sprawling Brooklyn Botanical Garden. Along with the massive main branch of the Brooklyn Public Library, they form a striking European-style boulevard that stretches out from Grand Army Plaza along Eastern Parkway. There, the 15-story Richard Meier building, all glass panels and modern lines, seems to announce Prospect Heights' arrival into the designer condo market. Beyond this strip, Prospect Heights has the main shopping and dining strip of Vanderbilt Avenue and a wealth of brownstones. They were recently under threat by plans to develop Atlantic Yards and tear down many of this community's loveliest stretches to make room for new development. Locals breathed a sigh of relief when the flailing economy canceled many of those changes—at least for now.

Gowanus, which was formerly an industrial area surrounding the famed canal, has recently had an explosion of condo conversions, gallery launches, concert spaces, and small, cool restaurant openings that make it worth including in the book.

Al di La Trattoria, 248 5th Avenue between Carroll Street and President Street; (718) 783-4565; Subway R to Union Street; aldila trattoria.com; $$$. This popular no-reservations spot is known for its long waits, but one bite of its northern Italian dishes (and a peek at the check) and you'll understand its popularity. Put your name on the list, then take a seat in the next-door bar-cum-waiting room with everyone else who's dying for a little comfort food and wait your turn for an invitation to the limited space of the intimate dining room. The menu is divided Italian-style into antipasti, primi, and secondi, but 3 courses here would be way too much. Better antipasti include an escarole salad with Jerusalem artichokes, pancetta, and walnuts, and the *malfatti,* a gnocchi filled with swiss chard and ricotta that's served in a brown butter sauce. There are also tagliatelle in a meaty ragout and spaghetti with clams, garlic, and olive oil. Meats (including a tangy hanger steak cooked in balsamic) and sides (grilled swiss chard, polenta, roasted brussels sprouts) are equally hearty. As for dessert, which supposedly includes a reputable panna cotta and rave-worthy ricotta fritters—well, I've never gotten that far.

Applewood, 501 11th Street between 7th Avenue and 8th Avenue; (718) 788-1810; Subway: F, G to Seventh Avenue; applewoodny .com; $$$. This locavore haunt lives by all the rules of farm-to-table dining, using only hormone- and antibiotic-free meats and wild seafood. The menus are seasonal, changing every day based on what organic ingredients are at their peak. In the morning, a Southern leaning shows through with the fact that many dishes come with rich grits, comforting and made with heavy cream, and a biscuit served with house-made strawberry preserves. Brunch dishes include grilled grass-fed steak served with sunny-side-up organic eggs; an omelet stuffed with green kale, bacon, mild white cheddar, and the salty bite of bacon; or a lobster and pea-shoot omelet. Lunch choices might have fish-and-chips that are gussied up with Long Island bluefish and artichoke aioli. Even the bathrooms are farmhouse inspired and homey, with kitchen towels instead of paper ones to dry your hands. The highlight of dinner here: the "Meet the Farmer" special meals they host regularly with local farm owners and communal tables full of neighborhood fans eagerly getting into the question-and-answer session with the restaurant's chef.

Bark Hot Dogs, 474 Bergen Street between Flatbush Avenue and 5th Avenue; (718) 789-1939; Subway: 2, 3 to Bergen or Q, B to Atlantic; barkhotdogs.com; $. You know from the minute you walk in that Bark isn't going to serve your average midtown cart dog. The walls are lined with reclaimed wood and subway tiles, the stools and tables are streamlined and sleek. And the frankfurters themselves don't disappoint. House-made from a mix of pork and beef, their casing has a snappy bite. These griddled dogs take the wiener to a whole new level: Basted with house-made smoked lard butter, they're topped with house-made pickles, relish, and oak barrel-aged sauerkraut. Bark also makes their own chili, which you can get on top of a frank for a memorable chili cheese dog. Order yours with their namesake **Sixpoint** (p. 75) Bark Red Ale, a light concoction that's only sold here. Or make the caloric splurge on a milk shake in either malted chocolate (which is both really malty and really chocolaty) or one that's a decadent mix of crème fraîche ice cream and fresh blueberries. The shakes are made from Manhattan's Il Laboratorio del Gelato, and they are creamy, rich perfection. Come at breakfast time on a weekend, and treat yourself to an egg sandwich made with their house-smoked ham or bacon. See recipe for Bark's **New York Style Sweet & Sour Onions** on p. 296.

Blue Ribbon Brooklyn, 280 5th Avenue between 1st Street and Garfield Place; (718) 840-0404; Subway: R to Union Street; blueribbonrestaurants.com; $$$$. This is the Brooklyn outpost of the popular Manhattan chefs' hangout, which is known for having a kitchen that stays open until 4 a.m. to feed throngs of hungry kitchen crews when they get off work. The menu here is similar, and therefore equally pricy and encyclopedic. The dining room is all shiny wood and dim lighting—and the service is so polished and smooth you could almost forget you're in Brooklyn. ("Look," exclaimed my husband, "The host remembered my name!") They serve all the French classics—escargot in garlic-herb butter, *foie gras* terrine, steak tartare, chicken liver pâté with toast points, and comforting onion soup gratinée. But the bone marrow with chunky oxtail marmalade and sea salt steals the show—it's unforgettably rich and satisfying. There's also a sushi and raw bar, which means that in addition to buying crab claws, oysters, and clams by the piece you can also order spectacular silver trays piled high with ice and crustaceans. The menu of main dishes is, if nothing else, eclectic. It includes everything from paella to lobster with corn on the cob to whole grilled fish and tasty duck confit over greens—perfect for a group of late-night noshers with different appetites. Unfortunately for local toque-wearers, the kitchen closes at midnight—the restaurant's one nod to being in Brooklyn.

Brooklyn Fish Camp, 162 5th Avenue between Degraw Street and Douglass Street; (718) 783-3264; Subway: R to Union Street or 2, 3 to Bergen or B, Q to 7th Avenue; brooklynfishcamp.com; $$. This is another Brooklyn outpost of a Manhattan favorite, in this case, Mary's Fish Camp, the popular and perennially packed lobster roll and seafood joint in the West Village. At Brooklyn Fish Camp, it's only marginally easier to get a table, but it has all the same highlights of the Manhattan menu—especially the much-lauded, lightly dressed lobster roll and the whole grilled Maine lobster served with green pea pancakes and drawn butter. You'll also find crab beignets, oyster po'boy sandwiches topped with plenty of pickles, and fried clam rolls, all of which serve as satisfying tastes of the sea on a night when you just can't get away from the city. There's also a lovely backyard, in which they sometimes show movies in the summer, and a children's menu. Tip: If you are not dining with little people, take the hint and come late.

Convivium Osteria, 68 5th Avenue between St. Marks Place and Bergen Street; (718) 857-1833; Subway: 2, 3 to Bergen Street or 4, 5, B, D, N, Q, R to Atlantic Avenue; convivium-osteria.com; $$$. This European-style hideaway makes you feel whisked away from the moment you walk in the door. Follow the waiter through the charming main dining room, past the boisterous families and groups seated at large tables, to the quieter enclosed garden in back. There, exposed brick walls are decorated with copper pans, banged-tin gas lanterns, and wrought-iron pot holders. A fountain and quiet conversation are the only sounds you'll hear, adding to the sense that you've been transported far from 5th Avenue.

And the food—which is equal parts Italian, Spanish, and Portuguese—is truly inviting. Appetizers may include grilled sardines, which are crusted with garlic, rock salt, and parsley and grilled to perfection, then served on a rustic piece of country bread. The briny scent of the fish fills the air as soon as they arrive at your table. Pasta dishes are highlights here: The hearty spinach gnocchi sit in a rich, buttery Asiago cream sauce, and apple-cinnamon ravioli are topped with duck ragout—a play on the warmth of the cinnamon that works like a charm. Entrees lean toward the hearty and braised, like tender Berkshire pork belly ribs served in a delicate tomato sauce on a bed of polenta. The charming waiter had suggested picking them up, mimicking nibbling them like corn on the cob, but they fall right off the bone.

It's all rich, as are the desserts, including a buttery shortbread topped with Frangelico and dark chocolate, then enrobed in a thick white icing and topped with a maraschino cherry. The waiter rattled off the name for this candylike dessert in rapid Italian, which he explained, tweaking his fingers in the air for emphasis, translates to the "Nipple of Venus"—a naughty ending to a heavenly meal.

Dram Shop, 339 9th Street between 5th Avenue and 6th Avenue; (718) 788-1444; Subway: F, R to 4th Avenue-9th Street; $. This place is mostly a bar: The pool table and full-size shuffleboard are popular spots, as is the long bar where drinkers groove to the iPod mix of alt rock that's DJed by the bartender. (Here, the new Wilco album might follow an oldie-but-goodie by the Violent Femmes.) The booths are big and often packed, especially on weekends, when groups keep squishing in to make room. It doesn't seem like the kind of place to have great food, but it is. Great bar food that is: The menu ranges from chicken wings (meaty, fried well, and with a nice kick of spice) to nachos and big, juicy double cheeseburgers piled with lettuce, pickles, mustard, and mayo. Made with griddle-seared square patties, the burgers are huge, and designed to absorb all the beer you'll drink that night—which, with a beer list this long, could be more than you'd like to admit.

Flatbush Farm, 76 St. Marks Avenue between 6th Avenue and Flatbush Avenue; (718) 622-3276; Subway: 2, 3 to Bergen Street or B, Q to 7th Avenue; flatbushfarm.com; $$$. Perhaps more than any of Brooklyn's farm-to-table restaurants, Flatbush Farm's menu reflects what is organic, local, and seasonal. Each ingredient is sourced so carefully that it's a who's who of regional farming. That means the herbs and greens are from Satur Farms; the cheese and game are from Vermont Fancy Farming; the fruit and tomatoes are from Blooming Hill Farms; apples, cider, and potatoes are from Stone Ridge Orchard. Of course, that also means what's on the docket is what's in season in the Northeast, and whether or not you'll be interested has more to do with the weather than the chefs themselves, who keep things quite simple. Appetizers might be a cold poached asparagus salad, and in peak asparagus season two or three other dishes may feature these green stalks—the same goes for rhubarb or foraged mushrooms when they are at their best. It's a fitting introduction to the pleasures, and limitations, of this Michael Pollan–led movement.

Four & Twenty Blackbirds, 439 3rd Avenue between 7th Street and 8th Street; (718) 499-2917; Subway: F, G to 4th Avenue/9th

Street or D, N, R to 9th Street; birdsblack .com; $. Come to this adorable Gowanus cafe for one thing: pie. It's not just any pie, but some of the best in the city. The sell by the slice in the shop, or you can order ahead for a whole pie, which is especially popular during the holidays. In fall, look for salted caramel apple, brown butter pumpkin, and bourbon pear; in summer, the standout is strawberry balsamic.

Franny's Pizza, 295 Flatbush Avenue between Prospect Place and St. Marks Place; (718) 230-0221; Subway: 2, 3 to Bergen Street or B, Q to 7th Avenue; frannysbrooklyn.com; $$. Opening this simple, little Prospect Heights pizza place was a bold move in a pizza-loving town. But the risk has paid off in spades, and Franny's has become a local favorite, both for its tasty pizzas and for its commitment to eco-friendly practices. The husband-and-wife duo who opened Franny's goes way beyond local, organic ingredients, fair-traded coffee, and hormone- and antibiotic-free meats, though of course they follow those tenets as well. They also do a lot of things the customer doesn't see: They use renewable energy (made up of 35 percent wind power and 65 percent small hydroelectric power), convert kitchen grease into biodiesel fuel, and use mostly paper products made from recycled, biodegradable materials. Oh, and the pizza is really tasty, too. The crust is charred nicely, and then topped with a simple, sweet tomato sauce and buffalo mozzarella as well as anchovies, sausage, or clams. They also serve salami plates

Park Slope Food Co-op

Joining this massive grocery store co-op is no laughing matter. The organization enjoys such popularity that they have new-member orientations four times per week, each one lasting 2 hours. Sit through the spiel, and then you have to submit two forms of ID, a passport photo, and pay $125 in order to start shopping. After that, you must volunteer to work there for 2 hours and 45 minutes each month. Those are the rules—nonmembers can't even enter the store.

So, with that much hassle and so many good grocery stores in Brooklyn, why join? Well, the benefits are numerous, which is why they have more than 14,000 earnest members, thank you very much. They focus on local and organic produce, artisan cheese, pasture-raised and grass-fed meat, free-range and organic poultry, and wild and sustainable fish. They also have aisles full of fair-traded chocolate and coffee, and bulk grains and spices at low prices. Certainly if you have a family, the savings (which the co-op claims range from 20 to 40 percent) add up quickly. Plus, the co-op has babysitting for members to take advantage of while they work, and they offer nutrition, recycling, and occasionally cooking classes, too. 782 Union Street between 6th Avenue and 7th Avenue; (718) 622-0560; Subway: F to 7th Avenue or R to 4th Avenue; foodcoop.com.

and seasonal crostini topped with buffalo ricotta and spinach or pancetta and garlic butter. Of course, the pizza should be enough, but the waits can be killer so by the time you're seated you may want to order the whole menu.

Geido, 381 Flatbush Avenue between Prospect Place and Park Place; (718) 638-8866; Subway: 2, 3 to Grand Army Plaza or Q, B to 7th Avenue; $$. It's nice to stumble into a place that feels like an ex-pat hangout, and this dinner-only Japanese restaurant always seems to count many Japanese youth among its regulars. The walls are covered with graffiti, some of it of cartoon characters, and much of it not in English; the vibe is fun and casual. Sit at the sushi bar, or plan to make a meal off the comfort food menu, which includes house-made gyoza dumplings, udon noodles, and pork *katsu*. On any given day, the enormous marker board of specials might include tempura, special rolls, and *kushiyaki,* which are skewered meats that are often marinated and then broiled—you can choose from these daily treats without ever opening a menu.

James, 605 Carlton Avenue between St. Marks Avenue and Prospect Place; (718) 942-4255; Subway: B, Q to 7th Avenue or 2, 3 to Bergen; jamesrestaurantny.com; $$$. This refined little restaurant serves up three trends in one: seasonal cuisine, posh cocktails, and small plates. The space is a nice mix of elegant (dramatic chandelier, architectural flower arrangements) and comfortable (the long dark wood bar has cushioned stools, and the service is warm and friendly). Start with cocktails, mixed with fresh juices

house-made vanilla ice cream sprinkled liberally with fresh, sweet summer blueberries.

Rose Water, 787 Union Street between 5th Avenue and 6th Avenue; (718) 783-3800; Subway: R to Union; rosewater restaurant.com; $$$. Like **Applewood** (p. 104), Rose Water lives by a mission of sustainability, so the menus change daily here, too, with savory appetizers like poached duck egg with lamb bacon or fried goat cheese with black mission figs, prosciutto, and honey. Dinner entrees might be roast leg of lamb with fava bean puree and sorrel pesto or grilled polenta with porcini mushrooms and nettles. Brunch is a highlight: The blueberry pancakes are fluffy and come topped with roasted cashews, an interesting pink peppercorn butter, and grade B maple syrup; crepes may come filled with rhubarb compote and topped with sliced strawberries and crème fraîche. The brunch menu lists interesting beverages, including a spa-worthy cucumber mint *agua fresca* and hibiscus ice tea.

Stone Park Cafe, 324 5th Avenue between 2nd Street and 3rd Street; (718) 369-0082; Subway: R to Union Street or F to 4th Avenue; stoneparkcafe.com; $$$. This market-focused restaurant, one of the better choices in the Slope for a refined night out, can be a bit pricey for what you get. A $14 braised short rib

appetizer on a mini brioche bun, topped with a quail egg, left me wondering, "Where's the beef?" (How small was it? The petite chunk of short rib barely exceeded the width of the quail egg.) Fortunately, they have a $32 fixed-price menu that's a spectacular value. Dishes focus on whatever's in season and fresh but could include a grilled octopus and frisée appetizer salad topped with preserved lemon and tempura-fried squash blossoms that are so delectable, they'll make you wonder if you could order a whole plate. Entrees might be pan-seared diver scallops, browned to perfection on the top, or a well-marinated skirt steak with garlicky mashed potatoes. Desserts are just as good: Order the peach cobbler or the key lime pie, and ask to swap out the standard vanilla ice-cream scoop for whatever they've made fresh that day. The mint chocolate chip is memorable, but the caramel will have you licking the melted splotches off the plate—or at least sucking them off your finger when no one is looking.

The Sunburnt Calf, 611 Vanderbilt Avenue between St. Mark's Avenue and Bergen Street; (347) 915-1000; Subway: B, Q to 7th Avenue or 2, 3 to Bergen Street; moolifegroup.com; $$. The Aussie restaurant started on the Lower East Side of Manhattan, and opened an Upper West Side location before venturing into Brooklyn. It's not a cuisine that's easy to find in the borough, and don't come expecting Vegemite sandwiches, sausage rolls, lamb served several ways, and lamingtons for dessert. Instead, the Calf serves up Australia's take on Southeast Asian fare like shrimp toast, satay, and pad thai. A good example: You can get beer-battered barramundi, but don't be surprised when it's served over vermicelli rather than with chips.

Taro Sushi, 244 Flatbush Avenue between St. Marks and Prospect Place; (718) 398-5240; Subway: 2, 3 to Bergen Street; tarosushi brooklyn.com; $$. This once unassuming little Japanese-owned Dean Street spot—a surprise fave of neighborhood sushi lovers—has relocated to a larger, grander space. Locals in the know go for the *omakase*, or chef's choice, which starts at a mere $20 per person and includes plenty of fish that has been flown in from Tokyo. Or order your pieces a la carte, paying special attention to the list of daily specials.

The Vanderbilt, 570 Vanderbilt Avenue between Bergen Street and Dean Street; (718) 623-0570; Subway: B, Q to 7th Avenue or 2, 3 to Bergen Street; thevanderbiltnyc.com; $$$. Instead of additional speakeasies, Brooklyn needs more small-plate restaurants, and they should all be as good as The Vanderbilt. The cocktails are tasty, the beer list is interesting, and the food, which comes out as it's finished in a parade of tasty morsels, will make you want to linger. Consider the crispy Serrano ham croquettes (a dish you will need more than one of if you're with a group), the duck *rillettes* with quince paste, the *boudin blanc* with potato puree, and the crispy pork belly with lentils. You can move on from the charcuterie—to braised short ribs, steamed mussels, or perhaps a hanger steak—but it's tempting just to continue ordering small plates of rich and fried treats and forgo the entrees and desserts.

Zuzu Ramen, 173 4th Avenue between Degraw Street and Sackett Street; (718) 398-9898; Subway: R to Union Street; zuzuramen.com; $$. Noodle bars have been popular in Manhattan for a few years, but Brooklyn is getting in on the act. Start with pan-seared pork dumplings, edamame, or pork shoulder–filled  steamed buns topped with cucumbers, scallions, and Sriracha sauce, before slurping down a big bowl of ramen noodles swimming in a pork- and vegetable-filled green curry–miso broth. Or choose the shrimp in a hot and sour broth with Thai basil and lemongrass. At first, from the menu to the bar stools and simple Asian decor, Zuzu may feel like a derivative of Manhattan's Momofuku Noodle Bar—and then you'll probably just let that thought go and be glad to have it in the neighborhood.

Landmarks

Tom's Restaurant, 782 Washington Avenue between Sterling Place and St. Johns Place; (718) 636-9738; Subway: 2, 3 to Grand Army Plaza; $. This popular Prospect Heights diner, circa 1936, may just have the best breakfast in the borough—and that's why the line is so darn long. Fortunately, they make it easy for you to wait, offering glasses of ice water and mugs of coffee as well as orange slices and strawberries with whipped cream. The menu takes all the basics and turns them on their ears, with harvest pancakes (filled with corn and dried cranberries) and blueberry-cheese "Danish" pancakes; pumpkin-walnut Belgian waffles and sweet potato ones; eggs Florentine with deep-fried deviled crab cakes. The condiments—a caddy of strawberry, cinnamon, and lime butters—are flavorful enough to brighten your morning, as are the drinks: cherry-lime rickeys, whipped ice coffees, and chocolate egg creams served in frozen fountain glasses. The eggs aren't anything special, but for sweet breakfast dishes the place might just be perfect—especially since they decided to open on Sunday, too.

Specialty Stores, Markets & Producers

Bagel Hole, 400 7th Avenue between 12th Street and 13th Street; (718) 788-4014; Subway: F to 7th Avenue; bagelhole.net. There's a surprising dearth of great bagels in Brooklyn, but there's a reason why this little spot—which has no seats and modest decor—often has a line out the door. They hand-roll their bagels on-site, and they make all the classic flavors—plain, onion, cinnamon raisin—and nothing newfangled. Shout your order over the crowd (don't worry, everybody does it) and ask for whatever is hot from the oven. Then, clutch your hot little brown bag in your hands, and get out of the crowded little space as fast as you can. The warm, doughy bagels are great used in an egg sandwich or slathered with cream cheese. Just consider yourself warned: If you don't like dessert in the morning, avoid the raisin-walnut schmear. It's almost as sweet as frosting and, when combined with a hot bagel, forms an icing-like glaze that's fantastic or cloying, depending on your taste.

Bierkraft, 191 5th Avenue between Berkeley Place and Union Street; (718) 230-7600; Subway: R to Union Street; bierkraft.com; $. Yes, you can buy beer here—and plenty of it. Beer lovers from all over the borough come here when they can't find a beloved brew somewhere else. They have more than 500 labels, and you  can buy growlers and kegs, too. A quick look at the list shows more than a dozen countries are represented, in addition to seasonal choices and oddities, like banana bread beer, and chocolate beer for Valentine's Day. But there are plenty of things here for the non-beer lover, including a lovely array of cheese and a menu of carefully composed sandwiches. Build your own from their choices, including house-roasted organic turkey and Wagyu beef that you can top with one of 45 types of cheese, including 4 bries, 4 Goudas, and 2 cheddars. They also added tables and benches, and now serve pints along with the sandwiches.

Bklyn Larder, 228 Flatbush Avenue between Bergen Street and 6th Avenue; (718) 783-1250; Subway: 2, 3 to Bergen Street; bklyn larder.com; $$. Owned by the same folks who do Prospect Park's most popular restaurant, **Franny's** (p. 110), Bklyn Larder is one-stop shopping for the borough's locally made products. Stock up on **McClure's** (p. 249) mustard and spicy garlic pickle spears (which come in giant family-size jars) as well as **Lioni Latticini** (p. 215) mozzarella and ricotta, and the Larder's own gelati and sorbetti. Many of the meats are house-made, and the cheese counter seems to cover the globe. Stocking up on everything you want would cost a small fortune, so Bklyn Larder may be best at lunchtime, when you can get grilled sandwiches made with their artfully sourced ingredients, such as grilled cheese, porchetta, and tuna with anchovies and egg, all on locally made artisan bread. Or go on a weekend, when you can pick up bread, pâté, salad, and sweets for the perfect Prospect Park picnic.

Blue Apron Fine Foods, 814 Union Street between 7th Avenue and 8th Avenue; (718) 230-3180; Subway: 2, 3 to Grand Army Plaza and B, Q to 7th Avenue. There are lots of little gourmet shops in the Slope, but this tiny shop somehow manages, in very little square footage, to outshine them all. They carry an impressive collection of locally cured and smoked fish from **Acme** (p. 159) in Greenpoint, and meat from Salumeria Biellese in Manhattan and Karl Ehmer in Queens. Their pastries hail from **Margaret Palca Bakes** (p. 69) in the Columbia Waterfront District and **Baked** (p. 60) in Red Hook, and the chocolate is from **Jacques Torres** (p. 28) in Dumbo. Of course, not everything is local—the salted caramels, olive oil, and many cheeses are flown in from Europe.

Christie's Jamaican Patties, 387 Flatbush Avenue between 8th Avenue and Sterling Place; (718) 636-9746; Subway: Q to 7th Avenue or 2, 3 to Grand Army Plaza. Finding good patties this far north on Flatbush Avenue is a pleasant surprise. And they sure are good: The dough is flaky and the beef filling is soft and smooth and well spiced. (They also make chicken patties that have their own following.) You can order yours tucked inside traditional coco bread, too. The shop sells plenty of other Jamaican specialties— from jerk chicken to callaloo loaf and puffy coco bread—but the patties are so satisfying (especially with a douse of hot sauce) that you may find it hard to order anything else.

Colson Patisserie, 374 9th Street between 6th Avenue and 7th Avenue; (718) 965-6400; Subway: F to 7th Avenue; colsonpastries .com; $. This Belgian bakery waves its flag proudly, from Belgian ice creams to Belgian pastries. The small shop itself has just as many tables on the sidewalk as it does inside, but there's plenty here that's worthy of a trip if the chairs are all occupied. Start the day with something rich and buttery—an almond croissant, buttery raisin brioche, pain au chocolate, or Belgian waffles called *gauffres*—and a big cafe au lait. Lunch might be a pâté, brie, and apple sandwich, or *jambon* on a baguette with cornichons; quiche lorraine; or a *salade niçoise* followed by house-made currant ice cream that's more intense than it is creamy. Whatever you do though, plan to walk out the door with some proper pastries—the meringues with raspberries, pistachio *financier* cookies, and blueberry tarts are too delicate to pass up. It's all such a perfect taste of francophone Europe that you won't be surprised that the owners have a similar shop in Belgium.

Culture: An American Yogurt Company, 331 5th Avenue between 3rd Street and 4th Street; (718) 499-0207; Subway: R to Union Street; cultureny.com. This frozen yogurt shop made a big splash with their pie-like toppings. Their yogurt (which is as rich and tart as plain Greek yogurt and packed with probiotics) comes topped with a wide variety of combinations, from fresh peach pie, blueberry pie, or pumpkin pie filling, to maple and candied nuts.

Eagle Provisions, 628 5th Avenue between 17th Street and 18th Street; (718) 499-0026; Subway: R to Prospect Avenue. This minigrocery store on the southern edge of the Slope has all your Eastern European foodstuffs—loops of kielbasa hanging over the meat counter, cold cases full of pierogi, shelves weighed down by large jars of sauerkraut and spicy mustard in shocking quantities, and bakery bins lined with poppy-seed strudel, dark breads, and other baked goods. If you want Polish jams and box mixes, this is the place for those, too. But the secret find here is the beer selection. It's surprisingly worldly, and separated by country and state. The 1,500 different beers run the gamut from true cheapies (like Schlitz, Lionshead, and Pabst) to local beer (**Brooklyn Brewery**'s [p. 162] Local 1 and Local 2) to rare finds (like Polish and Latvian imports). What's really impressive though is the sheer breadth of choice—a good beer store will have Belgian Lambics and American regional beers, but this place has everything, including some very obscure finds. Who would think you could get elderberry black ales from Scotland and an oatmeal stout from Montreal at an Eastern European shop? You can find them here, and so much more. You'll also want to leave time to peruse their soda selection, which is almost as big and carries local faves like **Manhattan Special** (p. 167) coffee soda.

Fleisher's Park Slope, 192 5th Avenue between Sackett Street and Union Street; (718) 398-6666; Subway: R to Union Street or 2, 3 to Bergen or B, Q to Seventh Avenue; fleishers.com. This locally sourced meat market takes artisan butchery to the next level, with a sleek storefront that looks more boutique than grocer. The butchers follow the nose-to-tail philosophy that so many restaurants have adopted in an effort to not be wasteful, and they sell every part of the cows and pigs they butcher. Meats here are grass fed, organic, antibiotic free, and hormone free, and the animals they butcher were sustained on a vegetarian diet. Want to learn more about their philosophy? They teach classes, and offer lectures and demonstrations in their store.

Gorilla Coffee, 97 5th Avenue between Park Place and Prospect Place; (718) 230-3244; Subway: 2, 3, 4, 5, N, Q, R to Atlantic-Pacific; gorillacoffee.com. When a friend who lives in the Slope said, "I get excited about summer because Gorilla brings out their ice coffee," I knew I had to try it. And she's right—it is darn good coffee. Their organic, fair-traded beans, which they roast in Brooklyn daily in small 30-pound batches, make a brew that's dark, rich, and strong enough to hold up to being iced, which is why the regular coffee is popular for its high quality, but controversial because many find it too strong for their palate. The solution? Get yours in milky latte form—they even make a maple latte with New York State syrup—or buy their beans and make it at home.

Grab Specialty Foods, 438 7th Avenue between 14th Street and 15th Street; (718) 369-7595; Subway: F, G to 7th Avenue; grab specialtyfoods.com. Another small but well-edited food store, this one focuses squarely on cheese and beer. Cheeses include Salvatore Bklyn from Cobble Hill and several New York State offerings, as well as plenty of French and Italian choices and a wide array of blues. These are complemented by cured meats, the highlight of which is the local Salumeria Biellese picante sopressata. Their beer comes in a well-edited selection of bottles (lined up alongside equally interesting cocktail mixers and a wide selection of **Gorilla Coffee,** p. 125, beans) including local, Belgian, craft brews, and many large fermented ales, but most beer lovers come here for the filled-to-order growlers of beers like local **Sixpoint** (p. 75) Sweet Action, Fire Island Lighthouse Ale, and Québec's Unibroue La Terrible. Their sweets include cupcakes and brownies from **Baked** (p. 60) in Red Hook and dark chocolate bars with almonds and sea salt from Williamsburg's **Mast Brothers** (p. 169). The cold sections also include **Sahadi's** (p. 29) hummus, so you don't have to run to Brooklyn Heights and wait in line to get this local treat.

Grand Army Plaza Greenmarket, Grand Army Plaza at the Northwest Entrance to Prospect Park; Subway: 2, 3 to Grand Army Plaza or B, Q to 7th Avenue; grownyc.org/grandarmygreenmarket. This Saturday-only, year-round green market gets more and more crowded—especially with strollers and adorable little dogs on leashes—as the thermometer climbs, and the options for locally grown produce expand. Year-round, though, you'll find Vermont maple syrup, sausages from beautiful rare heritage piggies at the upstate Flying Pigs Farm, cheese from Cato Corner (they give their cheese funny names like Drunken Hooligan, Drunk Monk, and Womanchego, but you should still take them seriously), pickled beans and other vegetables from Rick's Picks (he also gives them funny names

like Phat Beets and Smokra, but you should take him seriously, too—he makes a mean bread-and-butter pickle), free-range and certified organic turkey (a sold-out stand at Thanksgiving time, so be sure to order ahead) from DiPaola Turkey Farm in New Jersey, and baked breads and pies, too. In the summer you'll also find gorgeous flowers (which people carry away by the back-breaking armfuls) and spectacular local produce that changes with the crops.

In early summer, rhubarb and those small, sweet Jersey strawberries are in season. As the summer progresses, enormous bunches of Long Island spinach, ears of Jersey yellow corn, and big fat Jersey tomatoes become highlights, too. Make a tomato sauce with local Jersey tomatoes that are crimson red, tiny heads of purple garlic, and onions that are so fresh they still have the stems and leaves on and a knife goes through them like butter, and suddenly you'll understand what all the fuss is about.

The Islands, 803 Washington Avenue between Eastern Parkway and Lincoln Place; (718) 398-3575; Subway: 2, 3 to Grand Army Plaza; $. This Jamaican restaurant is tiny as can be, but in the summertime you can sit outside at their sidewalk cafe tables, which come with a dramatic view of the fountains at the Brooklyn Museum. Order a plate of the well-seasoned jerk chicken, and ask for a splash of the super-hot scotch bonnet sauce they make themselves. Even the sides are tasty here, including the fried plantains, and the beans and rice cooked with coconut milk. Time your visit right, and you may luck into a glass of house-made "lemonade" that is Jamaican style, with just-squeezed limes.

Ladybird Bakery, 1112 8th Avenue between 11th Street and 12th Street; (718) 499-8108; Subway: F to 7th Avenue; ladybirdbakery .com; $. This little bakery on 8th Avenue looks truly homespun, with hand-painted flowers on the windows and walls and a few simple wooden tables, but the desserts are clearly from the hand of a professional. You'll find rich peanut butter cookies and iced sugar cookies in glass jars, and a glass-front countertop filled with peach pies, raspberry tarts, red velvet cakes with classic cream cheese frosting, and buttercream-covered children's birthday cakes, made to order. But the real standout here is the Brooklyn Blackout cupcake, a spin on an old recipe by a long-gone Brooklyn bakery called Ebinger's. The cupcake is comprised of a thin layer of dark chocolate cake encasing a dark chocolate pudding. The whole thing is topped with fudge frosting and chocolate cake crumbs, and it's a spectacular masterpiece.

Little Miss Muffin, 174 Park Place between Carlton Avenue and Vanderbilt Avenue; (718) 857-4963; Subway: 2, 3 to Grand Army Plaza or Q, B to 7th Avenue. Yes, they sell muffins in this tiny side-street shop, made up of a glass-front bakery case, an oven, and a fridge full of drinks. And they're rumored to be quite good. So are the cookies and the Caribbean sorrel punch. But once you eat one of the Jamaican patties, hot from the oven and wafting with steam, you will only have eyes for them. These yellow-tinged pastries, flaky

Prospect Park Foraging Tours

Ever wondered if those red berries you see growing in Prospect Park are edible? Well, the answer is probably yes, but you can find out for sure on one of forager Steve Brill's monthly tours. Sign up (wildmanstevebrill.com) to spend the morning with Steve, and you'll gather vegetables, herbs, mushrooms, and berries, right from this public park. His website has a plethora of information on what to wear (layers!), what to bring (bags for taking your edibles home!), and how to sign up. He also posted a calendar with tour dates marked and information on his other tours of Central Park in Manhattan, Forest Park in Queens, and the Montgomery Pinetum in Connecticut. Oh, and those berries you were tempted to munch on in the past: probably elderberries, and most definitely safe. According to Brill, even the flowers are edible and tasty, especially when sautéed into a pancake.

and scented with curry, come with several tasty fillings, from savory jerk chicken and curried chicken to rich spicy beef. Just don't ask for hot sauce—they don't carry it.

Park Slope Farmers' Market, 5th Avenue between 3rd Street and 4th Street; communitymarkets.biz. This seasonal, Sunday-only market is a fraction of the size of the Grand Army Plaza one, but you can get the basics. Open from 11 a.m. to 5 p.m., the stands spread out along J. J. Byrne Park. Offering mostly vegetables, vendors sell many varieties of organic lettuces, including monster heads of romaine, as well as radishes, little orange beets, and more interesting salad ingredients like nasturtium flowers. Alex Farm in Milford, NJ, has herbs like peppery basil, pesticide-free cilantro, and Italian parsley as well as lovely Jersey blueberries. There are also treats from Doc Pickle, Breezy Hill Orchards' apples, Bombay Emerald chutneys, and Made by Molly breads.

Russo Mozzarella and Pasta, 363 7th Avenue between 10th Street and 11th Street; (718) 369-2874; Subway: F to 7th Avenue; $. Locals looking for Italian-style sandwiches for picnics in Prospect Park need look no further than Russo's. This sibling to the East Village original sells some of the best sandwiches in the Slope. The long list of offerings (including the #2, a classic Philadelphia-style "hoagie," even if they don't call it that) come on long, seeded Italian rolls packed with sliced-to-order meats like mortadella, sopressata, and capocollo (ask for yours extra thin if that's how you like it) as well as Italian cheeses like provolone and fresh mozzarella and house-made toppings like roasted red peppers. They come dry, but you can ask for yours with lettuce, tomato, olive oil, and vinegar, as well as ground black pepper. You can also buy their cold cuts to go, as well as stock up on olives from their bar, and imported Italian foodstuffs like canned tuna and jarred anchovies. Like the Manhattan store, Russo's specializes in house-made sauces and pastas.

Sweet Melissa Patisserie, 175 7th Avenue between 1st Street and 2nd Street; (718) 788-2700; Subway: 2, 3 to Grand Army Plaza or F to 7th Avenue or Q, B to 7th Avenue; sweetmelissapatisserie .com; $$. Sweet Melissa started out as a tiny neighborhood bakery specializing in desserts and wedding cakes. Then the owner won a Food Network bake-off and a *Brides* magazine contest for the most beautiful wedding cakes in America. And while the breakfast treats (like quiche and oatmeal) are perfectly lovely, they also have afternoon tea that includes finger sandwiches and scones with clotted cream, but it's still the desserts that steal the show. Order a few brown-butter madeleines or a slice of hazelnut cake to go, or take a seat and watch the neighborhood go by.

Tarzian West, 194 7th Avenue between 2nd Street and 3rd Street; (718) 788-4213; Subway: F to 7th Avenue. This small houseware store is crowded with every cookery item you can imagine. For decades it has been the go-to spot in the Slope for all things culinary. From whisks and spatulas to Wusthof knives, All-Clad pots, pans, ramekins, and aprons, it's all here—piled high on shelves and stacked up to the ceiling in a colorful, vaguely chaotic kaleidoscope. If you live here, it's a relief to know there's a cheese grater waiting for you should yours break, and a housewarming gift within arm's reach. If you don't live near here, you'll have a quick flash of realization that you'd be here a lot if you did.

The Treats Truck, (212) 691-5226; treatstruck.com. Many Saturday mornings, this shiny silver truck parks on Union Street, right near the Greenmarket. Children and grown-ups alike line up for all sorts of bake sale–style sweets like chocolate chip and oatmeal cookies, sugar cookies covered in icing and sprinkles, and peanut butter sandwich cookies filled with raspberry jam or chocolate cream. Order a bar, including an espresso brownie or a butterscotch blondie with pecans, and you'll be asked if you want a middle or an end. It's such a nice touch—everyone has a preference.

Trois Pommes Patisserie, 260 5th Avenue between Carroll Street and Garfield Place; (718) 230-3119; Subway: R to Union Street; troispommespatisserie.com. No, this bakery's wares may not be precious—the devil's food whoopee pies are a little lopsided, and the

little peach fruit pies look decidedly more homemade than professional—but the fruit is fresh from the green market and everything tastes just right. In fact, some of it tastes even better than just right. Miniature chocolate-caramel tarts are humble looking, but they melt in your mouth with rich flavor, as do the tiny lemon meringue tartlettes, despite looking a bit banged up. The house-made ice creams are wonderful, too, including the unforgettable caramel praline crunch and the blueberry-buttermilk sorbet, both of which taste more like French ice cream than the more-creamy American stuff. Best of all, the cones are house-made, too. This is one place that's proof positive that you shouldn't judge the book by its cover.

Wafels and Dinges Truck, (866) 429-7329; wafelsanddinges .com. Many weekends, this Belgian waffle truck parks at the corner of 7th Avenue and Carroll Street. Come in the morning for *liège* (round, soft) or Brussels (rectangular, crisp) waffles, topped with fruit (sliced strawberries or bananas) or a creamy, sweet spread (Nutella, Belgian fudge, caramel-like dulce de leche, or gingery *speculoos*). Or ask for their secret, off-menu dish: waffles filled with bacon. The thin, watery hot cocoa is a rare misstep, but you can also get coffee. Schedules can change, so check their website or sign up for their Twitter feed to track their whereabouts, and find out about specials, which often include free toppings.

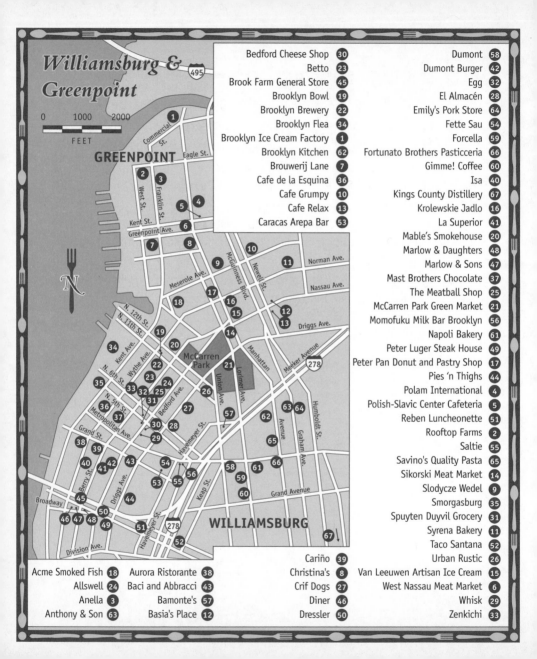

Williamsburg & Greenpoint

GREENPOINT

WILLIAMSBURG

Broadway

Division Ave.

0 · 1000 · 2000
FEET

Bedford Cheese Shop	30
Betto	23
Brook Farm General Store	45
Brooklyn Bowl	19
Brooklyn Brewery	22
Brooklyn Flea	34
Brooklyn Ice Cream Factory	1
Brooklyn Kitchen	62
Brouwerij Lane	7
Cafe de la Esquina	36
Cafe Grumpy	10
Cafe Relax	13
Caracas Arepa Bar	53

Dumont	58
Dumont Burger	42
Egg	32
El Almacén	28
Emily's Pork Store	64
Fette Sau	54
Forcella	59
Fortunato Brothers Pasticceria	66
Gimme! Coffee	60
Isa	40
Kings County Distillery	67
Krolewskie Jadlo	16
La Superior	41
Mable's Smokehouse	20
Marlow & Daughters	48
Marlow & Sons	47
Mast Brothers Chocolate	37
The Meatball Shop	25
McCarren Park Green Market	21
Momofuku Milk Bar Brooklyn	56
Napoli Bakery	61
Peter Luger Steak House	49
Peter Pan Donut and Pastry Shop	17
Pies 'n Thighs	44
Polam International	4
Polish-Slavic Center Cafeteria	5
Reben Luncheonette	51
Rooftop Farms	2
Saltie	55
Savino's Quality Pasta	65
Sikorski Meat Market	14
Slodycze Wedel	9
Smorgasburg	35
Spuyten Duyvil Grocery	31
Syrena Bakery	11
Taco Santana	52
Urban Rustic	26
Van Leeuwen Artisan Ice Cream	15
West Nassau Meat Market	6
Whisk	29
Zenkichi	33

Cariño	39
Christina's	8
Crif Dogs	27
Diner	46
Dressler	50

Acme Smoked Fish	18
Allswell	24
Anella	3
Anthony & Son	63
Aurora Ristorante	38
Baci and Abbracci	43
Bamonte's	57
Basia's Place	12

Williamsburg & Greenpoint

Williamsburg is a neighborhood that changed dramatically—and fast. More than a decade ago, the artists and creative types started moving into this once-blue-collar area, and the scene began to morph. Trucker hats and ironic tees emerged as the 'hood's icons of hipster style. Debates began about whether all of these skinny "starving" artist types were actually struggling or whether they were "trustafarians," twentysomethings supported by trust funds. Waterfront, glassy high-rises were developed for successful creative types hoping a little of Billyburg's "cool" factor would rub off. These new condo constructions were successful at classing up the neighborhood—or destroying it, depending on your perspective. Either way, this new spirit has imbued the neighborhood with renewed energy as well as restaurants, galleries, and shops on bustling Bedford Avenue. On summer nights, Bedford is packed with revelers—in many ways, it has become Brooklyn's answer to

Manhattan's Bleecker Street, with bars as well as pizza shops to sate the late-night munchies. But, off the main strip, life feels very much like it always has: A mix of immigrants—from Italians to Puerto Ricans and Hasidic Jews—form close-knit communities in which everyone seems to know one another.

Working-class Polish Greenpoint has been historically cut off from Manhattan by poor train service. (The main subway line, the G train, runs only between Queens and Brooklyn.) Perhaps that has protected Greenpoint from the gentrification that other neighborhoods have faced—that, a lackluster housing stock, and a middle-of-the-last-century oil spill that contaminated Newtown Creek. That is, until now. During the building boom of the last few years, Greenpoint has seen its share of newcomers flocking to rehabbed artist lofts in former warehouses and flashy new-construction condo buildings spilling over from Williamsburg. With them, these newcomers add to the mix small, sophisticated bars and restaurants that offer lower price points than their Manhattan counterparts. But, though old-timers may gripe that the hipsters are changing everything, Greenpoint has maintained much of its Old World flair. On Manhattan Avenue, Polish butchers abut Polish bakeries, and signs are often in both Polish and English. Just off Manhattan Avenue, there's a wealth of Polish-style cafeteria restaurants, where you may have to have the woman at the counter translate the specials for you, and each table has a trio of seasonings: salt, pepper, and paprika. Greenpoint, at its best, feels far from the glam of Manhattan, even though you can see the city skyline looming just across the East River.

Allswell, 124 Bedford Avenue between N. 10th Street and N. 11th Street; (347) 799-2743; Subway: L to Lorimer Street; allswellnyc .tumblr.com; $$$. There are all-too-few gastropubs in New York for the swelling Anglophile community, and this one, opened by former Spotted Pig chef Nate Smith, certainly looks the part. Settle into a booth and order a pint and a snack of sausage pie or Welsh rarebit, which is white toast topped with a beer-tinged cheese sauce. Or, plan on a more fancy dinner of rabbit *rillettes*, ricotta dumplings with chard, or scallops with saffron risotto. Either way, you can't go wrong.

Anella, 222 Franklin Street between Huron Street and Green Street; (718) 389-8100; Subway: G to Greenpoint Avenue; anellabrooklyn .com; $$. This market-fresh restaurant serves up whatever's in season, using as much produce from nearby **Rooftop Farms** (p. 173) as possible. Start with oysters, then move on to a perfectly al dente pasta and a seasonal dessert, such as blueberry sorbet in the summertime.

Aurora Ristorante, 70 Grand Street between Wythe Avenue and Kent Avenue; (718) 388-5100; Subway: L to Bedford Avenue; auroraristorante.com; $$$. This seasonal Italian spot, a spin-off of Manhattan's Soho location, serves up romance in its candlelit garden, along with house-made pastas. The menu changes frequently, but start with a salad: Choose from peppery greens topped

with sweet summer peaches and toasted hazel-nuts, or a watermelon salad mixed with feta, basil, and olives and topped with sea salt. Then, share a plate of pasta and enjoy a moment straight out of *Lady and the Tramp:* The pappardelle with roasted rabbit and olives is hearty and flavorful, as is the tagliatelle with meat ragout. Or skip the pasta and go right to the meats, like a grass-fed skirt steak served with fingerling potatoes or a seared pork chop with mustard greens.

Baci & Abbracci, 204 Grand Street between Bedford Avenue and Driggs Avenue; (718) 599-6599; Subway: L to Bedford Avenue or G to Metropolitan Avenue; baciny.com; $$. This lovely Italian spot has a pretty dining room, with exposed brick walls and a built-in wood-fired pizza oven, but come summer the flower-filled garden is still the place to be. Start with a caprese salad of chopped local tomatoes (both red and the low-acid yellow ones) mixed with torn basil leaves and milky house-made mozzarella. Then, choose a pizza (such as the fragrant one topped with crispy prosciutto and fresh wild arugula) or one of the many house-made pastas, from gnocchi with tomato and more of that wonderful mozzarella to a spinach-ricotta ravioli topped with mushrooms and truffle-scented brown butter sauce.

Basia's Place, 167 Nassau Avenue between Diamond Street and Jewel Street; (718) 383-0276; Subway: G to Nassau Avenue; $. It's hard to take this small restaurant seriously. On a hot summer day, from the outside, it looks closed. But open the door, and you'll see a crowd of locals watching the Polish satellite news on the flat-screen TV and enjoying the cool, air-conditioned darkness. Sure, it's a comfortable atmosphere for homesick Polish ex-pats, but they're also here for the food. Dishes are served up cafeteria style, on bright orange trays reminiscent of elementary school lunches. You order from a list on the wall and grab your own silverware, then wait for your order to be called out in Polish. Fortunately, the home-style fare is far from institutional: House-made pierogi are light, with thin dumpling-like wrappers that are filled with a creamy mashed potato-and-American cheese mixture or a well-seasoned ground beef, then crimped by hand and topped with caramelized onions and a dollop of heavy sour cream. They're so tender, they may just be the best in town. There are plenty of other items on the menu—from goulash to cutlets, cabbage rolls stuffed with meat called *galupke,* and pork chops. The soups are extremely popular, and I have watched people pick up to-go orders of plastic tubs filled with chicken noodle soup that looks so comforting I wished that I weren't already full.

Betto, 138 N. 8th Street between Bedford Avenue and Berry Street; (718) 384-1904; Subway: L to Bedford Avenue; bettonyc.com; $$. The team behind Manhattan's 'inoteca and 'ino restaurants have opened their first Brooklyn location in Williamsburg, helmed by former Corsino chef Shaunna Sargent. Picture similar rustic Italian flavors, with shared small plates of cured meats like soppresata and speck and cheese, such as local Camembert as well as crostini, topped with a variety of options, including apple and pecorino, chicken liver mousse, and cannellini beans. More substantial fare is equally expected for fans of the chainlet, from *panelle* to roasted acorn squash, pork belly meatballs in tomato sauce, and spaghetti with broccoli rabe.

Brooklyn Bowl, 61 Wythe Avenue between N. 11th Street and N. 12th Street; (718) 963-3369; Subway: L to Bedford Avenue or G to Nassau Avenue; brooklynbowl.com; $$. First and foremost a hipster bowling alley and cool music venue, this rock 'n' roll–fueled hot spot took Williamsburg by storm when it opened. The best news for food lovers? The **Blue Ribbon** (p. 105) folks are handling the dining. They designed a comfort food menu that's tasty and worth the trip alone. Order up shareable trays of crunchy fried chicken (yes, the hint of Old Bay seasoning is controversial), platters of barbecue chicken wings, big bowls of macaroni and cheese, or french bread pizza. (The spicy one topped with pulled pork and smoked jalapeños is especially tasty.) Just don't miss the praline-and-Nutella milk shake they serve with a shot of bourbon—it may even be worth skipping the local **Brooklyn Brewery** (p. 162) and Kelso beers for, and that's saying a lot. Worried about the greasy finger food messing up your game? Take a break and order your dinner at one of the restaurant-style booths by the bar, or eat with your non-bowling hand, as the menu suggests.

Cafe de La Esquina, 225 Wythe Avenue between 4th Street and 3rd Street; (718) 393-5500; Subway: J, M, Z to Marcy Avenue or L to Bedford Avenue; esquinabk .com; $$$. From the team behind the Soho restaurant by the same name, this upscale  Mexican taqueria and hipster hangout serves up ceviche, quesadillas, tostadas, and tacos. While everything is way pricier than what you'd pay in Sunset Park, you'll also find plenty of atmosphere and cool cocktails.

Cafe Relax, 68 Newell Street between Nassau Avenue and Driggs Avenue; (718) 389-1665; Subway: G to Nassau Avenue; $. This small luncheonette is not as pretty as Karczma, with its theme-park style setting, or even feminine Lomzynianka, which is lined with dainty lace curtains and lit with old-fashioned tabletop lamps, but the food is better. There's a menu board above the counter, with handwritten signs detailing the specials. Entrees are enormous, served with 2 sides, and mostly under $6, but you could make a whole meal out of the white borscht, a beet-free potato soup topped with kielbasa slices, hard-boiled egg, and dill and served with a side of rather dense mashed potatoes. (Consider yourself warned: It is only served on Wednesday and Saturday.) The pierogi, potato pancakes, and cutlets are good too.

Caracas Arepa Bar, 291 Grand Street between Havemeyer Street and Roebling Street; (718) 218-6050; Subway: L to Bedford

Avenue or L to Lorimer Street or G to Metropolitan Avenue or J, M, Z to Marcy Avenue; caracasarepabar.com; $$. Getting a table at Manhattan's East Village location of this casual Venezuelan spot can be tough since you have to compete with bargain-hunting NYU students. Fortunately, Caracas Arepa opened this Williamsburg location, with twice the space and far fewer college students. If you've never had an *arepa* though, you'll see right away why they are popular. These thick griddle-seared corn pancakes are warm and comforting, and you can get them filled with creamy cheese and shredded beef. Order sides of fried plantains, black bean empanadas, or guacamole, and you have a feast for less than $20, even if you get a banana or coconut milk shake to round out the meal. Turns out those undergrads were on to something.

Cariño, 82 S. 4th Street between Berry Street and Wythe Avenue; (718) 384-8282; Subway: J, M, Z to Marcy Avenue or L to Bedford Avenue; carinonyc.com; $$. Few New York City neighborhoods have great Mexican restaurants, the kind with fresh tacos served prop-

erly, radishes and limes, tasty tamales, and enchiladas doused in a rich, flavorful sauce that put the suburban chains to shame. Cariño has all that—and they serve up *aguas frescas* in fresh flavors like mango, watermelon, and hibiscus. Sure, the service can be a little slow but it's as friendly as it is casual. Plus, with *chilaquiles* and house-made chorizo with eggs, Cariño is as good at brunch as it is in the evening, when an impressive tequila menu steals the show.

Christina's, 853 Manhattan Avenue between Milton Street and Noble Street; (718) 383-4382; Subway: G to Greenpoint Avenue; $. This reliable Polish diner on Manhattan Avenue serves up all the classics. Start your day with a hearty plateful of food here, served in their large booths (natch) with bottomless cups of coffee and fresh-squeezed orange juice. Choose from potato pancakes, babka french toast, cheese and fruit blintzes, or make a caloric splurge and order up a plate of their "fantasy" blintzes, topped with hot fudge and whipped cream.

Crif Dogs, 555 Driggs Avenue between N. 7th Street and N. 8th Street; (718) 302-3200; Subway: L to Lorimer Street; crifdogs.com; $. This East Village hot dog shop now serves up their all-beef, pork and beef, and vegetarian dogs to, well, roughly the same crowd in Williamsburg. Look for fun topping combinations like cream cheese, scallions, and everything bagel seeds and a bacon-wrapped dog with teriyaki sauce and pineapple.

Diner, 85 Broadway between Berry Street and Wythe Avenue; (718) 486-3077; Subway: L to Bedford Avenue or J, M, Z to Marcy Avenue; dinernyc.com; $$. This hipster take on a diner actually looks like an old-fashioned one. Located in a rehabbed 1920s dining car, the narrow front room has a long bar with chrome bar stools, and the equally narrow back room has just one row of tables. Your waitress writes down the menu on a butcher paper tablecloth, which is not always as successful in practice as it is in concept. (On one occasion, my waitress gave long descriptions of each dish, and then wrote one word each on the paper—"egg" or "soup"—so after she had left we couldn't remember most of what was on offer.) But like many Brooklyn spots that are cooler than they are efficient, the food itself is memorably good. The menu changes every day but could feature salads like grilled duck hearts with watercress and rhubarb butter, soft-shell crabs over asparagus and hollandaise, or roasted asparagus with shaved Parmesan and a fried egg, as well as a pasta-like house-made pappardelle with broccoli, garlic, and bacon. Fortunately, the offerings usually include a juicy, delicious grass-fed burger topped with cheddar cheese and served on a buttery brioche roll with perfect french fries. It is clearly, at this diner like many others, the best thing to order.

Dressler, 149 Broadway between Driggs Avenue and Bedford Avenue; (718) 384-6343; Subway: J, M, Z to Marcy Avenue; dresslernyc.com; $$$. This gorgeous little special-occasion spot is a showstopper. The high ceilings are lined with mahogany panels and mirrors rimmed with metal carved into vine patterns. And the seasonal menu often lives up to the promise of the decor.

Appetizers of duck confit over greens come with navel orange segments and sweet honey-poached black mission figs; rich braised oxtail ragout is served with fresh ricotta over handmade pasta. For entrees, sophisticated takes on the warm and comforting continue to reign, with a grilled Long Island

Dumont Burger, 314 Bedford Avenue between S. 1st Street and S. 2nd Street; (718) 384-6127; Subway: L to Lorimer Street or G to Metropolitan Avenue; dumontburger.com; $$. This younger, even more casual sibling of **Dumont** (p. 145) on Union Avenue looks like a bar (with no real tables save for a few on the sidewalk come summertime), so the high quality of the food is a pleasant surprise the first time you come here. The burger alone is worth the trip: Juicy and served with Bibb let-tuce, tomato, and house-made pickles, it comes in regular (on brioche) or a minisize (on cia-batta), and you can get it with classic toppings (cheddar, American, Jack, caramelized onions, bacon, mushrooms) or with more interesting ones (gruyère, blue cheese, avocado). Order fries, salad, onion rings, or a milk shake for the  perfect retro treat. Since this is Williamsburg, they also have, for the neighborhood's many non-red-meat-eaters, fish sandwiches, chicken sandwiches, and a chickpea version of a veggie burger, plus specials like a creamy tomato soup or a spicy black-bean chili (perfect on a cold day) as well as fried clams that are perfect on a sunny summer day.

Egg, 135 N. 5th Street between Berry Street and Bedford Avenue; (718) 302-5151; Subway: L to Bedford Avenue; pigandegg.com; $. No matter when you come, you can expect to wait for a table at this popular comfort food spot that's packed from morning through night. Add your name to the list on the marker board, and cool your heels on the sidewalk for a while. But most think it's worth the wait. Brunch dishes include delectable biscuits served with gravy or country ham, stone-ground grits, and great french toast; dinner brings fried chicken and kale. They're dedicated to using local, organic ingredients—they even bought their own farm upstate, complete with a smokehouse. For updates on how their crops are doing, check the note cards on your table and the chalkboard on the back wall, which often details specials made with ingredients from the latest haul.

El Almacén, 557 Driggs Avenue between N. 6th Street and N. 7th Street; (718) 218-7284; Subway: L to Bedford Avenue; elalmacennyc .com; $$. This Argentine restaurant is homey as can be. In the summertime, diners fill the backyard, where twinkling white lights illuminate the night sky and sangria keeps the conversation going; in winter everyone moves into the rustic dining room with its exposed brick walls and chalkboard menus. The menu is convivial, too, as most things beg to be shared. Order plates of empanadas filled with spinach-and-corn and beef-and-olives, and breaded avocado "fries." Then dig into a *parrillada* tray—a heaping plate of grilled meats, including short rib, rib eye, chorizo, and truffled potato wedges. For dessert, which you might as well share, too, you'll want to go with the hot *churros,* which come with chocolate and dulce de leche dipping sauces. Okay, I take that back—you won't want to share those at all.

Fette Sau, 354 Metropolitan Avenue between Havemeyer Street and Roebling Street; (718) 963-3404; Subway: L to Lorimer Street; fettesaubbq.com; $$. For barbecue lovers, this is Brooklyn's best bet. Get in line for your food, which is served cafeteria style, by the pound. The actual meat offerings change every day but include both classics (beef brisket, pulled pork, pork ribs, hot links) and more interesting options, including lamb shank and pork belly—and, yes, the belly is both fantastic and a coronary waiting to happen. (The name of the restaurant does translate to "Fat Pig" after all.) The meat is uniformly very smoky, tender, and flavorful. Unfortunately, the seating is family style at long picnic tables, and the sides (cold broccoli salad, uninspired potato salad) are as bad as the meat is spectacular. The flavor of oak, hickory, and cedar runs through just about everything you want to eat, including the one passable side, the baked beans filled with burnt ends. Fortunately, the bar serves lots of bourbon and whiskey, as well as several local beers on tap, including Brooklyn-based **Sixpoint** (p. 75) Vienna Pale Ale, so you can wash your 'cue down with a proper drink.

Forcella, 485 Lorimer Street between Powers Street and Grand Street; Subway: L to Lorimer Street; (718) 388-8820; forcellaeatery .com; $$. Neapolitan pizza is rarely this good in the US, so it's not a surpise to hear that the owner, Giuio Adriani, is a double-certified pizza master. Menus at the Manhattan location on the Bowery and this Brooklyn outpost are similar, with antipasti, salads, pizzas and white pizzas, and a Nutella-filled dessert made of pizza dough.

Isa, 348 Wythe Avenue between 2nd Street and 3rd Street; (347) 689-3594; Subway: L to Bedford Avenue; isa.gg; $$$. Nominated for a James Beard award in 2012, Isa is polarizing in its very Brooklyn-ness. The space is rustic yet chic, with communal tables, exposed brick, an open kitchen, and walls of windows that open in the summer months. The menu is equally organic, with seasonally driven dishes like raw scallops with apples and celery as well as sardines with olive and mackerel with cauliflower.

Krolewskie Jadlo, 694 Manhattan Avenue between Nassau Avenue and Norman Avenue; (718) 383-8993; Subway: G to Nassau Avenue; krolewskiejadlo.com; $. Don't let the decor fool you—once you get past the statues of armored guards at the front door and the swords on the wall, the food isn't cheesy at all. Come here for heavy but comforting Polish classics, served by Polish waitresses to mostly Polish customers. It's all pretty carefully prepared: The pierogi are tender and light, and in the summer include a fresh blueberry filling choice, in addition to all the traditional fried savory ones (meat, potato and cheese, mushroom and sauerkraut). The potato pancakes are tasty, with a smooth texture, and the kielbasa is heavily smoked. (Ask for the good strong mustard—that stuff can cut through any back flavor.) The goulash, a beef stew filled with vegetables, tastes as much like bell peppers as it does the more traditional paprika and caramelized onions. Most dishes come with 2 sides: cucumbers in a creamy dill-cucumber sauce and a carrot-cabbage slaw. Together, they're a meal in themselves.

La Superior, 295 Berry Street between S. 2nd Street and S. 3rd Street; (718) 388-5988; Subway: G to Lorimer Street or L to Bedford Avenue or J, M, Z to Marcy Avenue; lasuperiornyc.com; $$. There's so little good Mexican food in this part of Brooklyn that La Superior gets any superiority by default. The food, though, will transport you to a Mexico City street cart. Order as though you were munching as you walk, rather than in courses, since the food comes out randomly anyway. Start with blender-frothed *agua frescas*—the pineapple, prickly pear, and watermelon are good. The tacos, served one-per-order, can be topped, among other things, with pork, chipotle-spiced shrimp, or sliced tongue. (If you're an adventurous eater, try the pig brain taco special—the texture is pleasantly soft.) The enchiladas suizas are more entree size, and you may find yourself tiring of the tangy green sauce and wishing you had stuck to the array of smaller dishes. Instead, go for the quesadillas—they're made from masa, not flour tortillas, filled with interesting savory stuffings and then fried, so they don't look at all like what you're used to. Complement your tacos and quesadillas with the *queso fundido,* a rich pot of melted cheese topped with crumbled chorizo and served with warm corn tortillas to spoon it into. It's comforting, but the dish that gets the most raves is the *torta ahogada,* a sandwich on sourdough bread filled with pork *carnitas,* then smothered with refried beans and a spicy red chile sauce. As for the decor, well, that part really is superior to Brooklyn's other Mexican restaurants. The room itself is decorated minimally (with a Mexican wrestling doll, movie posters, and faded wallpaper) but stylishly, just like the patrons.

Mable's Smokehouse, 44 Berry Street between N. 1th Street and N. 12th Street; Subway: L to Bedford Avenue; (718) 218-6655; mablessmokehouse.com; $$. From the brisket to the ribs and pulled pork, the meats are all good here. Unfortunately, like primary competitor **Fette Sau** (p. 149), the sides (too-sweet candied sweet potatoes, a too-mild mac and cheese) feel like a bit of an afterthought. Get in line to place your order, and then take a seat at a table and your 'cue will be brought out to you on cafeteria trays that feel appropriate for the largely just-out-of-college crowd that frequents the place.

Marlow & Sons, 81 Broadway between Berry Street and Wythe Avenue; (718) 384-1441; Subway: J, M, Z to Marcy Avenue or L to Bedford Avenue; marlowandsons.com; $$$. Marlow & Sons, which—like **Diner** (p. 143)—is affiliated with the **Marlow & Daughters** (p. 168) butcher, has a seasonal, hoof-to-tail theology that infuses everything they do. They get some of their produce from nearby **Rooftop Farms** (p. 173). Salads change daily depending on what's in season, and could be greens topped with thinly sliced stone fruit or corn on the cob, lightly fried then rolled in aioli, grated cheese, and cilantro. The liver pâté with toasted baguette slices is a winner, as are the oysters they ship in from all along the East Coast.

Entrees feel like a creative use of seasonal produce or a random one, depending on your perspective. Anyone who has ever spent a summer trying to use up boxes of CSA produce week after week will be impressed with their inventiveness. A braised beef (they don't say which cut, and you can bet it's not the short ribs) sandwich comes topped with corn relish when there's plenty of corn, and tagliatelle with sausage may have kale, tomato, and peppers as well as a bit of mint thrown in. Desserts include some seasonal items (plum-ricotta tart, anyone?) but the standards are hard to pass up—the bourbon-soaked chocolate cake comes with mint ice cream, a clever nod to a mint julep, and the chocolate-salted caramel tart is so good that one night, tables on either side of me had come in just for that. Served on a warm plate and oozing caramel, it tastes just right, whatever the season.

The Meatball Shop, 170 Bedford Avenue between N. 7th Street and N. 8th Street; (718) 551-0520; Subway: L to Bedford Avenue; themeatballshop.com; $. Known for its two Manhattan locations and the cookbook they spawned, The Meatball Shop joins the fleet of Lower East Side restaurants to cross the Williamsburg Bridge into the borough of Kings. The restaurant specializes in—you guessed it—meatballs, and they come in 5 flavors (including heritage pork and beef ground with proscuitto and mixed with ricotta) that are customizable with your choice of 5 different sauces. Get your balls alone (they call it "naked"), in a sub, in sliders, or atop a salad. On a recent visit, the flavorful sides of cheesey polenta and corn risotto were even better than the balls themselves.

Pies 'n Thighs, 166 S. 4th Street between S. 5th Place and Driggs Avenue; (347) 529-6090; Subway: J, M, Z to Marcy Avenue or L to Bedford Avenue; piesnthighs.com; $$. When the original Pies 'n

Thighs shut down a few years ago, locals held their breath as the owners built a new location. In the meantime, devotees flocked to **Roberta's** (p. 247), where chef Carolyn Bane fried up her chicken in the interim. But the highly anticipated location is open, and locals can once again get the crispy fried chicken served up with biscuits, hot sauce, and sides, without trekking out to Roberta's. In addition to some of the city's best fried chicken, you can order pulled pork sandwiches and fried catfish. Tip: Go at an off hour, or be prepared to wait and wait.

Polish-Slavic Center Cafeteria, 177 Kent Street between Manhattan Avenue and McGuinness Boulevard; (718) 349-1033; Subway: G to Greenpoint Avenue; $. This, the prettiest of the cafeteria-style restaurants, is as feminine as **Basia's Place** (p. 138) is masculine. Instead of men sitting mostly in the dark watching news and talking politics, here you'll find couples and friends basking in the light—and, of course, watching the news. The bright dining room has many windows, as well as several skylights and a pleasant street-front terrace with umbrella-topped tables. Because it is located in the Polish-Slavic center, set back from the street, it feels a bit like a private club. (Note: They close early in the evening, and they are closed on Sun.) But the pierogi, filled with the traditional meat, cheese, or sauerkraut fillings, as well as strawberry and blueberry in summertime, are solid, and it's one of the most pleasant atmospheres to eat them in.

Saltie, 378 Metropolitan Avenue between Havemeyer Street and Marcy Avenue; (718) 387-4777; Subway: G, L to Metropolitan Avenue-Lorimer Street; saltieny.com; $. An artisanal sandwich shop with just a few seats, Saltie was opened by several **Diner** (p. 143) alumnae. At breakfast, you'll find egg sandwiches; at lunch, a killer sardine sandwich called the Captain's Daughter, layered with capers and perfectly boiled eggs. But the snacks and desserts merit a look too, including a dark chocolate pudding made with olive oil and topped with sea salt, and a creamy salted caramel ice cream you're sure to find addictive.

Taco Santana, 301 Keap Street between S. 5th Street and Broadway; (718) 388-8761; Subway: J, M, Z to Marcy Avenue; $. When I read a rumor online that this Bushwick taco shop was serving burritos as good as those in California, I couldn't believe my eyes. Everyone I had ever known who has lived in LA or San Francisco, the promised land of tasty burritos, had given up looking for such a thing in New York and resigned themselves to rolling their eyes whenever an ignorant East Coaster (myself included) would confess to liking Chipotle. I made the trek out to Santana on a cold fall night, fully expecting to be disappointed. The place was empty, but the owners (a husband-and-wife team) were busy putting together a large to-go order. I ordered my *al pastor* burrito and settled in with an imported Mexican Coke to wait, amusing myself by trying to translate the soccer game on the TV. The burrito came out, steaming hot and football size, and I was offered red and green hot sauce, which I accepted, expecting to need them. I took a bite

and was suddenly in San Francisco. It was spicy, rich, and flavorful, and any nibble of beans or rice had enough chilies or pork to keep it interesting. I knew, right away, what all the fuss was about, that I would be back, and that—for once—no hot sauce was necessary.

Zenkichi, 77 N. 6th Street between Wythe Avenue and Berry Street; (718) 388-8985; Subway: L to Bedford Avenue; zenkichi .com; $$$$. From the second you step in the unmarked door at this Japanese restaurant, you are transported to another place that's far from the drunken hipsters and club kids on the street. You wait in a bamboo-walled garden, and then are taken to your table, up dimly lit stairs, down dark hallways that are lined with stones. Groups of up to four are given booths with bamboo shades that the waiters close every time they leave; larger parties are given their own walled-off areas. (Your space feels so isolated that there's a button on the table, should you need to summon your server.) The menu is a mix of modern Japanese small plates, and most people get the *omakase,* a 5-course meal that's just under $50 per person and changes seasonally. Yours might start with barbecued eel served on a soup spoon, bluefish sashimi that is rich enough to make you wonder why it isn't more common, Madagascar shrimp that's miso-marinated and served with cucumber, and a savory poached fig stuffed with sesame cream. The next courses are similar riffs on clean flavors and restraint: a salad topped with roasted pumpkin, Japanese eggplant, and pork wrapped in a shiso leaf and tempura-fried, thin slices of roasted duck breast, and soy-marinated tuna sashimi served over rice. It's all flavorful and artfully prepared, if not as surprising as the decor. You'll have to go somewhere else for green tea ice cream, though: Desserts are custard-like plays on savory mixed with sweet, such as frozen black sesame mousse, miso cheesecake, and a dark chocolate pudding studded with shockingly bitter raw walnuts.

Landmarks

Bamonte's, 32 Withers Street between Union Avenue and Lorimer Street; (718) 384-8831; Subway: G to Metropolitan Avenue or L to Lorimer Street; $$. This 109-year-old stalwart serves up nostalgia along with Italian red-sauce classics. The bar area is lit with red lights; the dining room has Dodgers memorabilia butting up against photos of the Yankees in the early days. And the tuxedoed waiters take their time catching up with the many regulars. Start with clams casino, 6 meaty clams topped with smoky, thick-cut bacon and a spicy marinara sauce, or the ever-popular fried zucchini, which manages to stay bright and juicy despite being egg battered and plunked in the fryer. Locals also go for the linguini with clams in a red or white sauce, gigantic house-made cheese ravioli, and big, sloppy plates of sausage-filled lasagna. Of course, as with any old-timer, the history can be flashier than the present. (The chicken scarpiello, a classic of chicken cooked on the bone and bathed in a garlicky lemon and white wine sauce, can be way overcooked.) Fortunately, the tiramisu is perfection—and if you decide to share, they'll serve it on two separate plates for you.

Peter Luger Steak House, 178 Broadway between Driggs Avenue and Bedford Avenue; (718) 387-7400; Subway: J, M, Z to Marcy Avenue; peterluger.com; $$$$. This old Brooklyn steak house, located in an unlikely spot under the shadow of the Williamsburg Bridge, is considered by many to be the best in New York, and therefore quite possibly the world. But the first time you come, you're immediately struck by how, well, uncomfortable it is to dine here compared to other steak houses. Reservations are hard to come by, yet you must wade through a dense crowd at the bar to get to the host stand, and then shout your name over the din. Unless you're in the back room, you may find yourself continuing to shout once you're seated in the beer-hall-style room.

It's annoying, yes, but this place isn't about a comfortable atmosphere, it's about the food. The meal is rich from the beginning to the end: Appetizers, which mostly come in portions made for two, include sizzling strips of extra-thick broiled Canadian bacon as well as a tomato salad topped with Luger's wonderfully flavorful steak sauce, redolent of horseradish and tamarind. The highlight of the menu is the prime porterhouse for two, which is marbled and dry aged to perfection then served broiled in a scalding hot cast-iron pan. Sides like creamed spinach and hash-brown-like German fried potatoes fulfill your steak-house fantasies of caloric decadence. Desserts, though they seem daunting after all that meat, include cheesecake, hot fudge sundaes, and apple strudel with whipped cream, which they list on the menu as the German *schlag,* a nod to the family's heritage.

Specialty Stores, Markets & Producers

Acme Smoked Fish, 30 Gem Street between N. 15th Street and Meserole Avenue; (718) 383-8585; Subway: G to Nassau Street or L to Bedford Avenue; acmesmokedfish.com. This smoked fish manufacturer, on an industrial block in Greenpoint, is not open to the public, except on Fri from 8 a.m. to 1 p.m., when they offer locals some of the same deals that their restaurant and store customers get every day. (They are the suppliers for Russ and Daughters and Zabars.) Sample a few different types—from the mild cold-smoked Nova to the more flavorful hot-smoked salmon, sable, sockeye, coho, whitefish, and chubbs—then make your selection from the prefilled vacuum-packed sleeves. They also sell smoked fish salads and a few herring dishes (pickled herring, herring in white sauce, and herring and onions). Just don't forget your wallet: They're cash only, and the deals are good.

Anthony & Son Panini Shoppe, 433 Graham Avenue between Frost Street and Withers Street; (718) 383-7395; Subway: L to Graham Avenue. There are several spots in the Italian part of Williamsburg that make their own mozzarella, but it is this unassuming deli that makes some of the creamiest in the borough. Sold in balls, it's perfect layered with tomato and basil in a caprese salad or melted atop a homemade pizza. Unusually creamy and well salted, the cheese, which is made daily in the shop, doesn't last long at all. It's best the day you buy it—in this case, it seems, perfection is fleeting.

Bedford Cheese Shop, 229 Bedford Avenue between N. 4th Street and N. 5th Street; (718) 599-7588; Subway: L to Bedford Avenue; bedfordcheeseshop.com. Way more than a cheese shop, this small grocery store sells local treats and imports alike. Start with the large mustard selection, make your way to the olive oils and vinegars, and it could be awhile until you even see the cheese. Of course, they carry **Mast** (p. 169) and **McClure's** (p. 249), but they also carry Vienna's Staud's preserves and plenty of British imports like cans of spaghetti hoops and curried baked beans. The cured meat selection includes *bresaola* from Manhattan's Salumeria Biellese; the cheeses are a mix of European and domestic. Pick up an earthy brie de meaux from France or a nutty Spanish Garrotxa. Occasionally, they also get a delivery of a runny cow's-milk cheese made in the neighborhood, on the sly. Ask for it when you're there—and ask about their cheese appreciation classes as well.

Throwdowns and Showdowns

In the last few years, cooking competitions have taken hold of Brooklyn. And no Pillsbury Bake-offs are these. Instead, an actor named Matt Timms runs some of the best-known events—the Chili Takedown, which has now spawned Bacon, Tofu, and Fondue Takedowns. For potential food vendors, it's also a great place to ramp up some interest—and publicity—for a new business. These packed-to-the-rim events, which often take place in a Williamsburg bar to much fanfare, feature amateur contestants (rather than professionally trained chefs) creating innovative dishes. The winner of the bacon competition was a bourbon-bacon ice cream; the winner of the tofu throwdown was tofu empanadas. And Mr. Timms isn't the only one doing it. Each year, a cookbook author hosts a Casserole Party, and there are also Jell-O Throwdowns, Beer Cookoffs, and something called the Park Slope Pork-off, as well as a whole host of similar events that raise money for charities. Of course, in a town known for people cooking up innovative dishes, it should be no surprise that competitions were a natural evolution of the food-making trend.

Brook Farm General Store, 75 S. 6th Street between Berry Street and Wythe Street; (718) 388-8642; Subway: J, M, Z to Marcy Avenue or L to Bedford Avenue; brookfarmgeneralstore.com. This pretty little shop, hidden away on a side street, is full of lovely things for your kitchen, as well as the rest of your home. Stock up on French bistro water glasses, those tough-to-break stalwarts that are made of tempered glass, as well as oversize white porcelain latte bowls. The selection is well edited, with practical items like sturdy woven market totes, luxe linens, and stoneware teapots sitting next to quirkier items like stainless steel drinking straws, porcelain egg coddlers, stovetop popcorn makers, and assorted food stuffs, like jars of hard-to-find New York State maple sugar. Be sure to check out their own line of organic bath soaps and oils.

Brooklyn Brewery, 79 N. 11th Street between Wythe Avenue and Berry Street; (718) 486-7422; Subway: G to Nassau Street or L to Bedford Avenue; brooklynbrewery.com. Sure, you can buy this locally made beer bottled around town and on tap at many area bars. But you should still come here, to their Williamsburg brewery. You're not here for the tour either, though they are solid, free, and take place between 1 and 4 p.m. on Sat and Sun. No, you're here for the Brewmaster Reserves, two small-batch beers that they rotate every 2 months and that are otherwise difficult to find. Buy a few tokens (the $4 tokens buy you a pint) and settle into their taproom to taste, for example, the Surachi Ace or the Intensified Coffee Stout, made with Red Hook's **Stumptown** (p.  77) coffee. The taproom is also open (and hopping) on Friday night, and at the holidays you can get their secret limited edition Black Opps brew here, too. If you can't get to the source, try the ShackMeister amber ale they make for **Shake Shack** (p. 91) or the Blue Apron Ale they made for Thomas Keller's Manhattan special-occasion showstopper, Per Se, and his California jewel, French Laundry. Or track down the beers they bottle in large champagne-size bottles, Local 1 and Local 2, the latter of which is made with New York State honey.

Brooklyn Ice Cream Factory, 97 Commercial Street between Manhattan Avenue and Box Street; (718) 349-2506; Subway: G to Greenpoint Avenue. The last place you'd expect to find a warm and homey little ice-cream shop is here, on the first floor of a rehabbed building full of artists' lofts, on the block that is literally the end of the road for Greenpoint. (Manhattan Avenue ends in a cul-de-sac just a few feet away, and on the other side of the water is Long Island City, Queens.) Unlike their Dumbo location (p. 25), which feels like the perfect marriage of need and opportunity, this one feels a bit random. Still, the ice cream remains unequivocally good. The red-and-yellow striped awning is a homey invitation (picture exposed brick walls, big windows, and comfy chairs with striped cushions), and the eggless, creamy ice cream—which comes in fresh flavors like peaches-and-cream, strawberry, and chocolate—always hits the spot.

Brooklyn Kitchen, 100 Frost Street; enter on Meeker between Frost Street and Leonard Street; (718) 389-2982; Subway: L to Lorimer Street or G to Metropolitan Avenue; thebrooklynkitchen .com. This kitchen supply shop has all the basics—ricers, ladles, cake pans, salad spinners, candy thermometers—and they do knife sharpening, too. But they're best known for their cooking classes, which often fill up the day they are announced. It's not just that there are few cooking classes in Brooklyn, though that's true. It's mostly that they hire locally famous food makers to teach these evening classes. Bob McClure of McClure's Pickles teaches his students how to can; Tom Mylan, formerly the butcher at Marlow & Daughters, demonstrates how to cut up a half pig or a lamb—and, yes, students get to take home the meat; Ben Van Leeuwen, local ice cream maker extraordinaire, teaches a chemistry-driven ice cream class with plenty of tastings. For the local foodie, a gift certificate here is the perfect gift. Brooklyn Kitchen teamed up with the Meat Hook, and now there's a butcher shop in their enormous Frost Street space, complete with gorgeous house-cured bacon and house-made sausages in flavors like banh mi and bulgogi.

Brouwerij Lane, 78 Greenpoint Avenue between Franklin Avenue and West Avenue; (347) 529-6133; Subway: G to Greenpoint Avenue; brouwerijlane.com. This small out-of-the-way shop opened in 2009, but from the beginning it has had coolers and racks lined with 170 rare bottles of beer that make an impressively well-edited collection. Still, most come here for the growlers. Pick a beer from one of the 19 taps—the friendly owner will gladly explain the options and give you tastes—then watch as they fill your growler with your brew of choice. The taps rotate frequently, but they often include several from the Austrian brewery Gösser, and the website is kept constantly up to date—look for a coffee stout made with milk, called Joe Mama's Coffee Milk Stout, if they have it. The fee includes a small deposit for the growler, which is returnable and reusable.

Once you have one, you'll want to keep it filled and in the fridge at all times. It's a pleasant experience from start to finish: Take your selections to the counter and revel in the old-fashioned cha-ching of their antique register.

Cafe Grumpy, 193 Meserole Avenue between Diamond Street and Newell Street; (718) 349-7623; Subway: G to Nassau Avenue; cafegrumpy.com. Grumpy is exactly how I felt when I first arrived here. Laptops filled every available space, despite signs requesting that customers not use them during peak hours. Whole four-top tables were taken up by hipsters who had spread out books or jackets in order to make their space less inviting to interlopers. And it was strangely loud, perhaps due to the number of people on their cell phones—which, of course, included the people crowding the benches out front. And then I drank my flat white, which (the barista explained to me) is basically a small latte made with beans roasted in the back of the Greenpoint location. (Cafe Grumpy also has shops in Park Slope and Manhattan's Chelsea neighborhood, but only the Greenpointers have their own roaster.) The foam on the top was thick and creamy, the leaf shape swirled into the top a thoughtful touch. It was, perhaps, one of the best lattes I have ever had. Suddenly, I felt much less grumpy. In fact, I sort of envied these Greenpoint hipsters for having such a great coffeehouse in their midst. I could see why they wouldn't want to share.

Emily's Pork Store, 426 Graham Avenue between Withers Street and Frost Street; (718) 383-7216; Subway: L to Graham Avenue.

Emily's makes its own sausages, including caul-fat-wrapped patties and broccoli-rabe-filled sausages that beg to be incorporated into your next Italian cooking venture. They also source some of the better products from around the borough, including **Lioni Latticini** (p. 215) mozzarella and ricotta as well as **Pastosa** (p. 219) ravioli. And just how good is their sausage? Motorino pizza uses it on their carefully crafted pies, if that's any indication.

Fortunato Brothers Pasticceria, 289 Manhattan Avenue between Devoe Street and Metropolitan Avenue; (718) 387-2281; Subway: L to Graham Avenue. The Fortunato family is from Naples, and while the menu seems to make its way around the boot, it's the rich southern Italian treats that shine. Come for the cannoli, dense Italian cheesecake, lobster tails, pignoli, and pistachio cookies, and you'll leave happy. Fortunately, the atmosphere is as rustically Italian as the menu—picture faux tin ceilings, slow table service, and *paisanos* who seem to hang out all day drinking coffee and debating politics. Best of all, the house cat will curl up sleepily in the chair next to yours, barely stirring the whole time you're there, just like in the Old Country.

Gimme! Coffee, 495 Lorimer Street between Grand Street and Powers Street; (718) 388-7771; Subway: L to Lorimer Street; gimmecoffee.com. It's a surprise to find such a small coffeehouse roasting its own beans, but roast they do in their Finger Lakes farm just outside of Ithaca. The tiny shop is part of a statewide chain of six locations. The decor is minimal and the small number of tables fills up quickly, but the brew is rich and strong, and the cold-brew coffee is powerful enough to hold up to ice.

Kings County Distillery, 35 Meadow Street between Bogart Street and Waterbury Street; Subway: L to Grand Street; kingscountydistillery.com. The original Prohibition-era distillery, Kings County makes moonshine and bourbon and sells them in flask-inspired bottles. In warm-weather months they offer informal tours several days each month on weekends, and they list details and a schedule on their website (where they explain that the street sign to Meadow is currently missing, so they can be hard to find). We'd say call ahead, but there's no phone. Fortunately, you can buy their spirits at shops around the borough and sample them at bars in just about every neighborhood.

Manhattan Special, manhattanspecial.com. Many people assume that this soft drink is named after Manhattan—but it is actually a Brooklyn treat. Manhattan Special was named after its plant in Williamsburg on Manhattan Avenue. In case you've never had it, it's a sweet iced espresso soda, popular with Italians in the neighborhood who are used to drinking their leftover brew on ice in the summertime. It was first produced in 1895. Today, it's made by fourth-generation Brooklynites, and you can find it all over the borough in shops and grocery stores. They also make a diet version, a decaf version, and flavored sodas, including hazelnut and vanilla.

It's a great caffeinated pick-me-up, and it also makes a fabulous *affogato*—the Italian version of an ice-cream float.

Marlow & Daughters, 95 Broadway between Bedford Avenue and Berry Street; (718) 388-5700; Subway: J, M, Z to Marcy Avenue; marlowanddaughters.com. The first thing you notice as you approach this small food store is that out front they have a large table piled high with locally grown fruits and vegetables. They're all so beautiful; they're a food stylist's dream. The sour cherries are plump and bright red, as are the small currants and the golden plums and apricots. The cherry tomatoes look ready to burst, and the corn sits in tight brightly colored green husks that look just-plucked from the fields. It's an apt introduction to what you'll find inside, which includes the well-edited, locavore-approved pantry list. A sign on the counter announces that they also have locally caught cod and sea scallops in the back. That said, it is primarily a butcher shop. Come for house-made duck confit, pâtés, and glass jelly jars of rabbit *rillettes* as well as house-cured spicy sausages. Their meat is delivered as whole and half animals, and then they butcher the pigs and cows down to smaller parts. Perhaps that's the secret to their impossibly bright red ground beef, which is sold at their nearby **Diner** restaurant (p. 143) in burger form. Take some interest in the different cuts, and the butcher may give you a lesson and sashimi-style tastes, sprinkled with sea salt.

Mast Brothers Chocolate, 105A N. 3rd Street between Berry Street and Wythe Avenue; (718) 388-2625; Subway: L to Bedford Avenue; mastbrotherschocolate.com. Based in the same building as their artisan chocolate factory (if you can call such a small, meticulous outfit that), this shop sells the company's namesake high-quality dark chocolate bars. It's as lovely a space (picture wood beams and a dark wood bar) as you would expect from a brand that takes such care with packaging. The artisan chocolate bars themselves are made with, among others, carefully sourced single-origin Venezuelan and Ecuadorian cacao beans that they roast and process themselves. The result: a deep, dark chocolate flavor that lingers on your palate. The bars come wrapped in twine and pretty hand-printed colorful papers in floral patterns and prints like fleur de lis shapes. (Some are imported from Italy; others are made by local artists.) You can buy these meant-to-be-savored chocolates plain, or studded with almonds, cranberries, and sea salt. At $7 to $12 per bar, they are a splurge, but they make lovely hostess gifts.

McCarren Park Green Market, Corner of Union Avenue and N. 12th Street; Subway: L to Bedford Avenue or G to Nassau Avenue; cenyc.org/greenmarket. This small green market takes place every Sat, but the best times to come are late spring through early fall, when the Northeast growing season hits its stride. Depending on when you go, you'll find vegetables and herbs from S. & S. O. Farms (red spring onions, horseradish greens, radishes, chamomile, and spinach), Madura Farms (several varieties of mushrooms, including oyster and maitake), and Garden of Eve (carrots, parsnips, rutabaga). You can also select fruit from Red Jacket Orchards (including raspberries, strawberries, and apricots in summer and apples in the fall), goat's-milk feta and chevre cheeses from Consider Bardwell Farm, and preserves and jellies from B & B Jams.

Momofuku Milk Bar Brooklyn, 382 Metropolitan Avenue between Havemeyer Street and Marcey Avenue; (347) 577-9504; Subway: L to Lorimer Street; momofuku.com. The dessert part of David Chang's Momofuku empire, Milk Bar has developed a national reputation for its playful, fun sweets. Chef Christina Tosi's signature cereal-flavored soft-serves, delectably custardy crack pie, toothachingly sweet candy-bar pie, birthday cake truffles, and pretzel-flavored milk shakes are served as fun endings to a meal of Chang's reknown cucumber- and scallion-topped pork buns. It's a small takeaway shop, but heaven-sent nonetheless.

Napoli Bakery, 616 Metropolitan Avenue between Leonard Street and Lorimer Street; (718) 384-6945; Subway: G, L to Metropolitan Avenue. This old-school Italian bakery isn't much to look at, and it doesn't sell pastries or sweets. Instead, they focus their energy on coal-fired bread, with stellar results. The sourdough loaves are tangy, the Italian baguettes are soft on the inside, the sesame breadsticks are crisp and almost nutty, and there are stuffed focaccia. Tip: The cashier says they freeze well, too. Who knew?

Peter Pan Donut & Pastry Shop, 727 Manhattan Avenue between Norman Avenue and Meserole Avenue; (718) 389-3676; Subway: G to Nassau Avenue; $. This venerable 58-year-old Greenpoint bakery has gotten a lot of attention for red velvet doughnuts, a tender cake doughnut glazed with a thin icing. It's special, to be sure, but I go for their yeast doughnuts, which are light and airy and filled with custard cream, whipped cream, and house-made jams in seasonal flavors like blueberry and raspberry, then topped with enough confectioners' sugar to ruin your shirt. All of their doughnuts are baked daily in the back. They have gorgeously light crullers (glazed with chocolate, vanilla, or strawberry icing), sour cream doughnuts, apple crumb doughnuts, and— miraculously—doughnut ice-cream sandwiches. They make other things like crumb cakes, muffins, pastries, bagels, and egg sandwiches on bialys, bagels, or toast that are served at their lunch-counter-style bar by uniformed waitresses in pink and turquoise smocks. I hear that all of their baked items are good, but you can't blame me for not tearing myself away from the doughnuts long enough to find out. Get lucky with your timing, and your doughnut may still be warm.

Polam International, 952 Manhattan Avenue between Java Street and India Street; (718) 383-2763; Subway: G to Nassau Avenue. Polam is so popular, you can barely get in the door on a busy Saturday, when the line to get meat butts up against the checkout line in the narrow store and you have to squeeze down the middle to take your place in the back. But it's worth the wait, as the locals (who scoop sauerkraut and pickles from enormous buckets into plastic bags as they wait their turn) well know. You can buy fresh meats (like racks of spare ribs), smoked meats (like the round hams and kielbasa rings hanging from the ceiling), and cold cut–style roasted meats for sandwiches, including a garlic-studded ham that's a real find. Just don't go when you're in a hurry—the selection is huge and you have to allow time for the staff to translate your English requests into Polish. Fortunately, you may luck out and find some Polish-Americans in line willing to help. Some drive from as far away as Connecticut for the pork, so it's in their best interest to keep the line moving.

Reben Luncheonette, 229 Havemeyer Street between Broadway and S. 5th Street; (718) 388-7696; Subway: J, M, Z to Marcy Avenue; $. This lunch counter under the elevated subway line in the South Side doesn't look like much. But their signature drink, the Dominican *morir soñando,* has gotten a lot of attention. Walk up to the to-go window and order one: Made with freshly squeezed orange juice, ice, sugar, and sweetened condensed milk that's shaken together until frothy, it's lighter and more refreshing than it sounds. It tastes a bit like a Creamsicle, with the added bonus of the bright freshness of just-squeezed orange juice. Plus, the guy behind the counter will give you a glass with the portion that doesn't fit in your Styrofoam cup so you can drink it before you go.

Rooftop Farms, 44 Eagle Street between Franklin Street and West Street; Subway: G to Greenpoint Avenue; rooftopfarms.org. Open most Sundays from 10 a.m. to 4 p.m., this miraculous organic farm—built atop a former bagel factory in Greenpoint, with spectacular views of the city—sells its wares to stroller-toting locals. Depending on the season, you may find several types of peppers, tomatoes, eggplant, and flowers, as well as a table full of other produce. It's all lovely and worth buying, and some Sundays they have educational programs where you can learn about how the farm works, and sign up to volunteer as well. You can also taste their produce

at **Anella** (p. 137) restaurant in Greenpoint and **Marlow & Sons** (p. 152) in Williamsburg. But if you come on a Sunday just for the farm stand, don't leave without climbing up another couple flights of stairs to see the farm itself, where rows and rows of produce reach up toward the sun and the city skyline. And remember: You can bring your food scraps here for composting, too.

Savino's Quality Pasta, 111 Conselyea Street between Leonard Street and Manhattan Avenue; (718) 388-2038; Subway L to Graham Avenue. This off-the-beaten-path pasta shop mostly does a wholesale business, so most of what's bagged and sold here is left over from what they made for Williamsburg's Italian restaurants. Go with an open mind, and get whatever they have—like pasta that is shaped like night crawlers for $2.75 per pound. Sure, they sell a lot of cheese ravioli, too—the big fat kind, frozen two trays to a box and stuffed with ricotta, but I like the element of surprise of just winging it. Oh, and the big jars of hard-to-find squid ink? Yeah, they won't sell those to you, no matter how nicely you ask. They get way too many orders for tagliatelle *al nero di sepia* to part with them.

Sikorski Meat Market, 603 Manhattan Avenue between Nassau Street and Driggs Avenue; (718) 389-6181; Subway: G to Nassau Avenue. This small meat market makes everything on-site, and their sausages have a rich pork flavor, with none of that chemically "liquid smoke" aftertaste. Come for the double-smoked *krajana* kielbasa, the bialy kielbasa (fresh white sausage that's not cured), or country-style *wiejska* kielbasa. If you arrive on a Saturday morning, remember that the kielbasa comes out of the smoker at 11 a.m. Just don't get so excited about your prized sausages that you forget to pick up the rye bread. There are boxes of crusty loaves, unwrapped, by the register. Hand yours to the cashier and they'll have it sliced for you. You can also buy a half-loaf instead of a whole, but regardless you won't want to pass this up. The mild rye bread, from the New Warsaw Bakery, which used to be next door, is the freshest in town.

Slodycze Wedel, 772 Manhattan Avenue between Meserole Avenue and Calyer Street; (718) 349-3933; Subway: G to Greenpoint

Avenue. You'll feel like a kid in a candy shop at this Polish import sweet store, where chocolates from more than 25 Polish manufacturers line the shelves. Not all of them are translated into English, so you have to look carefully at the pictures on the boxes to figure out what you're getting. Some chocolates are filled with vanilla or chocolate marshmallows; others are wrapped around orange or raspberry jellies.

Brands include Wedel, Solidarnosc, Kopernik, Olza, Wawel, Mieszko, Skawa, and Jutrazenka—names that are as familiar to Poles as Hershey and Whitman's. There's also a loose-candy area, filled with sold-by-the-pound treats like coconut and pistachio truffles. It's a great place to start if you're not ready to commit to a box.

Spuyten Duyvil Grocery, 218 Bedford Avenue between N. 5th Street and N. 6th Street; (718) 384-1520; Subway: L to Bedford Avenue. The word "grocery" in the name is ironic. This tiny, closet-size beer store, tucked into a shopping arcade, has a tiny but well-edited selection of beers and local foods. Look for maple-scented beer and bitter, dry Lambics with just a hint of sour cherry. ("We

Smorgasburg Joins the Scene

The **Brooklyn Flea's** (p. 97) summer-only, outdoor, food-only market may just be mecca for foodies (brooklynflea.com/smorgasburg). It's held along the riverfront from mid-May to mid-November, and it's the place to be on a sunny Saturday for people watching and grazing. Tables piled high with everything from Dough's blood orange–glazed doughnuts to Sichuan dumplings and cold sesame noodles from Shorty Tang & Sons surround a cluster of picnic tables. Come for lunch (preferably, it seems, with your dog) or pick up jars of Maiden Preserves jam and Rick's Picks pickles, bags of Crop to Cup coffee beans or Early Bird granola, and sacks of The Good Batch sandwich cookies and Whimsy & Spice handmade marshmallows to go. If you don't live near Boerum Hill, this may also be a better location for you to try one of **Mile End's** (p. 56) smoked meat sandwiches, and if you don't live near Red Hook be sure to sample the **Red Hook Lobster Pound's** (p. 73) buttery, lobstah-filled rolls, Solber's *papusas*, and **The Good Fork's** (p. 48) dumplings here.

don't sell any of that saccharine sweet stuff," says the owner.) You can also pick up **Mast Brothers** (p. 169) chocolate bars ("Great with the Kriek," we were told) and **Nunu Chocolates** (p. 70)

seconds. You may also be tempted by the long pink Polish hot dogs, which are made in-house and individually wrapped. They call out to be grilled at your next cookout.

Whisk, 231 Bedford Avenue between N. 3rd Street and N. 4th Street; (718) 218-7230; Subway: L to Bedford Avenue; whisknyc1. com. A charming little kitchenware and tabletop store if there ever was one, this spot has everything you could need to stock your kitchen—and unlike many Brooklyn kitchen shops, it's well-presented in a pleasantly uncrowded space, too. Browse through cast-iron and copper pans, colorful Le Creuset pots, spice racks, and small specialty tools like egg poachers, whisks (of course), and cannoli tubes, as well as cooler items like glam aprons and cookie cutters shaped like skull and crossbones. (This is Williamsburg, after all.) They also offer book signings by local cookbook authors.

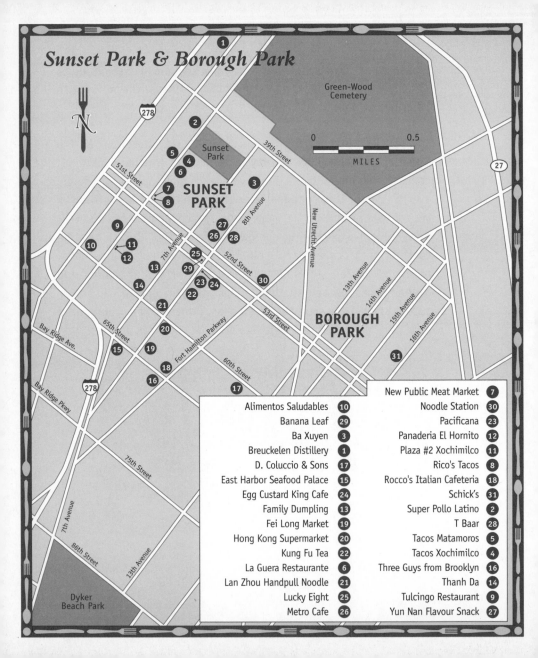

Sunset Park & Borough Park

Alimentos Saludables	10
Banana Leaf	29
Ba Xuyen	3
Breuckelen Distillery	1
D. Coluccio & Sons	17
East Harbor Seafood Palace	15
Egg Custard King Cafe	24
Family Dumpling	13
Fei Long Market	19
Hong Kong Supermarket	20
Kung Fu Tea	22
La Guera Restaurante	6
Lan Zhou Handpull Noodle	21
Lucky Eight	25
Metro Cafe	26
New Public Meat Market	7
Noodle Station	30
Pacificana	23
Panaderia El Hornito	12
Plaza #2 Xochimilco	11
Rico's Tacos	8
Rocco's Italian Cafeteria	18
Schick's	31
Super Pollo Latino	2
T Baar	28
Tacos Matamoros	5
Tacos Xochimilco	4
Three Guys from Brooklyn	16
Thanh Da	14
Tulcingo Restaurant	9
Yun Nan Flavour Snack	27

Sunset Park & Borough Park

Sunset Park is divided into two distinct and largely insular neighborhoods—a Chinese one, centered around 7th Avenue and 8th Avenue, and a Mexican one, on 5th Avenue. The Chinese community is largely self-sustaining. Many people live and work within a small radius and do all of their shopping, food and otherwise, here. The community runs its own shuttle bus that travels up and down 8th Avenue. As a result, small cookware shops that specialize in woks and noodle bowls sit next to to-go stores that serve up premade Hong Kong–style sandwiches and fancier restaurants with big chandeliers and formal dim sum service. All of the signs are bilingual (if not, it's English you won't find), and it's not unusual to meet waiters and cashiers who don't speak English at all. While not as well known as Manhattan's Chinatown and Queens' Flushing neighborhoods, this area has a lot to offer the lover of Asian cuisine. Be sure to explore the seafood stores, which are just as likely to sell frogs and unrecognizable crustaceans as salmon and grouper. Perhaps this is because many of the people in this area are Fujian and are used to eating a lot of seafood. The Mexican community has also created its own world on 5th Avenue, complete with street carts piled high with candy and roasted corn, shops that play Latin music, and casual restaurants that sell everything from roasted chicken to mole and tacos.

Borough Park has an authentic orthodox Jewish community, so you'll find synagogues, yeshivas, bearded men, playgrounds full of schoolboys in yarmulkes, and kosher food. It can be difficult for outsiders to visit this area, though, as most shops are closed from Friday afternoon until Sunday. Explorers should be especially aware of the Jewish calendar in the fall, when shops and restaurants close frequently in order to celebrate religious holidays.

Foodie Faves

Alimentos Saludables, 5919 4th Avenue between 59th Street and 60th Street; (718) 492-1660; Subway: N, R to 59th Street; $. This small sandwich shop seems to blend into the bodegas it's surrounded by, but the food here is worth seeking out. The room is decorated with pictures of the Pope and Jesus, as well as several large plastic containers of *agua fresca,* but is otherwise fairly simple. There are a few small tables in the front and a lunch counter, topped with Mexican pastries, that's home to a bustling to-go business. The shop sells plenty  of large sandwiches. Piled high with meats and cheese, they seem weighty enough to feed several hungry construction workers. But you are here for the tamales: The Oaxaca-style tamale is steamed in a corn husk and topped with a dark, complex mole sauce, but it's the pork tamale that's the star. Steamed in a green banana leaf that's tied with string like a present, it's topped with a rich, spicy red sauce that packs plenty of heat. Order a house-made *agua fresca* in tamarind, horchata, or *jamaica*—the large size is about a liter, so you'll have plenty of beverage to soothe your burning tongue.

Banana Leaf, 5216 8th Avenue between 52nd Street and 53rd Street; (718) 851-3818; Subway: N to 8th Avenue; $$. This Malaysian restaurant succeeds at bringing a taste of the Straits to Brooklyn's Chinatown, from classic *nasi lemak* to chicken rice and even chili crab. Many dishes have the hallmark flavors of curry, cilantro, soy, peanuts, rice noodles, and coconut milk that will transport you to Southeast Asia.

Ba Xuyen, 4222 8th Avenue between 42nd Street and 43rd Street; (718) 633-6601; Subway: D, M to 9th Avenue or R to 45th Street; $. This unassuming little sandwich shop on the edge of Chinatown turns out some of the best Vietnamese sandwiches in the city, which is saying a lot at a time when the *banh mi*'s popularity has skyrocketed. It's also one of the most authentic, and the least expensive, *banh mi* around. These heroes, served on tender baguettes made with rice flour, come topped with lots of different options, but the best may be the classic. The bread is smeared with rough pâté, then mayonnaise, then a squirt of Sriracha. On top of that goes two types of pork (ground and lunch meat) and a salad of marinated daikon, carrots, and cilantro. The meatball sub, made with soft pork meatballs, is equally popular, and the sardine sandwich has its fans, too. You may have to keep coming back to try them all to decide which you like best. You'll also want to make your way through the shake list: They are all made with sweetened condensed milk, and some include Asian fruit such as lichee, durian (a custardy fruit that smells a bit like gym socks), and sweet jackfruit.

East Harbor Seafood Palace, 714 65th Street between 7th Avenue and 8th Avenue; (718) 765-0098; Subway: N to 8th Avenue; $$. This may be the most popular dim sum parlor in Sunset Park. They have a free valet parking lot, but it fills up early. The wait can be so long that many people pick up a ticket with their number on it, go shopping, and come back later. If you do decide to stick it out, expect to hear dozens of numbers called out in Chinese before they call your number in English. Plus, since on weekends and holidays so many locals come in large groups and plan to spend time here, drinking tea and catching up, the turnover can be painfully slow for such a big space. But, of course, the dim sum is worth the wait. Tender *shu mai* (steamed shrimp crystal dumplings) are filled with fresh shrimp, and steamed *char sui* (steamed buns filled with barbecue pork) have a sweet and savory filling that's plenty meaty. They also have large fried shrimp wrapped with bacon, jalapeños stuffed with shrimp, and bun dough wrapped around Chinese sausage, a dish that tastes a bit like a pig in a blanket. Save room for the custard-filled steamed buns—a sweet ending to any dim sum. Or come for dinner and feast on Cantonese seafood like fried shrimp with broccoli and walnuts or *chow mai fun* topped with shellfish. Of course, since the restaurant specializes in Chinese banquets, you'll want to call ahead and make sure they're not booked before going out for dinner.

La Guera Restaurant (aka Rico's Tamales), 4603 5th Avenue between 45th Street and 46th Street; (718) 437-0232; Subway: R to 45th Street; $. The fluorescent lights may be off-putting, but the tamales are just right here. They keep a cooler of them by the front door, so you can order yours to go. The masa, steamed in corn husks, is rich and creamy—so rich, you have to wonder how much lard and salt goes into them. But no matter: Filled with chicken in a green chile sauce, cheese, or pork, they are a tasty treat and a worthy use of freezer space.

Lan Zhou Handpull Noodle, 5924 8th Avenue, enter on 60th Street between 7th Avenue and 8th Avenue; (718) 492-7568; Subway: N to 8th Avenue; $. This small shop carries one thing— noodle soup. The only decision you get to make is what goes in your bowl besides noodles (which, here, are thin, soft, and dreamy) and

CELEBRATE CHINESE NEW YEAR

Each January or February, Brooklyn Academy of Music and the Brooklyn Botanic Garden both mark the lunar New Year with celebrations. But the place to be to really celebrate the event with the local community is Brooklyn's Chinatown, where everyone turns out for a parade up 8th Avenue, sponsored by the Brooklyn Chinese-American Association. It's a fun and festive time to come out and see the neighborhood.It's not as polished as the Queens and Manhattan festivities, nor as crowded, but it's just as much fun. The neighborhood seems draped in red, including crimson balloons. Kids (dressed in traditional red silk garb) play drums, wave ribbons, and demonstrate martial arts and fan dancing. There are also dragon dancers and firecrackers. And there is plenty of food. Like other cultures, the Chinese have an array of symbolic foods to celebrate the New Year, many of which are said to bring longevity, wealth, prosperity, or happiness. Locals give each other tangerines and oranges as gifts, their hue symbolizing money. Restaurants have New Year menus, and the dim sum parlors are packed with families. Munch on sticky rice cakes (to tie your family together) and long noodles (for a long life). Slurp them whole—cutting them, as you can imagine, is bad luck (bca.net).

the fragrant beef broth, seasoned with Chinese five-spice powder. Go for the house special and you'll get a big bowl filled with a pork chop—which also soaks up that five-spice powder—beef tendon, tripe, a fried egg, and scallions. Or choose a single topping like pork or dumplings. Regardless, for $6 or less you'll get dinner that could serve four—and a broth that will warm you from the inside out on a cold night.

Lucky Eight, 5204 8th Avenue between 52nd Street and 53rd Street; (718) 851-8862; Subway: R to 53rd Street; $. The first things you see when you walk into this Chinatown restaurant are tanks. Large fish tanks line the front of the restaurant, and they're filled with fish puffing out their cheeks, tiny shrimp, and eels twirling around like black velvet hair ribbons. Whatever you thought you were going to order goes right out the window. You must have the seafood. Fortunately, they have many preparations to choose from including shrimp with candied walnuts, and the signature dish, Pride of Lucky Eight, a more complex mix of squid, abalone, shiitake, shrimp, and scallions with a punch of sesame oil and a pop of ginger.

Metro Cafe, 4924 8th Avenue between 49th Street and 50th Street; (718) 437-7980; Subway: R to 53rd Street; $. This small, brightly lit spot is the only Sichuan restaurant in Brooklyn's Chinatown. It has a whole separate menu of Japanese snacks and rice plates, but you can get those all along 8th Avenue. The real reason to come here is to chase the burn of Sichuan peppers and peppercorns. The husband-and-wife team is from the Sichuan province, and once you convince her (she runs the front of the house, he runs the back) that you can take the heat, they will certainly bring it. Order the beef with Sichuan special sauce, and you'll get a glass bowl full of braised, thin slices of beef swimming in a peppery, oil-tinged sauce that has a complex flavor with a clove-, cumin-, and anise-inflected aftertaste. The Chongqing chicken is a sautéed mix of flavorful marinated-then-fried chicken bits with dried red peppers and fresh green peppers. Start to show signs of wear (sweat along your brow, a new redder tinge to your face) and the owner will bring you a glass of house-made iced ginger tea to cool the burn. It only helps a little, but it's a thoughtful gesture just the same.

Noodle Station, 5224 8th Avenue between 52nd Street and 53rd Street; (718) 853-8588; Subway: N to 8th Avenue; $. There are plenty of similar-looking shops on 8th Avenue selling bubble tea, hot Chinese tea, steamed buns, cookies, and more solid lunch food like noodles. I like this one best because every time I walk in they seem to be unloading a new batch of buns from the back kitchen. The pillowy, white dough balls (made to be taken home and steamed or ordered already steamed in the restaurant) come in lots of different flavors, from sweet barbecue pork to creamy custard.

Pacificana, 813 55th Street between 8th Avenue and 9th Avenue; (718) 871-2880; Subway: N to 8th Avenue; $$. Brooklyn's most lauded Cantonese dim sum is on the second floor of a former bank and still retains the elegance of its previous incarnation. At lunchtime on weekends, the place fills up with local Chinese-American families who sit at large round tables under the vaulted ceiling. (Come with fewer people and you'll share a large table, which can be a little awkward as both groups pretend to be alone.) Take your places, and then the parade of silver carts begins to visit your table. First, you may get to choose from a variety of delicate steamed dumplings—say chicken *har gow* and shrimp *shu mai*. Then, perhaps steamed pork buns, called *char sui,* filled with fragrant and sweet barbecue pork or sweet ones filled with a yolk-rich yellow custard that, when cut open, makes the bun look like a hard-boiled egg. One cart brings rice noodles filled with plump, steamed shrimp and topped with a sweet soy sauce. The adventure is not knowing what taste will come next and the excitement of waiting to find out.

Ricos Tacos, 505 51st Street between 5th Avenue and 6th Avenue; (718) 633-4816; Subway: R to 53rd Street; $. Follow the mural of the pigs to this side-street find. You get your drinks right away, whether it's the house-made *agua fresca* or the Mexican-imported Coke in a glass bottle, but everything else is slow as molasses. Just when you have fidgeted and fiddled with the tabletop caddy of 3 salsas (red, green, and avocado) as much as you can imagine, and you're ready to leave, out come your tacos, steaming hot and just as good as you imagined tacos could be. Follow the advice of the mural (of three smiling pigs in a pot) and order the pork tacos, whether it's the fatty roasted pork *carnitas* (rich, moist, and meaty) or the heavily seasoned *al pastor* topped with onion, *queso fresco,* and cilantro. Both are served on small tortillas that are fragrant with the scent of roasted corn.

Rocco's Italian Cafeteria, 6408 Fort Hamilton Parkway between 64th Street and 65th Street; (718) 833-2109; Subway: N to Fort Hamilton Parkway; $. Get in line behind the regulars ("Where were you yesterday?" a cashier asked a customer when I was in line one day) for hearty Italian fare served by the pound that's as substantial as it is reasonably priced. The fried calamari, served with spicy or mild cocktail sauce, is the most popular order, but the stuffed artichokes, fried zucchini, croquettes, and ham-and-cheese-stuffed rice balls are popular, too. Don't leave without sampling the pasta dishes—from lasagna to chicken Parmesan over spaghetti; if you have room for dessert, check out the cannoli. They make plain and chocolate-dipped ones, and they fill them to order. Tip: If you're staying, rather than taking an order to go, you can still check out the dishes on the line before putting in your order.

Super Pollo Latino, 4102 5th Avenue between 41st Street and 42nd Street; (718) 871-5700; Subway: R to 45th Street; $. This little, no-frills Peruvian spot doesn't look like much, but the rotisserie chicken is spot on. Bathed in savory spices, and spit-roasted until tender and juicy, it's also a steal. For less than $10, you get a half chicken and a side of *maduros* (fried plantains cut to order then popped in the hot oil for a quick fry). They come out soft and warm and fresh, just as you knew they would be when you saw the guy behind the counter start peeling the plantain after you ordered. Take yours to go or eat it in the back room—which makes up in air-conditioning what it lacks in charm.

Tacos Matamoros, 4508 5th Avenue between 45th Street and 46th Street; (718) 871-7627; Subway: R to 45th Street; $. This is the most well-known of all the taco shops, and it's also the most comfortable to dine in. The room has wood moldings and is well air-conditioned, with a polite hostess, Spanish-language television on large flat-screen sets, and waitresses who speak English. The food isn't as perfect as the setting, but it's good enough to be worth the trade-off for some less-adventurous eaters. If you order the tacos, be prepared for a mild experience: The chorizo isn't spicy, the *al pastor* is missing heat and flavor, and the tongue hasn't been butchered properly. The quesadillas are a better choice. They're topped with a cool, crisp mix of shredded lettuce and sour cream—and they don't look anything like the quesadillas at your local Tex-Mex joint. Instead, they are deep-fried pockets filled with beef and no cheese. Wash them down with a Jamaica *agua fresca* or the mamey shake, which would be the perfect counterbalance to spice and heat, if only there were any.

Tacos Xochimilco, 4501 5th Avenue between 45th Street and 46th Street; (718) 435-7600; Subway: R to 45th Street; $. In the heat of summer, the ceiling fans don't quite cut it at this small, casual Mexican spot, which is decorated with family pictures, cowboy hats, and ropes, and a jukebox that plays Mexican bands like Liberación and Corridos Rancheros. Order a cold, house-made horchata (yes, that's cinnamon floating on the top) or an icy Mexican Coke. Start like everyone else does with a big bowl of pozole followed by a crispy beef chalupa topped with *crema,* cheese, and a green tomatillo sauce, *tortas* topped with fresh avocado, or pork tacos that are well spiced and topped with plenty of cilantro and onion.

Thanh Da, 6008 7th Avenue between 60th Street and 61th Street; (718) 492-3253; Subway: N to 8th Avenue; $. This Vietnamese shop serves breakfast and lunch. Start the day right with a Vietnamese coffee, thickened the traditional way, with sweetened condensed milk. Or come at lunchtime, when you'll want to stick to the *banh mi* sandwich (a steal at $3.75). The classic is filled with ground pork, pork lunch meat, and pâté, and topped with the pickled salad of daikon, cilantro, and jalapeño. They also have a second location on 8th Avenue, but it is smaller and less comfortable.

Tulcingo Restaurant, 5520 5th Avenue between 54th Street and 55th Street; (718) 439-2896; Subway: R to 45th Street; $. It's clear that the foodies have found this place. On my last visit, the restaurant was full—and about half of the diners were large groups of white Brooklynites who had clearly trekked here for the food. (The other half were Mexican locals, many of whom seemed to know the pretty young servers by name.) They had all come to the right place—the dining room is spacious, well lit, and comfortable, with paintings of Mexican tribal scenes, some of which are spiritual. And the food, from the enormous quesadillas that spill over the sides of the plates to the enchiladas doused in tangy green tomatillo sauce, is all tasty and hearty. The tacos may not be the best on the street, but even they are flavorful, and they're a rare misstep. Many of the dishes are topped with crumbled cheese, sour cream, radishes, and shredded lettuce—lending freshness to the well-seasoned roasted pork, chicken, and beef inside the tortillas.

Yun Nan Flavour Snack, 775A 49th Street between 7th Avenue and 8th Avenue; (718) 633-3090; Subway: R to 45th Street; $. This small Chinese shop has a counter built around the edges, with 6 little stools for lucky diners. Come for your noodle soup fix, and you'll be treated to a spicy broth filled with rice noodles with crispy pork (as well as other meats) and several different types of chiles. It's rich, flavorful, and interesting—but they don't speak much English, so don't expect to find out exactly what you're eating.

Specialty Stores, Markets & Producers

Breuckelen Distilling, 77 19th Street between 3rd Avenue and the Gowanus Bay (347) 725-4985; Subway: R to Prospect Avenue; brkdistilling.com. Good news for those who like to stock their kitchen with as many locally sourced ingredients as possible: This distillery makes gin and whiskey, right in Sunset Park. Better still, they offer tours and tastings on Saturday afternoons so you can try their products before you pick the bottle that's right for your liquor cabinet.

D. Coluccio & Sons, 1214 60th Street between 12th Avenue and 13th Avenue; (718) 436-6700; Subway: B, N to New Utrecht Avenue; dcoluccioandsons.com. This Borough Park importer is often called the best in the borough. Consider it one-stop shopping for all your pantry basics, from imported dry pasta in a variety of shapes, from common to uncommonly beautiful, to a wide selection of canned tomatoes for sauce, including the chef-preferred San Marzano ones as well as more unusual cherry tomatoes. In the canned aisles, you'll find tuna, olives, capers, and anchovies. They also have cheeses, dried meats, and fresh breads.

Egg Custard King Cafe, 5317 8th Avenue between 53rd Street and 54th Street; (718) 438-6808; Subway: N to 8th Avenue. You'll find egg custard tarts all over Brooklyn's Chinatown, but I suspect a lot of the smaller shops buy theirs here. And why wouldn't they? The crust is buttery and flaky; the custard is simple yet satisfying. They come in lots of unusual flavors—honeydew, almond, and coconut—some of which are brightly colored. But for those who love the rich egg taste of the original, there's just no substitute.

Family Dumpling, 5602 7th Avenue between 56th Street and 57th Street; (718) 492-0686; Subway: N, R to 7th Avenue; $. You don't come here for the atmosphere, which is simple as can be, or the service, which is polite if a bit gruff and hurried. You do, however, come for the dumplings—steamed-and-griddled pork-and-chive beauties. They're rich, flavorful, and unforgettable. The sesame pancake may be skippable, but the genre-defying scallion pancake, which puffs up with flaky goodness, is not at all greasy. It's unlike anything you've ever had before.

Fei Long Market, 6301 8th Avenue between 63rd Street and 64th Street; (718) 680-0118; Subway: N to 8th Avenue. This massive grocery store takes up a full block. In the front, you'll find bountiful vegetable, herb, and fruit tables, piled high and elbow-to-elbow crowded. Inside the main room, there's a full grocery store with rows and rows of boxed, packaged, and bottled Asian specialty goods. The seafood aisles have everything from fish to crabs, live shrimp, and turtles. Come for Chinese rice flour and sesame oil, and you'll probably also bring home Thai fish sauce and Japanese sweets. The refrigerator aisles are full of steamed buns, dumpling wrappers, and tofu—everything you need to replicate your favorite Chinese meal at home, from scratch or with a little help from pre-made products.

Hong Kong Supermarket, 6013 8th Avenue between 60th Street and 61st Street; (718) 438-2288; Subway: N to 8th Avenue. This large grocery store—with a parking lot, no less—looks plucked right out of the suburbs. It's one-stop shopping for Asian cooking ingredients, though it's not as inexpensive as some of the small food shops that line 8th Avenue. Here, you'll find every type of fruit, including non-Asian varieties like apples and pears, and aisles of sauces (like soy and peanut), ingredients such as sesame oil and rice noodles, and a whole row of Chinese and Japanese candies.

Kung Fu Tea, 806 55th Street between 8th Avenue and 9th Avenue; (718) 633-5588; Subway: N to 8th Avenue. This high-tech bubble tea place relies on sleek gadgetry to create tapioca-filled teas and tea lattes of unparalled deliciousness. (They come in flavors like passion fruit and winter melon, but I always like to stick to classics like milk tea and almond.) First, the barista places your tea of choice into a machine that shakes the liquid into frothy deliciousness, then he or she sits your cup into another machine to create an air-tight seal that prevents spilling. All you have to do is pierce the seal with an extra-wide straw and enjoy the chewy tapioca.

New Public Meat Market, 5021 5th Avenue between 50th Street and 51st Street; (718) 871-1188; Subway: R to 53rd Street. From the cow and pig heads in the window to the sawdust on the floor, this is an old-school butcher. Since 1940, the owners have served the Mexican community well with pig's feet, plenty of chorizo, honeycomb tripe, and lard. They also make entertaining easy: You can order *lechones,* whole roasted piglets for parties, with just a week's notice and they sell *al pastor,* preseasoned pork, ready to take home and fill your tacos, fuss-free.

Panaderia El Hornito, 5717 5th Avenue between 57th Street and 58th Street; (718) 439-7539; Subway: N, R to 59th Street. In the front of this small bakery and food shop, you'll find a treasure chest of Mexican cooking ingredients: The cooler is full of *queso fresco,* and the shelves are piled high with bags of dried chiles, bags of masa, and boxes of a Mexican hot chocolate called Abuelita. But the real find here is in the back of the store. Squeeze your way back, between the line and the refrigerator cases full of Jarritos sodas and Mexican Coke, and you'll see racks full of pastry-topped pans. Watch the other customers grab a pan and a pair of tongs, and start making their selections from the pastries cooling on the racks. Along with traditional sweet, eggy breads topped with colored sugar, you'll find turnovers filled with fruit like pineapple and super-sweet guava, and delectable custard-filled sugar doughnuts, sliced lengthwise and filled to the brim. Who knew that some of the best doughnuts in Brooklyn were hidden in the back of a tiny Mexican shop, unmarked and uncelebrated?

Plaza #2 Xochimilco Grocery Store, 5709 5th Avenue between 57th Street and 58th Street; (718) 439-1717; Subway: N, R to 59th Street. This little grocery store has everything you need to cook your own Mexican feast at home. The piles of fresh vegetables include tomatillos, ripe avocados, pods of amaranth seeds, and cactus paddles, as well as cilantro and bunches of herbs for soup. In the back, there are bags of every type of Mexican chile imaginable—from the dark ancho pods to the lighter *chile de arbol*—as well as several types of masa for tamales and thickening sauces. In the front, candies, packages of imported drink mixes and *agua fresca* mixes, and boxes of crisp fried pork skin called chicharrónes share space with heavy *molcajetes,* the mortar and pestles used for mashing guacamole.

Schick's, 4710 16th Avenue between 47th Street and 48th Street; (718) 436-8020; Subway: F to Ditmas Avenue; schicksbakery.com. This kosher bakery specializes in nondairy kosher baked goods, including challah breads and babka. The products are sold at Zabars in Manhattan and **Fairway** (p. 67) in Red Hook, but if you want to trek out here to get your sweets from the source, call ahead for hours. Next door to the small storefront, the commercial operation hums along, and you can watch racks of cakes and baked goods get piled into carts. Each Passover, they open a separate "Kosher for Passover" store, while most area bakeries close down. Tip: They make a tasty cheese babka, but consider calling ahead to order it in advance.

T Baar, 4823 8th Avenue between 48th Street and 49th Street; (718) 686-1380; Subway: R to 45th Street; tbaar.com. This bubble tea shop may just be the most polished of all the choices on 8th Avenue. They offer all the classic Taiwanese flavors, from black tea to green tea, coconut, almond, taro,

honeydew, and sesame, as well as their own twists on bubble tea mixed with slushies. All are filled with soft, gummy black balls of tapioca that you slurp up through an extra-wide straw. They also have fruit smoothies in every flavor imaginable, including mango, peach, and kiwi, and fresh fruit shakes made with bananas. And while it all sounds like beverages designed for tweens, just go with it—these sweet drinks are a lot of fun if you don't second-guess the merit of a beverage that starts with colored powder. You may even find yourself wanting one of their frequent drinker cards so that you get a free one for every dozen you buy. T Baar is a chain with other locations around the neighborhood.

Three Guys from Brooklyn, 6502 Fort Hamilton Parkway between 65th Street and 66th Street; (718) 748-8340; Subway: N to Fort Hamilton Parkway; 3guysfrombrooklyn.com. Should you ever need, say, a late-night peach fix, this fruit and vegetable store is open 24 hours, 7 days a week. They do such a brisk business that on weekends, cars are often double-parked along 65th Street. You'll find plenty of whatever is in season, at low prices, plus unusual Mediterranean treats like fresh almonds and plenty of Caribbean mangos and pineapples.

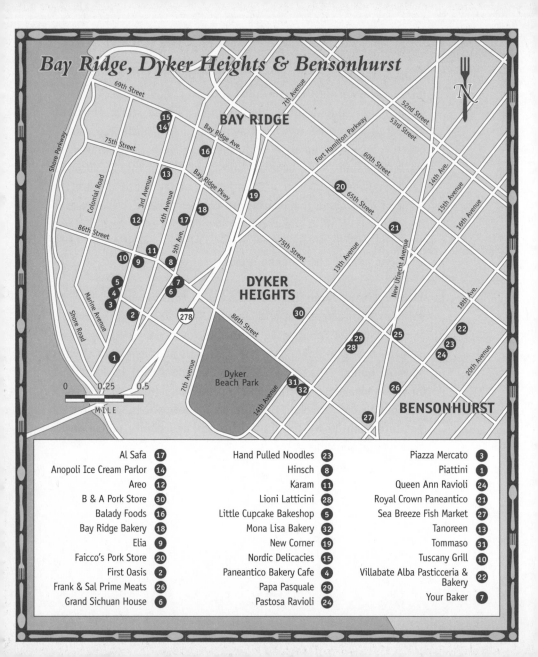

Bay Ridge, Dyker Heights & Bensonhurst

BAY RIDGE

DYKER HEIGHTS

BENSONHURST

Dyker Beach Park

0   0.25   0.5
MILE

Al Safa	17	
Anopoli Ice Cream Parlor	14	
Areo	12	
B & A Pork Store	30	
Balady Foods	16	
Bay Ridge Bakery	18	
Elia	9	
Faicco's Pork Store	20	
First Oasis	2	
Frank & Sal Prime Meats	26	
Grand Sichuan House	6	

Hand Pulled Noodles	23	
Hinsch	8	
Karam	11	
Lioni Latticini	28	
Little Cupcake Bakeshop	5	
Mona Lisa Bakery	32	
New Corner	19	
Nordic Delicacies	15	
Paneantico Bakery Cafe	4	
Papa Pasquale	29	
Pastosa Ravioli	24	

Piazza Mercato	3	
Piattini	1	
Queen Ann Ravioli	24	
Royal Crown Paneantico	21	
Sea Breeze Fish Market	27	
Tanoreen	13	
Tommaso	31	
Tuscany Grill	10	
Villabate Alba Pasticceria & Bakery	22	
Your Baker	7	

Bay Ridge, Dyker Heights & Bensonhurst

Bay Ridge sits in the shadows of the Verrazano-Narrows Bridge, which seems to loom around every corner. Bay Ridge was originally Scandinavian and Italian, and you can see residual signs of that in some of the businesses, including the pizzerias and cannoli-filled bakeries. (Most people think first of the John Travolta movie *Saturday Night Fever* when they think of Bay Ridge.) There are still plenty of Italian restaurants on 3rd Avenue (complete with valet parking and intricately folded cloth napkins), but in recent decades the dining scene has morphed to reflect the neighborhood's melting pot of other immigrant cultures, including Polish, Russian, Irish, and Greek. Most dominantly, you will find the Middle East represented here, which might mean seeing crowds of women in traditional dress and hearing the call to mosque.

Bensonhurst is best known outside these parts as a mafia hideaway for the Colombo and Gambino families. Talk about anything you saw and, at another time, you might have come down with a case of "Bensonhurst Amnesia." But with (as the saying goes) "everyone either locked up or dead," organized crime is no longer the defining characteristic of the neighborhood. Many homes have Italianate architectural influence, like striped awnings and juliette balconies. Come at the holidays and you'll see house after house covered in Christmas lights. Come in the summer, and the statues of the Madonna are surrounded by hydrangea, and clothing is drying on backyard lines. Brooklyn's Little Italy (one of the original destinations for first-generation Italian immigrants) still has some old-school red-sauce trattorias and Sicilian pastry shops, as well as a newer Chinese community.

Foodie Faves

Al Safa, 8002 5th Avenue between 80th Street and 81st Street; (718) 238-9576; Subway: R to 77th Street; alsafa-restaurant.com; $. The hospitality of Lebanese culture is alive and well at this small casual restaurant, where the owner will walk you through the menu himself. Start with a date juice cocktail, mixed with rose water and topped with pine nuts that grow pink in the liquid. Then order some small, baked pies, like the meat-filled *lahmejun* or the spinach-and-sumac stuffed one that sports a lemony tang. You should also try the *shawarma,* a lamb-and-beef mixture that's cooked on a vertical spit in the traditional cone shape, then quickly seared and served atop a pita with lettuce, tomato, onions, plenty of pickles, and a creamy tahini sauce. (It's juicy and more flavorful than at more well-known spots nearby.) The tongue sandwich is truly tender and comes topped with a fragrant garlic sauce. Just save room for dessert: the *moughleh,* a creamy pudding topped with whole pistachios, almonds, honey, and more rose water, is delectable. The owner will help with any explanations you need, but he won't tell you which dessert to choose. "That," he says, "would be like picking which of my sons I like best."

Areo, 8424 3rd Avenue between 84th Street and 85th Street; (718) 238-0079; Subway: R to 86th Street; $$$. You're best off here if you're a regular, as it seems that everyone is. Locals stream in, greeting the maitre d' by name, and other patrons, too. The menu is northern Italian, and there's a separate menu of specials that's as long as most restaurants' daily menus. Of course, if you aren't a regular, you may notice that you wait a bit longer for a table, for your food, and for service in general, as the sea of familiar faces are welcomed. The food itself is fine, if not groundbreaking, with heaping portions of fried calamari and more diminutive plates of baked clams with bread crumbs or, in summertime, stuffed squash blossoms filled with mozzarella in a delicate tomato broth. Entrees run from massive, tasty braised lamb shanks served on a bed of orzo and mascarpone (perhaps worth the trek, and the trouble parking, alone) and veal scaloppine with sautéed spinach and artichoke hearts in a lemony piccata sauce with capers. Most tables seem to start with a large carafe of white or red sangria and finish with huge hunks of cheesecake—and if you want to feel part of the crowd, you may consider doing the same.

Elia, 8611 3rd Avenue between 86th Street and 87th Street; (718) 748-9891; Subway: R to 86th Street; eliarestaurant.org; $$$. For a borough with astoundingly little Greek food (residents trek to Queens whenever they crave moussaka), this special-occasion restaurant (read: pricey) is impressive. The ingredients rely heavily on Mediterranean classics, but the preparations are tweaked just enough to be surprising. The crispy calamari appetizer is impeccably crunchy (the secret: it's crusted with cracker crumbs instead of flour) and served with a creamy parsley dipping sauce and a piquant tomato one. Entrees of grilled fish are served atop a bed of sautéed mixed greens with a bright lemon reduction; they often have several fish to choose from, but you want the sweet Australian barramundi if it's on the list. Lamb dishes are impressive too, including an enormous lamb shank served atop a bed of orzo. It's Flintstonian in size, but the flavor is surprisingly sophisticated.

First Oasis, 9218 4th Avenue between 92nd Street and 93rd Street; (718) 238-4505; Subway: R to 95th Street; firstoasisrestaurant.com; $$. A Syrian restaurant that was originally in Manhattan, First Oasis relocated to this space (closer to the owner's home) 5 years ago and now serves its broad menu in a lovely flower-filled garden. If you're not familiar with this cuisine, consider ordering the "Magic Combination" sampler platter, which comes in 2 courses. The first, a tray of *mezze,* includes garlicky hummus, tahini, smoky baba gha-noush, crisp doughnut-shaped falafel crusted with sesame seeds, stuffed grape leaves, a Mediterranean tomato-and-cucumber salad, and pickled turnips, presented with plenty of warm pita bread. The second course includes an array of kebabs (beef, chicken, lamb, and spicy sausagelike *kefta*), served with vegetables and rice. More experienced eaters of Syrian food go right for the raw *kebbeh,* a tartarelike appetizer, the kebabs, the couscous platters, and (of course) the super-thick coffee, which has the texture—at the bottom—of molasses.

Grand Sichuan House, 8701 5th Avenue between 87th Street and 88th Street; (718) 680-8887; Subway: R to 86th Street; grand sichuanhouse.com; $$. After you get over the surprise of finding an authentic Sichuan restaurant in Bay Ridge, hidden in an unas-suming location behind the Century 21 and not looking especially auspicious, pick your jaw up off the floor and start perusing the menu. This is the real deal, so come hungry and bring friends so you can try more dishes. Start with spicy dan dan noodles swimming in chili oil, scallion pancakes, or savory soup-filled pork dumplings.

Then move on to the crispy, cumin-crusted lamb (a dish that's a fiery and flavorful ode to cumin; it is sprinkled liberally with dried peppers), flavorful shredded duck stir-fried with string beans, and *ma po* tofu with pork. My advice: Order some egg fried rice or sautéed pea shoots with sliced garlic to soothe your taste buds.

Hand Pull Noodles, 7201 18th Avenue between 71st Street and 72nd Street; (718) 232-6191; Subway: D, M to 71st Street; $. The thudding sound you hear when you walk in the door is the sound of noodles being pulled. Order, then take a moment to watch the chef roll the dough on the table by hand, stretch and twist it in the air, slap his creation against the table, and repeat. The show is fun to watch, but it's just a prelude to the meal itself. Order a plate of pork dumplings—the fried ones are better than the steamed, but they're all big and meaty. Then, choose from a long list of noodle soups.

The noodles, which are thin spaghetti-like strands, are tender and served in a rich broth with bok choy and the meat of your choice. (The pork chop and the chopped bone-in lamb are the specialties here.) When your soup is served, then your job begins: Doctor the otherwise mild-but-flavorful dish with the array of sauces on the table. The black vinegar and garlic sauces are for the dumplings, but the soy and 3 types of chili (in oil, with garlic, and Sriracha) can be added to your soup for kick.

Karam, 8519 4th Avenue between 85th Street and 86th Street; (718) 745-5227; Subway: R to 86th Street; $. This extremely popular Lebanese shop has a few tables but does a brisk business in takeaway meals. Come for the beef-and-lamb or chicken *shawarma* (which can be dry or juicy, depending on the day), the grilled kebabs, and crispy, fried kibbe meatballs flavored with pine nuts. Be sure to pick up some honey-soaked baklava and rose water–scented rice pudding, too.

Piattini, 9824 4th Avenue at 99th street and Marine Avenue; (718) 759-0009; Subway: R to 95th Street; $$$. This Sicilian spot in the shadow of the Verrazano Bridge is friendly and perfect for a lingering, congenial dinner with friends, shared appetizers, and a couple bottles of vino, BYOB-style. Call ahead and ask them nicely to save a table for you—if you give them your name, you'll find they use it all night. ("What can we get you, Jeff? Would you like any gelato, Jeff? Can I get you some espresso, Jeff?") Start with the fried artichokes. They're perfectly cooked and almost sweet. In summer, order a plate of super-ripe cantaloupe wrapped in prosciutto. (Avoid the calamari and the porchetta—too bland.)

The best entree is also the most popular—the *bucatini con sarde* the unofficial house specialty. It's made with fresh sardines and bread crumbs, and you can smell the bowls from several tables away. The restaurant is also known for its house-made gelato— served sandwiched in a brioche roll or in an ice-cream glass topped with amaretto cookies. Gelato is the owner's true passion: Before opening this restaurant last summer, he actually served his frozen treats from the back of a tanning salon. And you can see right away where his pride comes in. The lemon tastes a bit like lemon meringue pie, and the hazelnut has a Nutella-like taste; the peach is a fresh ode to summer. Pistachio, ricotta, and espresso are much milder—which, after a plate of pungent fish pasta, may be just right. Luck into coming at the right time, when they're making the gelato, and they'll give you samples right out of the machine. And be sure to wave as they call out to you—"Have a good evening, Jeff!" Here, you're a regular after your first meal.

Tanoreen, 7523 3rd Avenue between 75th and 76th Street; (718) 748-5600; Subway: R to 77th Street; tanoreen.com; $$. After years of packing the devotees into a tiny area, Tanoreen has finally moved into its long-awaited larger space up the street. No longer BYOB, the restaurant is also taking reservations, a blessing for those who remember waiting longingly on the curb. The menu remains the same—a festival of highly seasoned lamb dishes, many made with their house-made spice mix, which includes plenty of cinnamon.

Tuscany Grill, 8620 3rd Avenue between 86th Street and 87th Street; (718) 921-5633; Subway: R to 86th Street; $$. In an area once known for red-sauce Italian spots, this northern Italian restaurant is a standout. Start with a bowl of warm olives marinated in red pepper flakes or white beans with spicy sausage (from nearby **Faicco's,** p. 214, butcher shop), and a glass of Sienese red like Montepulciano. Entrees, like the spaghettini with sausage, tomatoes, and a spicy red cream sauce or Tuscan herb-crusted grilled ribs, are hearty stick-to-your-own-ribs-fare, but the candlelight and soft music scream romance.

Landmarks

New Corner, 7201 8th Avenue between 71st Street and 72nd Street; (718) 833-0800; Subway: N to 8th Avenue or R to 77th Street; newcornerrestaurant.com; $$. New Corner is so authentically old school that it reminds you of how hard it is for nostalgic hipster restaurants to re-create this kind of atmosphere. The regulars, many of whom have been coming for more decades than I have been alive, know the waiters and maitre d' by name. The bar—with its old-fashioned lanterns, wood paneling, and customers ordering Dewars on the rocks with a splash of water—hasn't changed much in decades, nor has the booth-filled dining room with its digital board of Quick Draw numbers. Once you've settled into the 1960s, pick up the burgundy menu and you'll see that it, too, is a relic. And that's when you realize that you either embrace the Old Brooklyn in this red-sauce restaurant, or leave.

I embraced it and felt well rewarded. The classic Italian-American dishes reminded me of my childhood. Large oval platters come heaped with chicken Parmesan, pounded thin (but not too thin) and topped with a simple marinara sauce and an abundance of melted mozzarella, or veal cutlets filled with prosciutto and topped with a mushroom Marsala sauce. Dishes come with your choice of potato croquettes and steamed vegetables, or a bowl of pasta, served in whatever shape you like. True, the prices were probably lower back in the day, and the atmosphere must have felt current then. But for red-sauce Italian-American food, this spot remains the one to beat.

Tommaso, 1464 86th Street between Bay 8th Street and 15th Avenue; (718) 236-9883; Subway: D, M to 18th Avenue; tommaso inbrooklyn.com; $$. This 38-year-old Italian restaurant is as well known for its opera-singing chef-owner as for its classic Italian-American cuisine. Come on a weekday, and you can order the 3-course, fixed-price meal for $25, which comes with gelato or Italian cheesecake for dessert. Start with mussels steamed in a delicate tomato–white wine sauce with a hint of garlic, or a tasty *calzonetti* filled with spinach and ricotta and baked in a cornmeal crust. Entrees are slightly less successful, including the veal, which is pounded thin and wrapped around prosciutto and mozzarella, then

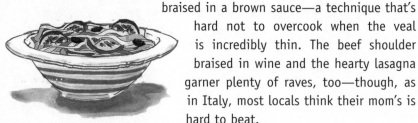

braised in a brown sauce—a technique that's hard not to overcook when the veal is incredibly thin. The beef shoulder braised in wine and the hearty lasagna garner plenty of raves, too—though, as in Italy, most locals think their mom's is hard to beat.

Anopoli Ice Cream Parlor, 6920 3rd Avenue between Bay Ridge Avenue and Ovington Avenue; (718) 748-3863; Subway: R to Bay Ridge Avenue; $. As old-fashioned and simple as can be, this ice-cream shop-cum-diner makes all its own ice cream, in retro flavors like cherry-vanilla, coffee, and butter pecan, then serves them (with house-made hot fudge, if you please) in equally retro metal dishes. The decor, with its soda fountain counter, vinyl booths, and old-time photos of Brooklyn, is equally rooted in the past. Whether or not you're happy here has much to do with whether you like your ice cream newfangled, or whether the malteds and egg creams of the past are your thing.

B & A Pork Store, 7818 13th Avenue between 78th Street and 79th Street; (718) 833-9661; Subway: D, M to 79th Street. Of course they sell a lot more than pork at this Dyker Heights butcher shop and meat market. Yes, they make a variety of their own sausage links and patties, but they also make their own mozzarella and roast their own beef, ham, and turkey for sandwiches. They sell **Queen Ann** (p. 220) pastas, which are made nearby, including the stuffed shells and manicotti. Their prepared foods include *arancini*, mozzarella sticks, and a spinach- and mozzarella-stuffed stromboli bread wrapped in pastry that's so flaky, you'll want to eat it for lunch every day. Just be prepared to fight off your coworkers when they smell the buttery richness.

The Lore and Lure of the Egg Cream

The first thing you learn about this soda fountain classic is that there are no eggs in this drink and there never were. Instead, you make an egg cream by mixing chocolate syrup (traditionally of the Fox's U-bet variety, which is still made in Brooklyn) with milk in a tall fountain glass and then spraying seltzer on top of the mixture and stirring with a long spoon until a foamy head forms. Then, you drink it through a straw rather quickly, since the head subsides with time. (See Fox's **Egg Cream** recipe on p. 279.) Proper egg creams—which always have chocolate syrup rather than vanilla, strawberry, or some newfangled flavor like hazelnut—are hard to find these days, even in Brooklyn.

Though there are several versions of the legend, the most prominent story dates back to 1890, when Louis Auster made one in his Brooklyn candy shop. According to folklore, the word *egg* in "egg cream" derives from the Yiddish *echt,* which means "real," as in the "real cream" used in the drink. Auster then became so famous that his candy shop sold 3,000 of these drinks per day. Is this the true story of the invention? Nobody seems to know. But for those who grew up in Brooklyn, it is a source of pride and frustration, because there are so few places that make proper ones.

Balady Foods, 7128 5th Avenue between Ovington Avenue and 72nd Street; (718) 567-2252; Subway: R to Bay Ridge Avenue. The Halal meat section is small in this Middle Eastern grocery store, but the shelves are piled high with everything else you need to create a feast at home. The pickles and olives look fresh and meaty, and the bins are full of dry goods like colorful lentils and couscous. There are also inexpensive bottles of pomegranate molasses, rose water, honey, and fig jam, and a refriger-  ated section packed with *labaneh,* yogurt, and cheese. On the way out, you'll find nuts and dried fruit, as well as sesame seed candy, nougat squares, and powdery cubes of Turkish delight.

Bay Ridge Bakery, 7805 5th Avenue between 78th Street and 79th Street; (718) 238-0014; Subway: R to 77th Street; bayridge bakery.com. This colorful bakery is packed to the rim with baked goods. You can tell they are trying to be everything to everyone— there are Danishes, Italian cookies and wedding cakes, and delicate French pastries. But the real find here are the Greek desserts, hidden in the back. "Is your chef Greek?" I asked the friendly Asian woman who came out from behind the tall counter to help me. "Yes. How did you know?" I knew because I have spent a lot of time in Greece, and these pastries looked just right, and went beyond the basic baklava. And they were as tasty as they looked: The *galakto-boureko* was filled with rich custard and rolled inside crispy, flaky phyllo dough, and the flaky *kataifi* was a light round of shredded phyllo (which looks a bit like shredded wheat cereal) sitting in a sweet pool of honey. There are also Greek butter cookies and, of course, fantastic baklava.

Faicco's Pork Store, 6511 11th Avenue between 65th Street and 66th Street; (718) 236-0119; Subway: N to Fort Hamilton Parkway. This butcher shop in Dyker Heights supplies the sausages to **Frankies 457 Spuntino** (p. 47) in Carroll Gardens for their sausage-pepper-and-onion sandwiches, and they are worth checking out for yours, too. In addition to making their own sausages, including fennel, provolone, sweet Italian, hot Italian, and broccoli rabe, they also make their own sopressata. If you want some pasta to go with your meat, they carry **Queen Ann** (p. 220) pasta.

Frank & Sal Prime Meats, 8008 18th Avenue between 80th Street and 81st Street; Subway: D, M to 18th Avenue; (718) 331-8100; frankandsal.com. This Bensonhurst grocer specializes in all things Italian, from the gorgeous tomatoes, zucchini, and other

seasonal produce out front (look for Mediterranean treats like fresh green almonds when they are in season) to a cheese and meat counter that's overflowing with imported Italian choices. Come

for sliced sopressata, Genoa salami, capocollo, prosciutto, mortadella, and provolone that have been sourced from Italy (you won't find any Boar's Head here, thank you very much). Pick up some imported canned, boxed, and jarred goodies (like Arborio rice, vinegar, olives, and olive oil) while you're at it, as well as Italian sodas like blood orange and Chinotto. Throwing a party? Their antipasto platters and 6-foot hero sandwiches are popular.

Hinsch, 8518 5th Avenue between 85th Street and 86th Street; (718) 748-2854; Subway: R to 86th Street; $. This luncheonette in Bay Ridge has a diner menu, but it is known for having the best egg creams in Brooklyn. You'll find the place right away, due to the enormous neon sign (circa 1948) that glows out front. The setting is certainly right: Sidle up to the lunch counter, with its blast-from-the-past vinyl bar stools and plastic-covered menus, and order your egg cream—they come in strawberry, vanilla, and chocolate flavors, but true nostalgics go for the original chocolate.

Lioni Latticini, 7819 15th Avenue between 78th Street and 79th Street; (718) 232-7852; Subway: D, M to 79th Street; lionimoz zarella.com. This small Bensonhurst shop is actually the front of their wholesale warehouse, but they'll stop the friendly card game in the back to sell you some of their cheese. The cheese is made in Union, NJ, and then shipped all over Brooklyn—it's sweet as the cow's milk it's formed from, and it's so fresh it's often made the day you buy it. At the glass counter, there's fresh and salted hand-pulled mozzarellas, as well as the smoked and dried (also known as scamorza) varieties; in the fridge, you'll find tubs of ricotta and the smaller sizes of mozzarella that are stored in water. The company makes everything from a tiny "pearl" size to a "cherry" size, the more popular bocconcini used in marinated salads with roasted red peppers or sun-dried tomatoes, and also an "egg" size that's often used sliced into the tricolor caprese salads with fresh basil and sliced tomatoes, though depending on the day of the week you may not find all of these available. The company also imports buffalo milk mozzarella from Italy.

Little Cupcake Bakeshop, 9102 3rd Avenue between 91st Street and 92nd Street; (718) 680-4465; Subway: R to 95th Street; little cupcakebakeshop.com. Brooklynites who love Manhattan's Magnolia Bakery (made famous by both *Sex and the City* and that *Saturday Night Live* ditty, "Lazy Sunday") need not trek into the city and get into a long, wrap-around-the-block line for their sugar fix. Here, at this white corner space with its pretty baby-blue-striped awning, you'll find similar little cupcakes (bright-pink strawberry, delicate coconut "cloud," and sunny yellow lemon) topped with sugary, brightly colored frostings. The countertop is covered in glass cake domes filled with full-size versions of their more nuanced cakes, such as the red velvet, walnut-laden apple spice, and hummingbird cakes filled with banana and pineapple and topped with cream-cheese icing and pecans. There are also homespun cookies in nostalgic flavors like chocolate chip, and rocky road bars, too. As at Magnolia, the banana pudding is a hidden gem, but unlike at Magnolia you can order a coffee, take a seat in the supremely feminine space (think frilly mirrors and pretty chandeliers), and tend to your inner girl.

Mona Lisa Bakery, 1476 86th Street between Bay 8th Street and 15th Avenue; (718) 837-9053; Subway: D, M to 18th Avenue;

monalisabakery.com; $$. It's hard to miss this massive, yellow Bensonhurst bakery. It has a distinctive terra-cotta tile roof and takes up a large chunk of 86th Street, sprawling along the road with an open-air bakery that includes a bread area, several pastry counters, cookies, gelati, and an enormous display of wedding cakes in the middle. There's so much to choose from, but it's hard to resist the allure of the Italian breads, including a braided, seeded one called "twist" bread, round peasant bread, and a lard ring filled with prosciutto and salami that many locals serve at Sunday supper. The cakes include cheesecakes in several flavors, including a classic Italian one that's made with ricotta and fragrant of orange, a New York–style cheesecake that gets a lot of attention, and rich takes on the American cream-cheese varieties swirled with hazelnuts, chocolate, or black cherries. Pastries include all the classics, like *sfogliatelle*, lobster tails, and cannoli—though the latter is prefilled. Instead, go for a cheese cone, a caramelized, slightly salted lattice cookie filled with sweet cream-cheese frosting—it's spectacular.

Nordic Delicacies, 6909 3rd Avenue between Bay Ridge Avenue and Ovington Avenue; (718) 748-1874; Subway: R to Bay Ridge Avenue; nordicdeli.com. If you're Scandinavian and you live in Minnesota, it's easy to find the foods of your homeland. But in Brooklyn? This little import shop is just about your only option. Inside you'll find jars of lingonberry and cloudberry preserves, boxes of Swedish pancake mix, Wasa crisps, and premade potato lefse (which look a bit like crepes), tubes of roe, and cans of fish balls. The shop also has chocolates and marzipan, and a refrigerated case of northern European cheeses, including Danish Havarti, Jarlsberg, and Gouda. They do a brisk mail-order business, especially at Christmastime. They also make house-made to-go meals and do plenty of catering, the highlights of which include, as you might imagine, fish pudding, herring salad, smoked sausages, Norwegian meatballs, and *kransekake,* which is a sweet marzipan-filled cake decorated with candies and flags. Just consider yourself warned: Like many Europeans, they take a month off in the summertime, often early July to early August.

Paneantico Bakery Cafe, 9124 3rd Avenue between 91st Street and 92nd Street; (718) 680-2347; Subway: R to 95th Street; $. This Bay Ridge bakery is as Italian as can be, and seems to cover all the bases. Owned by the **Royal Crown** (p. 220) folks, they make espresso and cappuccino, bake bread, sell cheese, and make massive sandwiches on their house-made bread and serve them in their sidewalk cafe. But don't skip the Italian pastries: The cannoli, filled to order, are crisp and filled with rich, simple ricotta cream studded with chocolate chips. The fruit tarts are equally spectacular and piled high with a mountain of sweet whipped cream that's then studded with berries.

Papa Pasquale, 7813 15th Avenue between 78th Street and 79th Street; (718) 232-1798; Subway: D, M to 79th Street; papapasquale ravioli.com; $. This small Sicilian pasta shop in Bensonhurst is best known for its five-cheese ravioli, which some think is the best in the borough, but you can also get stuffed shells, manicotti, and tortellini, as well as unfilled pastas like fettuccini, linguini, pasta sheets for lasagna, and pappardelle. They also sell sandwiches and imported Italian goods.

Pastosa Ravioli, 7425 New Utrecht Avenue between 74th Street and 75th Street; (718) 236-9615; Subway: D, M to 71st Street; pastosa.com. The flagship of this ravioli empire is in Bensonhurst. Here, the windows of the red-painted corner store are filled with hanging cheeses and meats. Inside, the shelves are home to many types of large round ravioli (from earthy mushroom to broccoli rabe to pumpkin with a hint of nutmeg and the most popular, the creamy cheese-filled ones that are made with Polly-O brand ricotta, a company that the owner used to work for and always believed in) and medium-size square ravioli stuffed with meat, spinach, or cheese. The house-made pastas also include

cheese-filled manicotti and stuffed shells; ricotta cavatelli; tortellini stuffed with spinach, cheese, or meat; and fresh cut pastas like linguine, fettuccini, ziti, and fusilli. Today, the store stocks imported cheese and cured meats like pepperoni, hot Italian dried sausage, and sweet sopressata. The Pastosa brand includes their own sauces (think vodka, Alfredo, marinara, pesto), house-made mozzarella cheese, an entire counter full of premade foods (like fried cheese ravioli, rice balls, and mozzarella sticks), and their own line of canned goods like tomatoes and roasted red peppers.

Piazza Mercato, 9204 3rd Avenue between 92nd Street and 93rd Street; (718) 513-0071; Subway: R to Bay Ridge Avenue. The place looks like one of the many specialty Italian food shops and caterers in the area, with bread, veal cutlets, house-made chicken parmesan, and meatballs that you take home and heat up on your own—I call it bachelor food. But the secret find here is that they make their own balsamic vinegar, and many of the shops in the area, carry it.

Queen Ann Ravioli & Macaroni Company, 7205 18th Avenue between 72nd Street and 73rd Street; (718) 256-1061; Subway: N to 18th Avenue or D to 72nd Street. This small pasta shop has a few fresh options, like the bins full of cut linguine and radiatore, and the stuffed ones in the fridge behind the counter, which tend to include the large round cheese ravioli. They make several types each day, but because the repertoire includes so many shapes, sizes, and flavors, much of the pasta here comes frozen, like the chicken tortellini and spinach gnocchi.

Royal Crown Paneantico, 6512 14th Avenue between 65th Street and 66th Street; (718) 234-1002; Subway: D, N to New Utrecht Avenue; royalcrownny.com. "I'll have two stone breads," says the man in front of me on a late Sunday afternoon. "They're the perfect thing for sopping up the last of the gravy—the red sauce—on your plate at Sunday supper." And he's right—the bread here is flavorful, and just the right mix of textures—crunchy on the outside, soft, chewy,

and porous on the inside. (It's those little holes that make it just right for sauce sopping.) If they're out of stone bread, consider a cakelike loaf of prosciutto bread, or a flavorful olive baguette. The pastries here may not compare with some of the other neighborhood shops—but that bread can't be beat.

Sea Breeze Fish Market, 8500 18th Avenue between 85th Street and 86th Street; (718) 259-9693: Subway: D, M to 18th Avenue. Most regulars speak Italian when ordering, but this is one spot where they'll take you just as seriously if you order in English. Here, the specialty is shellfish, and there are big tanks of lobsters in different sizes, cherrystone and littleneck clams, oysters, mussels, hard-shell crabs, shrimp, scallops, and clams (though the sign calls them VONGOLE). Just as many fish come whole as filleted, and they're well priced and clear eyed. Of course since the market serves the Sicilian community, there's also plenty of salt cod for baccalà.

Villabate Alba Pasticceria & Bakery, 7001 18th Avenue between 70th Street and 71st Street; (718) 331-8430; Subway: N to 18th Avenue or D to 71st Street; villabate.net. Possibly the best Italian bakery in Brooklyn, this Sicilian stunner seems to do everything well. Big and shiny, with copper finishes and velvet ropes separating the gelati and pastry lines, this is what I imagine heaven might look like. Trays of Italian cookies line the shelves, from toasted pignoli to soft ladyfingers, and sweetly iced lemon drops. Other counters are filled with marzipan shaped into fruit (cherries with delicate stems, strawberries, and oranges with the perfect rough texture) and vegetables (eggplants, onions, artichokes) and even hamburgers. Of course they also sell breads and rolls, bread crumbs, and boxes of Italian candies.

Cakes fill the windows. Pastries, most of which are filled with ricotta cream, sit beside them—and these are what really shine. There are cannoli in one of the glass cases, decorated with maraschino cherries and slices of candied orange peel, but if you like yours more crisp, you can also ask to have them filled in the back with either ricotta cream or zabaglione, a custard cream (Boston-Italian style), then dipped in chocolate. (They also serve ice cream–filled chocolate cannoli, too, stuffed with strawberry and pistachio.) There are éclairs, slices of rolled cakes, fruit-covered tarts filled with pastry cream and berries, and orange-scented ricotta cheesecakes.

The shop also sells lemon and coffee granitas and many flavors of gelati, including almond, pistachio, and custardy zuppa inglese. They also stay open an extra hour later in the summertime, so local families can come and get their cooling cones of gelati to help beat the heat of the evening.

Your Baker, 518 86th Street between 5th Avenue and Fort Hamilton; (718) 836-0022; Subway: R to 86th Street. It would be easy to walk past this little bakery on busy 86th Street, but don't. They make some of the best Danishes in Brooklyn, and they come in miniature sizes and large rings with flavors like lemon, cherry, and blueberry. The dough is soft and tender, and fragrant with cinnamon, and the fillings aren't too sweet, especially the rich cheese. They also make icebox cakes, in flavors like cream cheese–chocolate, and strawberry shortcake, which has fresh strawberries rather than gelatinous goo and whipped cream inside a rolled vanilla cake. Those, too, aren't too sweet but instead are the perfect summer afternoon treat.

Food Events

Feast of Santa Rosalia. This summertime street festival, organized by the Santa Rosalia Society (a local social club), stretches out on 18th Avenue in Bensonhurst, between 67th Street and 75th Street, over 10 evenings. Santa Rosalia is the patron saint of the Italian city of Palermo, and some consider her the patron saint of all of Sicily. As with many feasts, you'll find a cross and pictures of the saint lit by Christmas-style twinkle lights. And you'll also find plenty of food. Have dinner in the area, and then come for the zeppole (fried Italian doughnuts sprinkled with confectioners' sugar), boardwalk-style games, and carnival rides. Bakeries like **Villabate** (p. 221) stay open late, so you can feast on their gelato, or pick up some ricotta-filled cannoli, marzipan shaped into fruits, and tarts topped with whipped cream and summer fruit, like blueberries, strawberries, and fresh figs.

Norwegian Constitution Day, may17paradeny.com. Celebrated on May 17, this Independence Day is marked with an annual parade down 5th Avenue in Bay Ridge. There are bands and music, flag waving, and plenty of locals wearing either traditional dress or pins that say PROUD TO BE NORWEGIAN. The parade ends with the crowning of Miss Norway in Leif Erickson Park. Join the crowd in the park for Norwegian treats.

Midwood, Prospect–Lefferts Gardens & Flatbush

Midwood was the Brooklyn of Jewish yore—of kosher chocolate shops, penny candy, knishes, and egg creams, as well as stickball and Dodger mania. Today, it remains a beacon for the latest round of new arrivals. Midwood is currently home to a truly global mix, with Sephardic, Syrian, and Ashkenazic Jews living in clusters alongside Pakistani and Bangladeshi, Afghan, Syrian, and Turkish immigrants.

Flatbush (which includes lots of smaller neighborhoods, such as Ditmas Park, Kensington, and Prospect Park South) is equally diverse, but it has a more pronounced architectural style. The

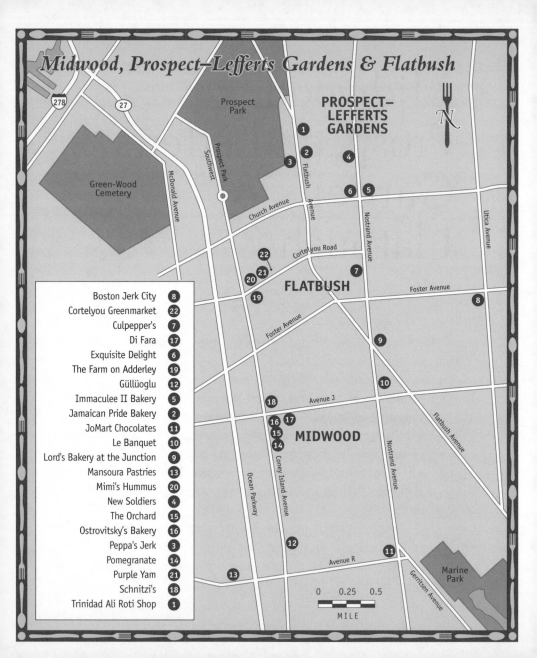

Midwood, Prospect–Lefferts Gardens & Flatbush

Boston Jerk City 8
Cortelyou Greenmarket 22
Culpepper's 7
Di Fara 17
Exquisite Delight 6
The Farm on Adderley 19
Güllüoglu 12
Immaculee II Bakery 5
Jamaican Pride Bakery 2
JoMart Chocolates 11
Le Banquet 10
Lord's Bakery at the Junction 9
Mansoura Pastries 13
Mimi's Hummus 20
New Soldiers 4
The Orchard 15
Ostrovitsky's Bakery 16
Peppa's Jerk 3
Pomegranate 14
Purple Yam 21
Schnitzi's 18
Trinidad Ali Roti Shop 1

most beautiful area in this part of the borough is widely known as "Victorian Flatbush," despite the fact that it is not all Victorian. Here you'll find suburban-size detached houses and mansions, many of which have bay windows, turrets, stained glass, and carefully manicured lawns with azaleas.

The rest of Flatbush is a study in contrasts of the West Indian and African-American communities, but even here you will find a mix of recent immigrant cultures. The main drag is Flatbush Avenue, a busy commercial street full of music and shops that culminates at the Junction, the intersection of Flatbush Avenue, Nostrand Avenue, and Avenue H. It is one of the busiest corners in the borough. On Flatbush and Nostrand, the centers of Caribbean life in New York, there are dozens of little restaurants. However, as many of these places exist on "island time," it can be hard to catch them open, even during their self-proclaimed business hours. Many of these places probably have spectacular renditions of, say, jerk chicken—you just have to have patience, or luck, to get it.

Foodie Faves

Boston Jerk City, 1344 Utica Avenue between Foster Avenue and Farragut Road; (718) 629-3002; Subway: 2, 5 to Newkirk Avenue; $. This unassuming little Jamaican sleeper sits on a particularly ugly stretch of Utica Avenue in East Flatbush that's filled with auto repair shops. It's a good 20 blocks from the subway, so for all but

the most dogged chowhounds, it is a destination you'll want to drive to. You'll know you're in the right place when you see the smoke coming from their sidewalk grill, filling the air with the scent of charcoal. Come here for the jerk chicken (though they also jerk pork and salmon), which you can order with a side of dense, casserole-like mac and cheese (that's crusted with a thick layer of cheddar), and a sweet ginger beer to wash it all down. Most locals seem to take theirs to go, but if you're far from home, you'll be happy to see that they have a comfortable (if oddly formal) dining room where you can dig into your juicy, fall-off-the-bone chicken. It's smothered in a Jamaican-style brown barbecue sauce (with plenty of tamarind), but the scotch bonnet–wary can ask for it on the side.

Culpepper's, 1082 Nostrand Avenue between Lefferts Avenue and Lincoln Road, (718) 940-4122; Subway: 2, 5 to Sterling Place; $. This place is hard to miss—an enormous awning in blue and yellow (the color of Barbados's flag) covers the corner shop. Well known within the Caribbean community for its Bajan fare, locals flock to this Prospect-Lefferts Gardens spot for the dishes that remind them most of Barbados. Even if you haven't been to the island, you'll enjoy the flying fish "cutters," fried fish sandwiches topped with lettuce, tomato, and mayonnaise and served on house-made salt bread. More interesting (or challenging, depending on your perspective) options include pudding and souse—a dish of black pudding served alongside pickled pig's feet—and oxtails with *coo*

coo, a polenta-like porridge made with okra. If you look confused by the menu, the friendly locals will invariably help you make your selection. Try it all with the appropriate beverages, sorrel (a sweet hibiscus punch) and *mauby* (a bitter brew made of tree bark). In the summer, skip the small, quiet dining room lined with photos of Barbados's prime ministers (like everyone else seems to) and take a seat at the picnic table in front of the restaurant—the regulars will happily move over to make room.

Di Fara, 1424 Avenue J between East 14th Street and East 15th Street; (718) 258-1367; Subway: Q to Avenue J; difara.com; $. The key to enjoying Di Fara's pizza? Patience. Get in line, order your pie, and then expect for the wait to feel interminable. (An hour, in the middle of a not-that-crowded afternoon, isn't unheard of.) The pizza maker here is the maestro, Domenico DeMarco, the largely undisputed king of Brooklyn pizza. He makes everything by hand (no gloves here, health inspectors be damned) down to tearing the basil leaves before placing them on your warm pie, topping the pizza with a drizzle of extra-virgin olive oil, and sprinkling with cheese on top. The pizza itself is spectacular, but you must decide if you are too type A to enjoy it. Will the inefficiency of waiting, while each pizza is slowly assembled by one man, drive you nuts? Will standing there for an hour (an hour!) for something that should take 10 minutes make you feel a little crazy? Can you distract yourself with a book, or with friends, or by texting people or surfing on your iPhone? If not, good as this pizza is, it is not for you. You will still walk out, shaking your head in wonder. But if you can get past the quirkiness and allow yourself to really taste your pizza, you may just find a little piece of heaven—in the form of thin crust, Neapolitan-style pizza—is worth the wait.

The Farm on Adderley, 1108 Cortelyou Road between Stratford Street and Westminster Road; (718) 287-3101; Subway: Q to Cortelyou Road; thefarmonadderley.com; $$. On a stretch of Cortelyou that's lined with new restaurants and shops, The Farm became a mecca for locavores and lovers of seasonal eating as soon as it opened. More than a decade ago, this part of Flatbush was sleepy, but now young professionals and families have moved in, after feeling priced out of closer-in communities, and they have brought mainstream American dining with them. The Farm has become the standard bearer for the new residents. It's a lovely space, with a pretty bar in the front and an even prettier garden out back. Food is carefully sourced ("We know everything about each animal we butcher," explained my waitress) and as local and

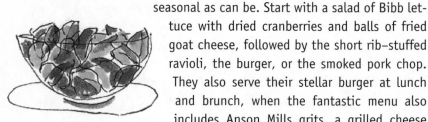

seasonal as can be. Start with a salad of Bibb lettuce with dried cranberries and balls of fried goat cheese, followed by the short rib–stuffed ravioli, the burger, or the smoked pork chop. They also serve their stellar burger at lunch and brunch, when the fantastic menu also includes Anson Mills grits, a grilled cheese with Grafton cheddar, and a chocolate brioche laced with sea salt. The local diners are rightfully thrilled to have a menu full of such pedigreed ingredients in their midst. See recipe for Chef Tom Kearney's **Stuffed Zucchini Blossoms** on p. 285.

Le Banquet, 2281 Nostrand Avenue between Avenue H and Avenue I; (718) 692-3666; Subway: 2, 5 to Flatbush Avenue; lebanquet restaurant.com; $. So many Caribbean eateries in Brooklyn forgo atmosphere for expediency, but not this Haitian restaurant. Here, the tables are topped with folded, colorful napkins, the paintings are by Haitian artists, and the music is a carefully selected mix that will transport you right to the islands. As with any good Haitian menu, the star is the fried pork *grillot* and, here, it's a knockout. The chunks of boneless pork are deep fried with the fat on. As a result, they become crispy but still retain their flavor and juiciness. The fat itself is a pleasure to eat—rather than being tough or chewy, it's thick enough that it becomes almost custard-like from its time in the fryer. The menu also highlights fried goat, stewed oxtails, and Creole chicken. They are all served with rice and beans, a flavorful take on the dish made with rice that's fluffy and light, fried plantains that are smashed and crisped, and *vinaigre piquant,* a vinegar-based hot sauce made with cabbage and carrots that's so good, you'll want to put it on everything.

Mimi's Hummus, 1209 Cortelyou Road between Westminster Road and Argyle Road; (718) 284-4444; Subway: Q to Cortelyou Road; mimishummus.com; $. This stylish little Mediterranean spot caters to a healthy, young neighborhood clientele with plenty of fresh vegetarian options. It offers regular chickpea hummus, drizzled with olive oil and sprinkled with parsley, as well as fava bean and mushroom versions. (There's also a meat version, which is topped with ground beef and pine nuts.) The Israeli salad—a mix of diced cucumber, tomato, and parsley—is bright and fresh as can be, and the pita is warm and comes (of course) in white or wheat.

New Soldiers, 1278 Nostrand Avenue between Parkside Avenue and Clarkson Avenue; (718) 284-4620; Subway: 2, 5 to Winthrop Street; $. This Prospect-Lefferts Gardens buffet-by-the-pound is a wonderful introduction to the full array of Jamaican cuisine, and all of it is fresh and well prepared. The fried chicken and conch fritters are crispy and tasty; the jerk chicken and beef may be less crunchy from having sat in a tray of wet jerk marinade, but the spicing is spot-on, with plenty of scotch bonnet, clove, and allspice. True adventurers dip their ladle into the kidneys in liver sauce (available only in the morning, when it promptly sells out), an iron-rich dish that tastes a bit like the inside of a steak-and-kidney pie; there are also plenty of sides and vegetables, including boiled plantains, yucca, and a bright sautéed medley of cabbage and peas. The bottles of hot sauce that they leave on the counter probably won't have you running for water, but you'll want to order a few bottles of Ting or *mauby*.

Purple Yam, 1314 Cortelyou Road between Rugby Road and Argyle Road; (718) 940-8188; Subway: Q to Cortelyou Road; purpleyamnyc

.com; $$. When Cendrillon, a Pan-Asian restaurant in Soho with lots of Filipino specialties closed, lovers of this less common cuisine mourned the loss. Fortunately, the owners soon opened this Ditmas Park location, which has a similar menu. Specials may not always be spectacular—one night a lamb dish sat in an unfortunately greasy sauce—but classics, like the *lechon kawali* (a fried pork belly with a crisp skin and succulent meat) and fresh *lumpia* (crispy spring rolls) are executed perfectly.

Schnitzi's, 1299 Coney Island Avenue between Avenue I and Avenue J; (718) 338-4015; Subway: Q to Avenue J; schnitzi.com; $. Follow the throngs of teenage boys to this sandwich shop where long warm baguettes are filled with hot-from-the-fryer breaded chicken cutlets (schnitzel, in German) and layered with fresh lettuce, tomato, pickles, and fresh or fried onions. The chicken comes with your choice of several types of breading: Spanish (with chili peppers), French (with Dijon mustard), Yemenite (with falafel seasoning), Greek (with garlic), and Polish (double breaded for extra crispiness). Once you order your schnitzel, and it's pulled from the fryer, it's time to pick your condiments. The young men tend to go for inter-esting combinations ("I'll have garlic mayo, spicy mayo, and *churrasco* sauce") and the guys behind the counter, furiously frying as fast as they can, get used to the multiples of condiments. ("Really—you only want horseradish mayo?") But don't let them make you think you've made a mistake by simplifying—these sandwiches are what every fast-food chicken sandwich aspires to be: hot, fresh, and tasty just the way they are.

Trinidad Ali Roti Shop, 589 Flatbush Avenue between Midwood Street and Rutland Road; (718) 462-1730; Subway: Q, B, S to Prospect Park; $. Of all the Trini restaurants in Brooklyn, this one has the nicest dining room, perhaps an easy accolade considering most don't have any seating. Here, you can take your order to a glossy wood table, and dine on comfy pleather chairs in a spacious, air-conditioned room. Best of all, the doubles are fantastic, with plenty of tamarind sauce and a light hand on the curry flavor. The wrappers themselves are unusually flavorful, too, with a rich egg flavor that you don't find elsewhere. They're a steal, as are the roti, which, for just a few dollars more, are burrito-size and stuffed with large chunks of potato and chicken in curry sauce. Warning: Go on a Sunday, and expect to get in line behind men filling large orders to take home and share as football-watching snacks.

Specialty Stores, Markets & Producers

Cortelyou Greenmarket, Cortelyou Road between Rugby Road and Argyle Road; Subway: Q to Cortelyou Road; grownyc.org/cortel yougreenmarket. Every Sunday, this green market sells locally produced foods. You'll find seafood  from Long Island's Gill's Seafood, which carries bluefish and fluke, as well as turkey cutlets, sausages, and burgers from DiPaola Turkey Farm; Knoll Krest Farm provides free-range eggs and eggy pastas; baked goods include hearty loaves from Bread Alone. You're sure to see apples, plums, and pears from Red Jacket Orchards, Madura Farm's maitake and shiitake mushrooms, and a smattering of vegetable farms' seasonal produce. In fall you'll find all the ingredients for a proper Thanksgiving cornucopia, including Indian corn, gourds, pumpkins, mums, and acorn squash.

Exquisite Delight, 2847 Church Avenue between Nostrand Avenue and Lloyd Street; (718) 693-4643; Subway: 2, 5 to Church Avenue. There's no atmosphere at this small takeaway stand, which consists mostly of an enormous grill covered in jerk chicken in various stages of char, a couple of stools, and (depending on when you show up) enormous metal barrels filled with chicken marinating in spice. You'll want to grab your bird and go, especially if you don't score one of the stools at the front of the store (which are located next to an odd painting that appears to be festooned with Chinese characters) overlooking busy Church Avenue. Other Jamaican dishes are available, but the patties are highly skippable, and the jerk is the specialty. Spicy and full of intense allspice flavor, the skin isn't quite as crisp as at other places and the grill flavor isn't quite as strong, but for jerk lovers it's hard to ignore the siren call of the strong peppery goodness.

Kosher Noshing

There are plenty of good things to eat in Brooklyn's Jewish enclaves, from sweet eggy challah breads and rugalach cookies to babka cakes. But, at times, the rules of being a customer can be different than in other neighborhoods. The first thing to remember is that the Sabbath is observed from Friday evening at sundown through Saturday evening at sundown, and that all stores and restaurants that adhere to Jewish law are closed during that time. On Friday afternoons before the Sabbath, and on Sunday after it ends, there is a flurry of activity as people do their shopping and run their errands. Stores are also closed on Jewish holidays, which are plentiful in fall.

To fit in among the crowds in more Orthodox neighborhoods, you'll also want to remember to dress modestly. In these parts, you'll see men in hats, long pants, and long sleeves, and women with head coverings, long sleeves, and long skirts. No, you don't need to go buy a hat, but if you come in shorts and tank tops, you will just be announcing that you don't belong here, and may receive some frosty looks. One more caveat: Remember that kosher food restrictions means that you will find no dairy in a store that serves meat, and vice versa. The result? Expect to find nondairy coffee creamer in your coffee in many restaurants, and meatless menus at pizza places.

Güllüoglu, 1985 Coney Island Avenue between Avenue P and Kings Highway; (718) 645-1822; Subway: B, Q to Kings Highway; gulluoglu baklava.com. This Turkey-based chain thrilled ex-pats when it opened a shop in Brooklyn a few years ago. The phyllo-and-honey pastries are more delicate than you'll find elsewhere, and more focused on pistachio. There are 12 types of baklava, including one filled with pistachio cream. Their savory treats include a surprisingly rich cheese pastry. Their Turkish delight, stored in glass jars on the countertop, is clearly fresher than what you usually find stateside. Want even more pistachio? Check out the freezer full of Turkish pistachio gelato.

Immaculee II Bakery, 1411 Nostrand Avenue between Linden Boulevard and Martense Street; (718) 941-2644; Subway: 2, 5 to Church Avenue. The experience starts with the drinks here. They make (and bottle) these Haitian specialties themselves. You'll want to try the Phoscao—a rich chocolate milk. The label says choco- late, sugar, and milk are the only ingredients, but there must be something else in that chocolate because it has a unique, aniselike aftertaste that will either repel or delight you, depending on how you feel about black licorice. The other house-made drink that you'll want to taste, if not finish, is the AK-100, which is thick—very, very thick—and made with corn, milk, and sugar. It tastes a bit like an undersweetened milk shake. Of course, you didn't just come for the interesting beverages. Immaculee bakes some of the city's best Haitian patties, which are very different from their Jamaican brethren. Wrapped in flaky puff pastry and filled with, for example, mild ground beef and onions, they have none of the spicy kick of the Jamaican variety and, in fact, taste like an appropriate marriage of Haiti's French and Caribbean cultures.

Jamaican Pride Bakery, 731 Flatbush Avenue between Clarkson Street and Parkside Avenue; (718) 462-9751; Subway: Q to Parkside Avenue. Since it's just across the street from **Peppa's** (p. 241), it would be easy to say that this small bakery benefits from being near Brooklyn's most famous jerk spot. But the Jamaican Pride Bakery turns out patties that, alone, would be worth the trip. Tender and flaky, the pale yellow pastry gives way to spiced beef or curried chicken fillings. Order yours with coco bread, and they'll wrap it around the pastry so both stay warm on the trip home.

JoMart Chocolates, 2917 Avenue R between 29th Street and Nostrand Avenue; (718) 375-1277; Subway: Q to Kings Highway; jomartchocolates.com. On a Saturday afternoon in Midwood, when it seems everything in this, a primarily Jewish area, is closed, JoMart stays open. This chocolate shop has 3 parts—a room full of baking and candy-making equipment, a room full of small gifts and cards, and the middle room—the most important one—which is full of glass cases filled to the brim with their house-made chocolates and truffles. Choices include a wonderfully savory dark chocolate–enrobed salted caramel, maple-marshmallow chocolates, and dried blueberries dipped in milk chocolate. The candies are a throwback rather than cool or trendy, and they are sweeter and milder than what new chocolatiers are experimenting with—a taste of childhood. At Christmastime, JoMart is a wonderland of chocolate Santas and other holiday treats.

Lord's Bakery at the Junction, 2135 Nostrand Avenue between Flatbush Avenue and Glenwood Avenue; (718) 434-9551; Subway: 2, 5 to Flatbush Avenue; lordsbakery.com. The enormous frosted birthday cakes in the window are the first thing you notice about this bakery (circa 1950). The icing may be hurt-your-teeth sweet, but it's also a throwback to childhood birthdays past. And while the birthday cakes—which include ice-cream cakes that fill a few freezers—may shout at the top of their lungs, Lord's also has some more subtle temptations. Consider the tender rugalach, or the flavorful red velvet cake, which is smeared with rich cream cheese icing that seems to dare you to find any better.

Mansoura Pastries, 515 Kings Highway between E. 2nd Street and E. 3rd Street; (718) 645-7977; Subway F to Kings Highway; mansoura.com. These Middle Eastern pastries are made by third-generation local Sephardic Jews. They serve their community honey-laden phyllo dough sweets. Choose from orange blossom–scented baklava with toasted walnuts or bright green pistachios, almond fingers, or *kataife* with walnuts or salted pistachios folded inside shredded phyllo dough. If you're not a fan of phyllo, consider the little squares of *basbousa,* a semolina cake perfumed with rose water and topped with sliced almonds and coconut zest, or the almond custard. In the candy case, there are glazed fruits dipped in chocolate, and nut clusters, too. In the fridge, you'll also find an almond milk drink served at celebrations, as well as cheese and spinach turnovers you can take home, bake, and serve as your own.

The Orchard, 1367 Coney Island Avenue between Avenue J and Cary Court; (718) 377-1799; Subway: Q to Avenue J; orchardfruit.com. Once named "the fanciest fruit shop in New York," this decades-old fruit boutique does most of its business in fruit trays, platters, and baskets for special occasions, both sad and happy. Perhaps that's why none of the fruits have prices on them. "They're all market price," I was told when I finally asked. "Those blackberries are $7.95 per pint." (Like at Chanel, if you have to ask you can't afford it.) When they do finally take your order, they'll cut your fruit to your specifications. Since none of it is labeled with the names of farms, nor is it marked organic or pesticide free or any of the other current ways of professing quality, you just have to believe that the bright hues of those gorgeous green grapes and blushing apricots speak for themselves.

Ostrovitsky's Bakery, 1124 Avenue J between East 12th Street and Coney Island Avenue; (718) 951-7924; Subway: Q to Avenue J. You can smell the powdered sugar from down the street, drawing you to the front door of Ostrovitsky's. Often considered the premier Jewish bakery in Midwood, this pretty wood-lined shop has racks full of chocolate and cinnamon babka, and glass cases full of prune-filled hamantaschen, rugalach, black-and-white cookies, and butter cookies swirled with chocolate and vanilla frosting. The cupcakes are pretty, too, and beg to be purchased for birthday celebrations; they sell challah and unseeded rye bread as well.

Peppa's Jerk, 738 Flatbush Avenue between Clarkson Street and Parkside Avenue; (347) 406-2515; Subway: Q to Parkside Avenue. This small, casual Jamaican take-out spot does one thing and one thing well. (Here's a tip: It's not the service.) Go for the jerk chicken charred over charcoal, and allow time, whether there's a line or not. The chicken itself, hacked into interesting bits by the counter staff, has a wonderful grilled flavor. Unlike at other jerk spots, the bird here is more about that open-flame taste than about heat or clove flavors. Grab a peanut punch or a pineapple soda and take your lunch to nearby Prospect Park, just a few blocks away. Just don't leave without adding some of Peppa's homemade vinegar-based hot sauce to your box. It, too, isn't as hot as it gets but it sure is tasty. Peppa's is actually open 24 hours a day, so you could also get your jerk fix as a late-night snack.

Pomegranate, 1507 Coney Island Avenue between Avenue K and Avenue L; (718) 951-7112; Subway: Q to Avenue M; thepompeople .com. This posh grocery store, which takes up a full city block and has valet parking and delivery service, is the largest kosher grocery store in the country. They make their prepared foods, which are plentiful throughout the store, in three separate kitchens in order to follow Jewish dietary laws. Start at the bakery, and then move through the airy, brightly lit aisles to produce (much of which is organic), the deli, and the grab-and-go meal area, which has traditional Jewish foods like brisket, pastrami, and corned beef but also harder-to-find items like a kosher sushi section. They have a wide variety of cheeses and olives, and plenty of hard-to-find kosher brands. Pomegranate also does kosher cooking demonstrations, a first for the area.

Food Events

West Indian–American Day Carnival, (718) 467-1797; wiadca .com. Perhaps Brooklyn's biggest event of the year, this annual celebration, a raucous street party that literally draws three million revelers, takes place every Labor Day weekend. There are preparties and a steel drum competition over the weekend, as well as events for kids, but the main event is the parade up Utica Avenue and Eastern Parkway (from Crown Heights to Grand Army Plaza in Park Slope), which takes place on Labor Day itself. It's full of costumed walkers and colorful floats, and many host bands, which might play calypso, soca, rap, or reggae.

For foodies, the parade is also a wonderful opportunity, if you're willing to brave the crowds, to eat your way through the Caribbean. Sidewalk vendors set up stands along Eastern Parkway, and you can smell the food as you approach the road. Makeshift grills are filled with corn, goat meat, jerk chicken, and kebabs as well as dishes of roti, beef patties, oxtail, and curried chicken being kept warm. There are also trays full of fried food (codfish fritters, plantains, flying fish, and a fried bread called *bake*), fruit (coconut, mango, breadfruit), and sugarcane. It sometimes seems like everyone is drinking beer, but you can also find rum punch, sorrel, ginger beer, and fresh coconut water to help you beat the summer heat and the spicy kick of the hot sauce that comes with jerk chicken. It's worth checking out this moveable feast, but one word of caution: The parade has had some problems with violence over the years (perhaps an inevitability when partying, high temperatures, and dense crowds are involved), so do keep an eye out for trouble.

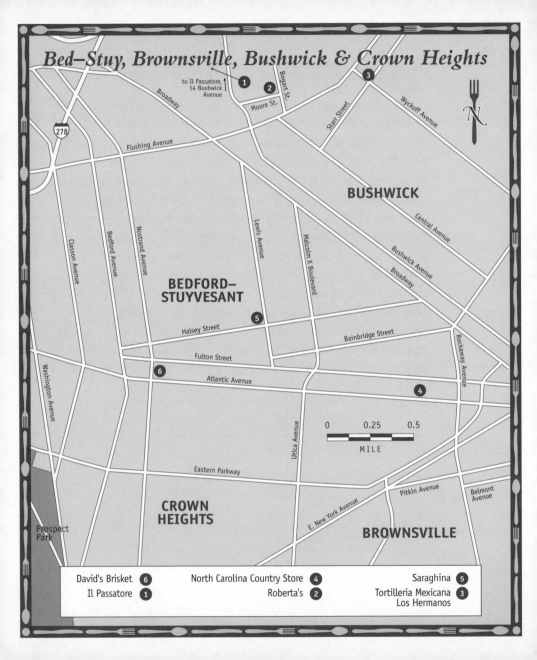

Bed–Stuy, Brownsville, Bushwick & Crown Heights

to Il Passatore,
14 Bushwick
Avenue

Broadway

Bogart St.

Moore St.

Starr Street

Wyckoff Avenue

278

Flushing Avenue

BUSHWICK

Central Avenue

Classon Avenue

Bedford Avenue

Nostrand Avenue

Lewis Avenue

Malcolm X Boulevard

Bushwick Avenue

Broadway

**BEDFORD–
STUYVESANT**

Halsey Street

Bainbridge Street

Rockaway Avenue

Fulton Street

Atlantic Avenue

Washington Avenue

Utica Avenue

0   0.25   0.5

MILE

Eastern Parkway

Pitkin Avenue

Belmont Avenue

**CROWN
HEIGHTS**

E. New York Avenue

BROWNSVILLE

Prospect
Park

N

| David's Brisket | 6 | North Carolina Country Store | 4 | Saraghina | 5 |
| Il Passatore | 1 | Roberta's | 2 | Tortilleria Mexicana Los Hermanos | 3 |

Bedford-Stuyvesant, Brownsville, Bushwick & Crown Heights

These predominantly African-American neighborhoods were, for decades, symbolic of poverty in Brooklyn. Once the home of Lena Horne and Jackie Robinson, these areas grew up around bustling Fulton Street and Nostrand Avenue, the central shopping routes—but eventually became dangerous, culminating in a low point in the 1970s and 1980s, when the name "Bed-Stuy" was often associated with vandalism and looting, particularly during the blackout of 1977. The stories told by black entertainers, including Spike Lee in his movie *Do the Right Thing* and Jay-Z in his rap lyrics, did nothing to change that reputation.

Today, an increase in property values has brought some change to these neighborhoods, especially Bed-Stuy. There are many hidden gems: Old African-American churches, some with gospel services, abound, as do unrenovated brownstones that still go for less than in other neighborhoods. The bustling thoroughfare of Fulton Street has a lot to offer. You'll find Southern-influenced fare (think fried chicken with collards and mac and cheese), as well as tasty West Indies spots that sell dishes from Trinidad or Jamaica. Although the exterior facades of these restaurants may be humble, there is often an inverse relationship between the comfort of the "restaurant" and the quality of the food in these parts. The takeaway: Be willing to trade air-conditioning for unforgettable flavor.

Foodie Faves

David's Brisket House, 533 Nostrand Avenue between Herkimer Street and Atlantic Avenue; (718) 789-1155; Subway: A, C to Nostrand Avenue; davidsbriskethouse.com; $. A Jewish-style deli in the middle of Bed-Stuy's Fulton Street Trini places? Surprise! Ignore the simple setting (and the big ATM 99¢ sign): The deli sandwiches, especially corned beef, pastrami, and beef brisket, are all steamed in house, and served on rye with mustard in overstuffed sandwiches.

Il Passatore, 14 Bushwick Avenue between Metropolitan Avenue and Devoe Street; (718) 963-3100; Subway: L to Graham Avenue;

ilpassatorebrooklyn.com; $. Hidden away on a quiet stretch across the street from a gas station, this small Italian restaurant has garnered a lot of attention. Start with a salad, a seasonal mix that could include (in late summer) a refreshing mix of watermelon, mint, and truffle oil, or mixed greens with strawberries, grapes, almonds, and balsamic vinegar. Follow that with hearty pappardelle with lamb ragout or a savory skirt steak—served on a bed of arugula and caramelized onions—that's flavorful and well marinated. The biggest surprise? The low, low number on the bottom of the bill.

Roberta's, 261 Moore Street between Bogart Street and White Street; (718) 417-1118; Subway: L to Morgan or J, M to Flushing Avenue; robertaspizza.com; $$. These are fighting words, but I mean them with all my heart: This is the best pizza I have had in Brooklyn. In fact, it's such a pleasant surprise to find that there's a Williamsburg pizzeria hidden among the projects and warehouses that you may actually forget that you are, as I like to say, on the corner of sketchy and dicey. Enter, and the scent of cheese and fresh dough will fill your nostrils as you take in the sight of a charming little restaurant located in an old garage space and filled with long family-style tables. (And that's before you even get to the oasis-like garden out back.) The wood oven–baked pies are amazing: Try the Specken Wolf, which is topped with crispy *speck* (an Italian ham), mush-rooms, and sweet red onions, or order a Margherita pizza with fragrant Berkshire pork sausage.

Saraghina, 435 Halsey Street between Marcus Garvey Boulevard and Lewis Avenue; (718) 574-0010; Subway: C to Kingston-Throop Avenue or A, C to Utica Avenue; saraghinabrooklyn.com; $. Run by recently immigrated Italians, this Bed-Stuy Neapolitan pizza shop feels like the real deal. The owner (a Milanese man who used to work for an Italian clothing line) was lured by the promise of inexpensive space, which he has decorated charmingly with a variety of unrelated commercial signs. The shabby chic garden, with its peeling paint, is packed on warm summer nights, with families dining on mismatched cafe tables underneath grapevines and twinkling lights. The main focus here is the Neapolitan-style pizza, which is topped with herbs from nearby Bed-Stuy Farm, as well as a few simple toppings, including prosciutto, capocollo, or

mushrooms. For those wanting more of a meal, start with squash blossoms stuffed with anchovies and cheese then fried, and follow that with one of the simple—yet undeniably authentic—pastas.

Tortilleria Mexicana Los Hermanos, 271 Starr Street between Wyckoff Avenue and St. Nicholas Avenue; (718) 456-3422; Subway: L to Jefferson Street; $. There are no hours listed anywhere for this Bushwick taco joint, so you feel lucky just getting in the door here. Because of its out-of-the-way location, the place feels like a secret club, despite already receiving a lot of critical acclaim. (Anthony Bourdain went there on his TV show *No Reservations;* the *New York Times* "$25 and Under" column gave Los Hermanos raves.) Snag a table at the long, luncheonette-style bar, or at one of the small tables in the main room (which is lit with strings of neon lights that line the room diner-style). Or walk out the long, narrow restaurant's back door and into the tortilla factory. There, just a few feet from where the industrial press is churning out fresh corn tortillas, another row of tables awaits. (You just have to be okay with the noise of the machine and of the music cranked up to drown out the press.) Order *tortas,* tacos, quesadillas, or tostadas. Just about everything is filled with your choice of savory meats (chicken, pork, beef, or chorizo), then topped with *crema.* Everything is flavorful if not as memorable as the setting.

Specialty Stores, Markets & Producers

McClure's Pickles, mcclurespickles.com. Bob McClure's family business is mostly run from his hometown, Detroit. But Bob moved here in 2006, set up shop in Bed-Stuy, and started pounding the pavement to get his pickle spears into local shops. They took off right away, and it's easy to see why: His spears are spicier, more garlicky, and crunchier than the big-box brands. The secret to their snap? The McClure family has a longstanding relationship with Michigan farmers, who send them their best cucumbers, which are then jarred between 24 and 48 hours from when they were picked.

Here in Brooklyn, he makes sauerkraut, mustard flavored with beer, and gallon-size containers of pickles for restaurants; all the smaller jars of pickles—like you see at the **Brooklyn Flea** (p. 97) in Fort Greene, **Bedford Cheese Shop** (p. 160) in  Williamsburg, and **Bklyn Larder** (p. 121) in Park Slope— are made in Michigan. If you fall in love with these zesty spears, you can learn to make them from the master him- self—Bob teaches pickling classes at **Brooklyn Kitchen** (p. 163). You won't get his parents' secret recipes, but you will learn how to pickle and jar, and get plenty of advice on which acids and salts pair best. The recipe is less key than sourcing great products, says Bob, who likes to get local pro- duce whenever possible, but prioritizes choosing the brightest, freshest products even if they aren't. Amen to that, Bob. See recipe for McClure's **Pickle Brine Bloody Mary Mixer** on p. 281.

North Carolina Country Store, 2001 Atlantic Avenue between Saratoga Avenue and Roosevelt Place; (718) 498-8033; Subway: C to Rockaway Avenue. When you don't know where to go for Southern staples, which can be hard to find in this decidedly Yankee town, come here. This small shop on the far reaches of Atlantic Avenue carries just about everything you need to make a Southern feast. Pick up some hush puppy mix, preseasoned dredge for frying chicken or seafood, flour for biscuits, and stone-ground grits. Then add to your armful jars of Duke's mayo (which the website says you can't even buy north of the Mason-Dixon Line), cans of premade chicken and dumplings, and fried apples. Turn to the meat case,

Fresh Direct Delivers Local Produce around the Borough

Early entrants into still-gentrifying neighborhoods often say the first things they miss are dry cleaners and grocery stores. Well, now you can cross grocery stores off your list. FreshDirect.com, an online grocery delivery service that launched in Manhattan in 2002, quickly spread to the outer boroughs.

You can choose local produce from their "farm stand," which has vegetables and herbs from Satur Farms and the Altobelli Family Farm, as well as from local providers including Coach Farm cheeses, Red Jacket Orchards juice, Ronnybrook Dairy, Old Chatham Sheep Cheese, Nature's Yolk Eggs, and Stile's Apiary.

So how does it work? Like any online retailer, you make your selections and put them in an online shopping cart. Then, you pick your time, and they deliver to your front door (up the stairs if necessary)—no need to lug groceries down the street or in the subway. For car-less Brooklynites, and neighborhood pioneers, it's a lifesaver (freshdirect.com).

and you'll see fresh tripe, leaf lard, all sorts of pork, and long links of liver sausage. It's a tiny shop, but it still holds all the flavors of the South.

Sweet Deliverance, (347) 415-2994; sweetdeliverancenyc.com. For busy locals who love to eat regional, organic produce more than they like to cook it, Sweet Deliverance is the answer. Kelly Geary, owner of this one-woman business, buys a couple dozen CSA shares—then turns them into a week's worth of meals, which you can sign up to have delivered to your home each Sunday. Operating out of a Bed-Stuy kitchen, which she shares with Bob McClure of **McClure's Pickles** (p. 249), this cookbook author is known for her homey comfort food made with fresh seasonal ingredients. Dishes include braised beef short ribs with gremolata, sweet potato–leek bread pudding, and bacon-cheddar-chive biscuits. Prefer to order your own CSA and do your own cooking, canning, and preserving? Kelly teaches weekly canning classes that include lessons on how to make jams (such as peach-lavender and cherry) and pickles (baby carrot pickles and zucchini relish), as well as an informative walk-through of the preserving process. Just be sure to sign up early: In the peak of summer, the classes fill up fast.

Food Events

International African Arts Fair, (718) 638-6700; iaafestival
.org. This July 4 weekend celebration of all things African draws
crowds of ex-pats from around the region. It sprawls out along
Commodore Barry Park, by the Naval Yards, with a flea market–style
fair of African arts and crafts (think carved wooden cheetahs and
tribal masks, and kente cloth headdresses), as well as entertainment including live music like reggae, dance troupes in colorful costumes, and spoken word performances. There are plenty of events
for kids, including puppet shows and face painting. Of course you
can also find plenty of African food. Look for African-American soul
food dishes, including fried chicken, collard greens cooked with
ham hocks, and mac and cheese, alongside more traditional African
dishes from the continent.

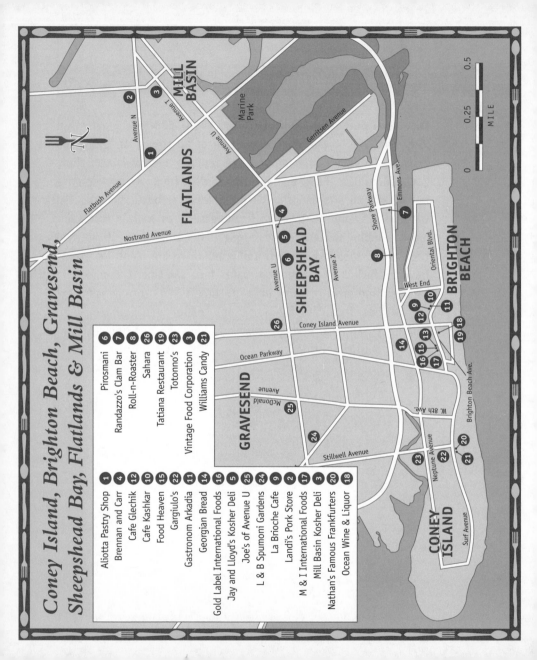

Coney Island, Brighton Beach, Gravesend, Sheepshead Bay, Flatlands & Mill Basin

Aliotta Pastry Shop 1
Brennan and Carr 4
Cafe Glechik 12
Cafe Kashkar 10
Food Heaven 15
Gargiulo's 22
Gastronom Arkadia 11
Georgian Bread 14
Gold Label International Foods 16
Jay and Lloyd's Kosher Deli 5
Joe's of Avenue U 25
L & B Spumoni Gardens 24
La Brioche Cafe 9
Landi's Pork Store 2
M & I International Foods 17
Mill Basin Kosher Deli 3
Nathan's Famous Frankfurters 20
Ocean Wine & Liquor 18

Pirosmani 6
Randazzo's Clam Bar 7
Roll-n-Roaster 8
Sahara 26
Tatiana Restaurant 19
Totonno's 23
Vintage Food Corporation 3
Williams Candy 21

MILL BASIN

FLATLANDS

Flatbush Avenue

Avenue N

Avenue T

Avenue U

Nostrand Avenue

Marine Park

Gerritsen Avenue

SHEEPSHEAD BAY

Avenue U

Avenue X

Shore Parkway

Emmons Ave.

West End

Oriental Blvd.

BRIGHTON BEACH

Coney Island Avenue

Ocean Parkway

GRAVESEND

McDonald Avenue

Stillwell Avenue

Neptune Avenue

W. 8th Ave.

Brighton Beach Ave.

Surf Avenue

CONEY ISLAND

MILE

0   0.25   0.5

Coney Island, Brighton Beach, Gravesend, Sheepshead Bay, Flatlands & Mill Basin

These four neighborhoods once combined to create a large resort area. Gravesend was a middle-class community, made up of Jews and Italians. Now it's predominantly Sephardic Jews, whose homes cluster around the synagogues, since they prefer to live within walking distance.

Sheepshead Bay, which (like Bensonhurst) has a Gambino family connection, is an old fishing village that originally had seaside bungalows and a horse-racing track. The main drag is Emmons Avenue, and from there you can see the sailboat-lined port. A few seafood restaurants remain, and for Brooklynites who can't get away for a summer weekend to the Jersey Shore or the Hamptons, it is a welcome chance to get a clam roll or fried oysters close to home.

Coney Island has always been New York's answer to the carnival, with freak shows and games of skee ball. The shore is lined with a long wooden boardwalk, and that's where you'll find arcade games and stands selling cotton candy and funnel cake, to the delight of flocks of seagulls. You'll also find the original wooden roller coaster, called The Cyclone (which has long been a symbol of the area), and the enormous Wonder Wheel, both of which have landmark status. Yes, there's also a popular aquarium, fireworks on Friday nights, and baseball games at MCU Park (home of the Brooklyn Cyclones). But the area is quieter than a century ago, except on July Fourth, when crowds flock to Nathan's hot dog–eating contest, and Memorial Day, when it seems all of Brooklyn comes for the Mermaid Parade. (This creative show is just what it sounds like—hundreds of people, many of them men in drag, dressed up as mermaids.)

Down the beach from Coney, Brighton couldn't be more different. Called Little Odessa, this beachfront community is a largely Russian nabe, which grew all the more Russian with the fall of the Soviet Union in the early '90s. This is the place to be for all the tastes of the motherland, from vodka to dumplings. Shop the many grocery stores full of Eastern European treasures, as well as the fruit markets packed with wonderful deals and impressively ripe produce. The stores stretch out underneath the elevated train line and, in the evening, baked goods are sold along the street. It's a feast for all the senses—assuming you can get parking.

Foodie Faves

Cafe Glechik, 3159 Coney Island Avenue between Brighton Beach Avenue and Brighton 10th Street; (718) 616-0766; Subway: Q, B to Brighton Beach; glechik.com; $$. This casual cafe is a comfortable place to try some inexpensive and traditional Ukrainian dishes, without committing to dressing up, taking in a show, or ordering a bottle of vodka, all of which are common nighttime activities in Brighton Beach. Order kvass, a soda that's similar to root beer, like everyone else. Then start with the red or green borscht (made with rice, eggs, and spinach); both are topped with plenty of dill and heavy sour cream. The *pelmeni,* delicate little dumplings boiled in chicken broth, can be filled with chicken or veal, or ordered Siberian style (which is a mix of ground pork and ground veal that's as delicate as the dumplings themselves). *Vareniki* are another type of dumpling, this time made with a thicker skin and boiled in water—they too come savory, but it's hard to resist the sour cherry option.

Cafe Kashkar, 1141 Brighton Beach Avenue between Brighton 14th Street and Brighton 15th Street; (718) 743-3832; Subway Q, B to Brighton Beach; $. Once you eat at this small BYOB restaurant, you'll join the crowds who've been seduced by Uyghur cuisine (the food of Turkic Muslims living in Uzbekistan and northwest China) and bemoan the fact that there aren't more Uyghur restaurants in America. Fortunately, this is a good one, and the staff is friendly and welcoming, even if you aren't one of the ex-pats who flock here. Much of the focus is on lamb. The lamb kebabs, whether you order the traditional or the lamb rib, are grilled (and served) on long metal skewers and plated with a chili sauce and sautéed onions. Of course, they also do veal and chicken kebabs, but the lamb is so tasty you may be tempted to order a second round. The *manty* (large round dumplings) and *samsa* (baked, stuffed rolls) are both filled with an onion and lamb mixture that's faintly seasoned with cumin. *Lagman* (a soup of noodles cooked in a flavorful lamb broth) is served in big Chinese-style bowls, and there are also salads topped with cold, roasted lamb. Come with a group and order plenty to share, or expect that it will take you a few visits to work your way through all the lamb preparations, though it will be time well spent.

Jay and Lloyd's Kosher Deli, 2718 Avenue U between E. 27th Street and E. 28th Street; (718) 891-5298; Subway: Q to Avenue U; $. At this deli, which opened in 1993, everything is pink—from the outside of the building to the inside walls and even the menus. Fortunately, that stops at the food. Join the retirees in the casual rose-colored dining room, and you'll be brought bowls of coleslaw and pickles, both sour and half sour, to munch on while you wait. Order a flaky spinach knish, followed by the house specialty, a corned beef sandwich. The meat is hand-cut, not overly spicy, and not too fatty nor too lean, nor is the sandwich itself huge at this kosher-style deli. Is it the best pastrami in the world? Maybe not. However, they serve mostly a conservative, older audience, who might be horrified if the sandwich were too rich or too large. But, unlike the Jewish delis in Manhattan, they don't charge you a sharing fee if you choose to split the thing.

Joe's of Avenue U, 287 Avenue U between McDonald Avenue and Lake Street; (718) 449-9285; Subway: F, N to Avenue U; $. Often called the best Sicilian in Brooklyn, this Gravesend restaurant looks a bit like a diner. The front is a takeaway counter, and the dining room is in the back. It's not fancy, but it is full of personality. The red vinyl booths have diner-style paper napkin holders, and the walls are adorned with maps of Sicily, a mural of Sicilian peasants, a pink flag for the Palermo soccer team, tambourines, and (quirkiest of all) plenty of *opera dei pupi* dolls (marionettes dressed like knights of the Roman Empire that were used in Sicilian puppet theater shows) hanging from the ceiling.

But you'll forget all about them when your food comes. Appetizers include croquettes, *panelle* (fried chickpea pancakes), stuffed artichokes, and *arancini* (rice balls filled with ground beef and peas). But you won't want to order too much of that, since many entrees are big enough to be considered family-style servings. The *pasta con sarde,* a heaping plate of spaghetti with sardines, wild fennel, and pine nuts, is savory and, well, fragrant. It's served with a big bowl of toasted bread crumbs, lest you forget that the Italians do not serve grated cheese on seafood pastas. Joe's chicken Parmesan is a large, very thinly pounded cutlet topped with mild, thinner than average tomato sauce and plenty of melted cheese, and served with a small pile of boiled potatoes. There's also lasagna, heaping plates of fried calamari, and meatball subs. The drinks of choice here? A carafe of iced red wine for the table, or bottles of **Manhattan Special** (p. 167) coffee soda.

Mill Basin Kosher Deli, 5823 Avenue T between 58th Street and 59th Street; (718) 241-4910; B41L Bus to Avenue N and E. 58th Street; millbasindeli.com; $. This out-of-the-way, decades-old Jewish deli in Mill Basin may serve the best corned beef sandwich in Brooklyn, an accolade that's not as contested as it once would have been. Order a corned beef, which is mild, sliced thin, with the fat carved off, and neither fatty nor dry (a difficult feat to accomplish, as deli lovers know), served on thick, crusty seedless rye bread with mustard and pickles. They also offer tongue, brisket, and pastrami, and you can get your sandwich Reuben-style (with sauerkraut) or with Russian dressing and coleslaw. A quirky find: egg rolls filled with pastrami and cabbage—a fusion experiment that's tastier than you might expect.

Pirosmani, 2222 Avenue U between E. 22nd Street and E. 23rd Street; (718) 368-3237; Subway: Q to Avenue U; $$. Catering to a crowd of couples on date night and large groups of Russian guys enjoying an evening out, this small Georgian restaurant has something for everyone. For the couples, there's a DJ with a synthesizer and microphone, singing an evening's worth of slow songs. If that's not the draw for the guys, then perhaps it's the BYOB (and the *B* in this case clearly stands for booze and not beer) policy, with its no-corkage fee leniency, and the reasonable prices for hearty food. The setting is more casual (murals of Cossacks feasting, paper napkins imprinted with the address) than the big banquet halls, and the menu is a la carte. It's a great opportunity to try Georgian specialties like spinach with walnuts and pomegranate seeds (a dish that's spreadlike without being creamy), Georgian salad (a Mediterranean-style mix of cucumbers, tomatoes, and parsley in a vinaigrette), and warm Georgian bread (a soft baguette-style loaf that widens in the middle). Entrees are rich, from a lamb stew served en croûte, to veal-filled dumplings the size of baseballs, warm stuffed grape leaves with yogurt sauce, and a vegetarian dish of fried potatoes and porcini mushrooms served under a cloud of dill. Tip: Come on a Saturday night, when sword-fighting demos outshine all the food put together. Just be sure to make a reservation, since the place is small and private parties abound.

Sahara, 2337 Coney Island Avenue between Avenue T and Avenue U; (718) 376-8594; Subway: F, N to Avenue U; sahara palace.com; $$. Sahara is enormous. It has 4 dining rooms, including

THE RUSSIAN NIGHTLIFE EXPERIENCE

The most outrageous meal you can have in Brooklyn? It's probably at a Russian supper club. On weekend evenings these enormous banquet halls come alive with Las Vegas–style revues; these places had vodka bottle service way before it was cool in Vegas. Grab a group of friends and reserve a table for the $80-and-up-per-person smorgasbord. (You could go just for the performance, but then you'd have to pay a cover charge, which is waived for those who are dining.) Dishes are served, family style, in rapid succession at your table and might include appetizers like borscht, caviar with blini, smoked fish, and pierogi filled with *foie gras;* entrees include chicken Kiev, rack of lamb, and beef stroganoff. Order a bottle of vodka or plan ahead and bring a few from home—many of these places don't charge a corkage fee, but they do inflate liquor prices.

The food is only part of the entertainment, of course. As you drink and dine and enjoy the company of friends, the curtains open and out come 12-piece bands, troupes of singers and dancers in full feather-lined showgirl costumes, and balladeers. Most of the shows are in Russian (save for American music sung in its original incarnation). Just plan to drop some coin (most cabaret dinners are over $100 per person on Saturday nights), be sure to call ahead (most only have shows on weekends), find out all of the charges and show information in advance so there are no surprise surcharges, and call a car service to take you home. This is one night that you won't want to sacrifice anyone's evening to the role of sober driver, and it is sure to be too late an evening to take the subway.

a casual one, flanked by 2 more formal ones, and an outdoor patio with a fountain; it also has valet parking and is a stop on a bus tour of Brooklyn. Ignore all that, though, and the Mediterranean food is surprisingly good. Locals have come since 1986 for the chopped shepherd salad, laden with Turkish feta, and the kebabs, grilled over an open flame and served with puffy bread, salad, rice, a charred pepper yogurt sauce, and hot sauce. The lamb is a specialty here, and the *shawarma,* spicy *adana* (seasoned with red peppers), and spicy lamb *beyti* (seasoned with garlic and parsley) are all seared to perfection.

Tatiana Restaurant, 3152 Brighton 6th Street between E. Boardwalk and Brightwater Court; (718) 891-5151; Subway: Q, B to Brighton Beach; tatiana restaurant.com; $$$. Going to this 15-year-old Brighton Beach stalwart is as much about sitting on their boardwalk terrace as it is about eating their Russian specialties. (Inside, there is a nightclub and dinner theater, but you came to enjoy the sea air, right?) The menu, even at lunchtime, is enormous and pricey, but you can't go wrong with the classics: piroshki, tongue salad, borscht with sour cream, potato salad, and chicken cutlet cooked Kiev-style, which means it's formed into an oblong shape that looks a bit like a baked potato, and filled with molten herb butter that gushes out satisfyingly when you cut into it.

Brennan & Carr, 3432 Nostrand Avenue between Avenue U and Gravesend Neck Road; (718) 769-1254; Subway: Q to Avenue U; $. This roast-beef-sandwich shop isn't a dive as much as a blast from the past. The first thing you notice about this Mill Basin institution, circa 1932, is that it's still in its original building, which was built to conform to the shape of the angled corner it sits on. The Tudor-style facade (picture stucco and wood beams) is consistent with the inside, which also feels like a period piece. Wood paneling lines the walls of the dark rooms, which are dimly lit by wagon-wheel light fixtures and, in wintertime, a fire in the mantled fireplace. The menu is listed on the original carved wood signs with the prices updated to the modern day with gold stickers.

Of course, nothing on the menu matters but the roast beef sandwiches. Roasted daily, the meat is served sliced, on a sesame-seed-crusted roll, then dunked in the jus it's cooked in. It's plain but comforting in its salt-and-pepper-seasoned simplicity. Ignore the sides, which include french fries and onion rings—they are all an afterthought. But do take a tip from the regulars' playbook, and ask for your roast beef with some of the cheese sauce that they usually serve on fries. It's a tweak that's not on the menu, but it seems to be on everyone's plate.

Gargiulo's, 2911 W. 15th Street between Mermaid Avenue and Surf Avenue; (718) 266-4891; Subway: D, F, N, Q to Stillwell Avenue;

gargiulos.com; $$. A grande dame landmark that celebrated her 100th birthday several years ago, this Italian special-occasion spot is as grand as it ever was. Park in the valet lot across the street (this is, after all, the modern-day badlands of Coney Island, and not the resort town it once was), and take your place in the dining room. Surrounded by fish tanks and vaulted ceilings, this formal space is home to many birthdays, anniversaries, and weddings, and holds a special place in the hearts of many Brooklynites as a result. The warm antipasto is a popular appetizer, as are the platters of prosciutto, roasted peppers, and fresh mozzarella. Follow that up with enormous platters of pasta, which come in full and half orders. Consider spaghetti with garlic, olive oil, and anchovies—a mild take on the oft-pungent specialty—or a seafood linguini piled high with mussels, calamari, and little clams. Or save room for the meat dishes, which are heavy on the Italian-American red-sauce classics, including chicken Parmesan and veal scarpariello, stuffed with prosciutto and topped with a Marsala sauce. You may not have room for dessert (Italian cheesecake, cannoli, tiramisu), but it's hard to turn down an after-dinner drink on the house when it's offered. Order a Baileys, an Amaretto, or a glass of port, and toast to many more meals like this one.

L & B Spumoni Gardens, 2725 86th Street between W. 10th Street and W. 11th Street; (718) 449-1230; Subway: N to 86th Street or D to 25th Avenue or F to Avenue X; spumonigardens.com; $$. This Gravesend pizza spot (circa 1939) is such a favorite of the locals that if you sit at one of the many picnic tables in front of the restaurant, you may feel acutely aware of the fact that everyone else at this "party" seems to know each other. Which, of course, is a wonderful sign of how this place continues to be embraced by the community. Order your square slices at the take-out window (don't get the round ones—my husband charitably compared them to the roller rink pizza of his youth) and take them to an umbrella-topped table. Follow the rules—don't get in the short line to the right unless you are ordering a whole pie, and remember that you can't order toppings if you buy by the slice. The pizza itself is Sicilian, which means that the crust is thick and puffy and the minimal cheese is under the sweet tomato sauce. Sprinkle on some pepperoncini flakes before taking yours to a table—the pizza is simple and benefits from the added heat.

Nathan's Famous Frankfurters, 1310 Surf Avenue between Stillwell Avenue and W. 15th Street; (718) 946-2705; Subway: D, F, N, Q to Stillwell Avenue; nathansfamous.com; $. This Coney Island hot dog stand really is world famous, and a major stop on many visitors' sightseeing list. Why? Well, in 1916, Nathan Handwerker, a Polish immigrant, borrowed $300 from friends Jimmy Durante and Eddie Cantor to open this Coney Island hot dog stand, where he sold each dog for a nickel. (Soda was also a nickel; malted milk shakes were six cents.) His wife, Ida, developed the recipe, and it remains nearly the same today. The stand is very much a part of New York history: Al Capone and Cary Grant were regulars, and President Franklin Roosevelt served these hot dogs to the King and Queen of England, Churchill, and Stalin.

Now, almost 100 years later, Nathan's is a chain that you can find at rest stops and shopping malls around the country, and you can also find their hot dogs in the grocery store. The menu has expanded, but it is still their hot dogs—which are skinless, well spiced, and come in both a kosher all-beef variety and a pork-and-beef combo—that people flock here for. This is the original, and it's still in its century-old location by the boardwalk, right near the amusement park. The crowds are big on holiday weekends, and there's not a lot of inside seating, so go at an off hour and stick to the hot dogs.

Randazzo's Clam Bar, 2017 Emmons Avenue between E. 21st Street and Ocean Avenue; (718) 615-0010; Subway: Q, B to Sheepshead Bay; randazzosclambar.com; $$. This bayside clam bar (circa 1958) has all the crusty appeal of a seaside seafood joint—there's a mirror etched with a Sheepshead Bay scene, with Randazzo's front and center, of course. The menu has steamed clams (littlenecks and cherrystones) and fried oysters, scallops, fish, and clam strips, all of which can be served with Randazzo's spicy marinara dipping sauce.

Where Have the Landmarks Gone?

When people talk about Old Brooklyn, the conversation invariably turns to the great landmark restaurants of the last century, many of which have closed. Locals bemoan the loss of the old Jewish delis, with their piled-high corned beef and pastrami sandwiches. And there are many other classics that have shuttered in recent years, too.

Some, like Lundy's, a bayside seafood palace that was a fixture in Sheepshead Bay from 1907 to 1979, fell out of favor when the neighborhood went through changes, and when the family who owned it went through changes, too. (It was once thought to be the largest restaurant in the country and was known for Manhattan-style clam chowder.) It reopened briefly for a few years recently, only to shutter again. Now, a grocery store sits in its space, taunting locals with its old signs still intact.

The same is true of the gas-lit Gage & Tollner, a downtown restaurant in a pillared brownstone that held court on Fulton Street from 1892 until 2004 and was thought to be New York City's oldest restaurant. Regulars at one time included Jimmy Durante and Mae West, and while the menu changed over the years, it was most well known as a steak-and-chop house and later as a Southern food establishment. After it closed, the space housed, to much dismay, a T.G.I. Friday's chain and, later, a fast-food restaurant. Patricia Murphy's, a Depression-era Brooklyn Heights favorite on Henry Street near Clark, closed for business in the 1970s. Locals who grew up in the area then still talk about the Shirley Temples they were introduced to there as children, and the warm popovers. These places, like the Brooklyn Dodgers, are now part of Brooklyn's history.

Roll-n-Roaster, 2901 Emmons Avenue between E. 29th Street and Nostrand Avenue; (718) 769-6000; Subway: Q, B to Sheepshead Bay; rollnroaster.com; $. This Sheepshead Bay fast-food joint retains its 1970-style throwback appeal. The restaurant, which has a glass greenhouse and parking lot that make it look like it was a former Wendy's location, has bright yellow-and-white striped awnings, wrought-iron lights, and distressed copper counter-tops. It specializes in roast beef sand-wiches on Kaiser rolls—and they're good enough to renew your faith in fast food. Get yours "double dipped" in gravy,  smeared with "cheez" sauce, or with extra gravy on the side; you also get to choose whether you like your meat rare, medium, or well-done. (Did the national chains ever offer such options?) Get your sandwich with round french-fried potato disks and, since this is the shore, fresh lemonade.

Totonno's, 1524 Neptune Avenue between W. 15th Street and W. 16th Street; (718) 372-8606; Subway: D, F, N, Q to Stillwell Avenue; $. This Neapolitan-style shop is one of Brooklyn's original coal-burning brick-oven pizzerias—it opened in 1924 and was operated continuously until 2009, when a fire shut it down for a year-long renovation. It's known for several things: simple coal-fired pies charred on the bottom and topped with sweet mozzarella, sauce made from imported Italian tomatoes, and being worth the trip out to Coney Island.

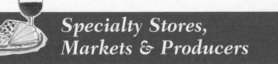

Specialty Stores, Markets & Producers

Aliotta Pastry Shop, 4522 Avenue N between E. 45th Street and E. 46th Street; (718) 252-4888; Subway: B41 Bus to Avenue N and East 58th Street. Aliotta is an Italian bakery of the most classic sort. Full of butter cookies covered in different colored sprinkles (sold by the pound, of course) and creamy ricotta-filled cannoli (with just a little candied pistachio at the ends, but no citrus peel or chocolate chips to break up the ricotta flavor), locals come here for holiday cookies and birthday cakes alike. The real find, though, are the fruit tarts and pies—carefully crafted, colorful gems topped with ripe fruits. Pies come lined with rows of blueberries; tarts may have fresh blackberries, blueberries, or strawberries that are glazed and piled atop a mound of lightly sweetened whipped cream and a cookielike crust.

Food Heaven, 239 Brighton Beach Avenue between Brighton 1st Street and Brighton 2nd Street; (718) 743-4700; Subway: Q to Ocean Parkway. Sometimes called the Russian Dean & DeLuca, this more manageably sized deli and gourmet grocery store sells everything from food gifts to precooked meals and ingredients. They sell meat chunked and ready to grill as a kebab, as well as premade sausage for grilling, and they even sell the long metal skewers. Just past the fresh meats, you'll find cured meats and cheeses, including mozzarella balls in a handful of different sizes, and squares of the creamy white Georgian cheese used in *khachapuri*. The upstairs cafe serves fancy teas—look up and you'll also see baskets hanging from the ceiling, ready to fill as hostess gifts and holiday presents.

Gastronom Arkadia, 1079 Brighton Beach Avenue between Brighton 12th Street and Brighton 13th Street; (718) 934-7709; Subway: Q, B to Brighton Beach. This by-the-pound buffet sells ready-made foods to take home and enjoy without a smidge of effort. Get your appetizers, entrees, and desserts here, or even supplies for a sort-of-catered brunch. They have just about anything you could get at area restaurants, from kugel to salads, crepes, smoked fish, and kebabs. You can also get soup, ladled straight from enormous metal pots. Relax if you don't speak Russian—everything is self-serve.

Georgian Bread, 265 Neptune Avenue between Brighton 5th Street and Brighton 6th Street; (718) 332-8082; Subway: Q, B to Brighton Beach. Flour fills the room at this tiny Georgian bakery, where a flour-covered man works at the large kiln that sits right behind the register. This clay oven–fired bread comes in two types: plain and cheese-filled, called *khachapuri* (which is a round of focaccia-like bread filled with a mild white cheese called *sulguni*). It is a revelation. Fresh from the oven, the porous bread is steamy and soft, and the cheese in the middle creates a contrast in textures that's reminiscent of American grilled cheese sandwiches. Of course, you can buy the cheese by itself in the shop, as well as a few Russian items, like bottles of tarragon-flavored soda, but you won't want to leave without as much of the cheese-filled bread as you can get your hands on. My advice? Go alone so you don't have to share.

Gold Label International Foods, 281 Brighton Beach Avenue between Brighton 2nd Street and Brighton 3rd Street; (718) 743-3900; Subway Q, B to Brighton Beach. This shop sells as much prepared food as groceries. Go to the take-out window, and you can pick up some Russian street food, such as piroshki (dumplings filled with cabbage or meat), *khachapuri* (a Georgian cheese bread), and poppy seed–stuffed strudels. Then, head inside for the rest of your shopping needs, from cold cuts (including a ham shaped like a little pig) to cheeses—they have over a dozen types of farmer's cheese alone.

La Brioche Cafe, 1073 Brighton Beach Avenue between Brighton 12th Street and Brighton 13th Street; (718) 934-0731 Subway Q, B to Brighton Beach. After wandering into store after store that seems to specialize in everything Russian, it's a pleasure to explore a smaller one with a narrow focus. The smell of sweet dough hits your nose as soon as you enter this Russian-Jewish bakery. Take in the racks of fruit Danish, poppy seed strudel, and tender chocolate-covered marshmallows. One whole case is devoted to Russian tea cakes with many frosted layers.

Landi's Pork Store, 5909 Avenue N between E. 59th Street and Ralph Avenue; (718) 763-3230; B41 bus to Ralph Avenue and Avenue N; brooklynporkstore.com. An Italian butcher shop that celebrates all things pork, this third-generation family-run shop is busy every weekend. Take a number, and wait your turn to place your order. Your butcher will walk you through the store, filling your requests for fresh meat, deli meats and cheeses, and prepared food. The highlights: Landi's makes several types of fresh pork sausage (hot Italian, sweet Italian, pepper and onion, cheese and parsley, broccoli rabe, and fennel) and several types of dry pork sausage (hot sopressata, sweet sopressata, and pepperoni) as well as plenty of pasta dishes laden with meat.

M & I International Foods, 249 Brighton Beach Avenue between Brighton 1st Place and Brighton 2nd Street; (718) 615-1011; Subway: B, Q to Brighton Beach. This massive 30-year-old grocery store has everything you could need to cook a Russian-style feast. Walk in the front door, and the first thing you'll see is their long deli counter, full of smoked sausages (pork, chicken, and beef) in very thin sticks and very fat ones and everything in between, as well as every shade of white, pink, red, and brown. Across from that, you'll find the bread counter, covered with loaves of soft ryes, wheats, and pumpernickels that can be sliced for you. Moving back, there are canned, jarred, and pickled ingredients as well as a pastry counter filled with meringues, cookies, and layer cakes with paper-thin layers filled with chocolate, vanilla, and mocha frostings. (These are for sale by the slice, chunk, or sheet.) There's even a large selection of Eastern European and Russian beers. In the back, there are cheeses and yogurt drinks and so much prepared food that you'll wonder why you ever thought you needed to cook at all, or why you need to pay restaurant prices. (The blintzes and pierogi look as good here as anywhere else.) Buy their chicken noodle soup, redolent of dill and richer than you could probably do yourself, a chicken Kiev, a cheese bread, and some sides and you'll be all set. On your way out, stop by the pickle counter and add some tangy goodness to your week.

Ocean Wine & Liquor, 514 Brighton Beach Avenue between Brighton 5th Street and Brighton 6th Street; (718) 743-3084; Subway Q, B to Brighton Beach. Many neighborhood restaurants are BYOB, so this is the perfect last stop before dinner. You can buy just about every type of liquor here, but it's vodka they really excel at. They carry more than 50 varieties, from the pricey to the trendy. There is also a wide range of flavored vodkas. Of course, you can get the common ones—lemon, raspberry, vanilla, and pepper. But where else can you find honey pepper, espresso, rose, tomato, pickle, and sweet tea vodka?

Vintage Food Corporation, 287 Brighton Beach Avenue between Brighton 2nd Street and Brighton 3rd Street; (718) 769-6674; Subway Q, B to Brighton Beach; vintagefood.com. This is a Turkish bazaar of bins full of nuts, seeds, dried fruit, spices, and candy. It's all inexpensive and high quality, which explains the crowds. There are 4 kinds of apricots in differing degrees of succulence, plenty of figs, and oddities like dried mulberries, as well as standards like pineapples in rings or chunks. You'll find rows of honey, nuts in the shell, as well as roasted (or unroasted) and salted (or unsalted) pecans, almonds, cashews, and walnuts, and even nut brittles.

Williams Candy, 1318 Surf Avenue between Stillwell Avenue and W. 12th Street; (718) 372-0302; Subway: D, F, N, Q to Stillwell Avenue; candytreats.com. On Surf Avenue, just a block from the boardwalk and a few steps away from **Nathan's** (p. 266), this 75-year-old Coney Island candy shop has become a bit of an institution. Ignore the bins of nonpareils and chocolate-covered raisins, and focus on the caramel- and candy-covered apples. These bright green apples are dipped in house-made glazes, then rolled in toppings like rainbow sprinkles, chocolate sprinkles, toasted coconut, and chopped peanuts, to add color and texture. The apples themselves, usually green-hued Granny Smiths, are fresh and crisp, with not a bruise in sight. They're chosen carefully for their freshness, so they're unusually sweet, too. How good are they? "I don't think I like caramel apples," said my sister. Then she took a bite, and her eyes lit up like Christmas morning. Can't eat a whole apple? They do similarly wonderful things with small, round house-made marshmallows.

Food Events

Nathan's Hot Dog Eating Contest. Every year, a highlight of the Fourth of July weekend is this hot dog–eating contest, which turns out the crowds down by the boardwalk. ESPN airs the event, which includes carnival-like performances from the likes of the Ringling Brothers acrobats and an enormous hot dog sculpture hanging over the stage. As competitors take their places, their accomplishments are listed. And, since you have to have won a regional competitive eating contest to qualify for this one (and most here have won several), the feats are impressive. (Tim Brown's world titles, for example, are in cannoli, tamales, and ramen noodles.) **Nathan's** (p. 266) makes 1,500 dogs in preparation for the contest, and these eaters can really put it away. As the 10-minute contest begins, newscasters share the strategies of the different contestants, like the fact that six-time winner Takeru Kobayashi from Japan "inhales" the bread and wiggles a little after each dog to settle it down in his stomach and make room for more. (He also dyes his hair—sometimes it is red and orange in homage to the hot dog.) Contestants have cups of water in front of them, in addition to the dogs, and some have requested that their water be at a specific temperature. They stuff the dogs in their mouth in different fashions (Joey Chestnut, for example, folds his in half lengthwise). Their cheeks puff out. In 2009, the 94th annual competition, Chestnut put away 68 hot dogs in 10 minutes—setting a world record—and won both The Mustard Belt and a $20,000 prize.

Recipes

Brooklyn's food scene has been defined in the last few years by young food entrepreneurs. Some of them have professional training and long resumes full of fancy Manhattan restaurants, but much of what they've gained fame for is their homespun, comforting fare. Here, you'll find a collection of recipes from local chefs, cooks, bakers, and entrepreneurs—and all are for dishes you can re-create at home.

Egg Cream

Brooklyn aficionados say it's hard to find a "proper" egg cream, but you can get pretty darn close with this recipe that comes from the source—Fox's U-bet Syrups.

**Fox's U-bet Chocolate Syrup
(available all over Brooklyn)**
Whole milk

**Seltzer made in a pressurized
cyclinder**

Spoon 1 inch of U-bet Chocolate Syrup in a tall, chilled 8-ounce glass. Add 1 inch of whole milk. Tilt the glass and spray seltzer (from a pressurized cylinder only) off a spoon, to make a big chocolate head.

Stir rigorously—then drink and enjoy!

Courtesy of Fox's U-bet Syrups, foxs-syrups.com

Lemon Verbena Soda

Here is a recipe for a very summery soda from Anton Nocito, owner of P&H Syrups (available at Brooklyn Farmacy, p. 40, and other locations). It's not something you can buy in a bottle from P&H very often: The lemon verbena, a fresh green herb, doesn't preserve very well, so it's only available at markets when it's in season.

2 cups sugar
2½ cups water
1 bunch fresh lemon verbena, stems removed and a few leaves reserved for garnish
Zest of ½ lemon

Juice of 2 lemons
Ice
Seltzer
Lemon slices or wheels, for garnish

In a saucepan, bring the sugar and water to a boil to dissolve the sugar.

Remove from the heat, add verbena and lemon zest, and steep for 20 minutes.

Add lemon juice, strain the mixture into an airtight container, cool, and refrigerate.

Will keep in an airtight container for 3 days.

To make a soda, add 1½ ounces to a 16-ounce glass with ice, top with seltzer, and stir.

Garnish with a lemon wheel and a leaf of fresh verbena.

Courtesy of P&H Soda Co., pandhsodaco.com

Pickle-Brine Bloody Mary Mixer

McClure's Pickles (available at Marlow & Sons, p. 152, in Williamsburg among others) sells their own Bloody Mary Mixer that's tart and vinegary and full of the garlicky brine from their pickles. Of course, it can be hard to get your hands on a bottle at any given moment, so here's Bob McClure's recipe for a similar mixer you can make at home in a pinch.

Makes about 32 ounces, enough for 4 (8-ounce) servings using 1 to 1½ ounces vodka over 1 ounce ice

½ cup distilled white vinegar, plus extra for poaching

2 or 3 cloves of garlic

1 or 2 small chile peppers

32-ounce mason jar with lid

⅓ cup water

1 tablespoon kosher salt

3 cups tomato juice

1 tablespoon chopped fresh dill

1 tablespoon chopped cucumbers or pickles, preferably McClure's

1 teaspoon ground black pepper

Pickle spears, for Bloody Mary garnish

In a small pot, bring to boil enough vinegar to cover 2 or 3 cloves of garlic and 1 or 2 small chile peppers. Boil them for about 3 minutes.

After boiling, let them sit for 5 minutes. Strain and run under cool water. Discard the vinegar.

In a quart-size (32 ounces) mason jar, mix together ½ cup distilled white vinegar, ⅓ cup water, and kosher salt.

Fill the rest of the mason jar with tomato juice (or if you want it thicker, use tomato paste and dilute to taste with water).

Chop the dill, chile peppers, and garlic. Add the finely diced McClure's cucumbers or pickles to the mason jar, then add about 1 teaspoon ground black pepper to the mix.

Seal the jar with a lid and chill the mix.

Shake well before serving. Garnish with a pickle.

Courtesy of Bob McClure of McClure's Pickles (p. 249)

Pork & Beef Dumplings

Classically trained chef Eton Chan (formerly of Asiate in Manhattan's Mandarin Oriental) quit the fancy restaurant business to open his own shop, Eton. He developed his recipes over time, practicing them at home with his wife, and as a result there's a modern twist to some of them, especially the vegetable dumplings, which are filled with glass noodles, green lentils, and tofu. Chan's dumplings are the perfect comfort food—flavorful yet steamed, and therefore relatively healthy. Because he uses cabbage in these pork-and-beef ones, they taste fresher and brighter than your standard pork dumplings. Chan makes his own wrappers, but you can get more foolproof results by buying them.

Makes 20–25 dumplings

For the filling:

1 pound ground pork
1 pound ground beef
2 cups chopped blanched cabbage

2 cloves blanched garlic, minced

For the dumplings:

1 pound dumpling wrappers

Vegetable oil

Combine all of the filling ingredients in a medium bowl. Mix well and refrigerate for 1 hour, until the meat absorbs most of the liquid.

To fill the dumplings, use a butter knife and scoop 1 tablespoon filling into the center of a wrapper. Fold wrapper in half and, starting on the right side of the semicircle, crimp the edges.

Lightly oil the pan and gently pan sear dumplings. Carefully pour 2 cups water into pan and cover (to steam) for 10–12 minutes. Remove lid and let water evaporate. Observe caramelization and take dumplings out of pan when protein begins to turn brown on the bottom of the pan. Serve with ginger vinegar or soy sauce.

Courtesy of Eton Chan, Eton (p. 46)

Stuffed Zucchini Blossoms

In the summertime, when the farmers' market tables fill up with big green zucchini, you can often find (off to the side) ziplock bags filled with delicate squash blossoms. Stuff them with cheese, dip them in batter, and then fry them, and you have an Italian summertime treat. The recipe, from Chef Tom Kearney of The Farm on Adderley in Ditmas, is served as an appetizer at the restaurant. "I like the contrast of hot and cold in this dish. Crispy flowers oozing with warm ricotta is also very gratifying," says Kearney. "I think it also epitomizes a bit of what our cooking is about, which is clean and seasonal." He gets his blossoms from a farmer in Lancaster, PA, but he's also had customers bring in those they've grown themselves.

Makes one dozen (about 4 servings)

12 zucchini blossoms

For the filling:

1 cup fresh ricotta cheese

1 egg

2 tablespoons grated Parmesan cheese

2–3 tablespoons bread crumbs

1½ teaspoons roasted garlic puree

Salt and pepper to taste

For the tempura batter:

1 egg

1 cup ice water

½ cup all-purpose flour

½ cup potato starch (or rice flour)

1 teaspoon salt

For the tomato water:

3 large tomatoes

Raspberry vinegar (or sherry vinegar or red wine vinegar), to taste

Canola or grapeseed oil, for frying

In a mixing bowl combine all ingredients for the filling. Using a wooden spoon or rubber spatula vigorously paddle the mixture to incorporate. The mechanical action of swiftly mixing will give the cheese a silky texture. Season with salt and pepper to taste.

Stuff each zucchini blossom with the mixture. A piping bag is ideal, although you can fashion a crude version using a ziplock bag.

For the tempura batter, combine the egg and water in a mixing bowl using a whisk. Whisk assertively, and a foam will develop on the surface of the water. Add remaining ingredients. Don't worry too much about lumps in the batter.

For the tomato water, cut tomatoes into quarters and crank them through a food mill. A food processor will work also; just pass the tomato through a strainer fine enough to catch the seeds. Season the tomato water with vinegar and salt and pepper.

For frying the blossoms, take a fairly large pot and fill it with about 3–4 inches of oil. Bring the temperature up to 350°F. Dip the blossoms into the tempura batter and pat them against the side of the bowl to shake off any excess batter. Holding the stem very gently, submerge the blossom into the oil halfway, hold it for about 5 seconds, and then release it into the oil. Do this one by one. The blossoms will bubble excessively in the oil. Use a spider to turn them over after about 30 seconds to cook both sides evenly. Take them out after about a minute or so.

Let the fried blossoms rest on a paper towel. They benefit by going once more into the oil and will get very crispy on the second run. Leave them in for another 30 seconds. Drain them on paper towels.

To serve, place a healthy portion of the tomato water in a shallow bowl and pile the blossoms directly on top.

Courtesy of Chef Tom Kearney of The Farm on Adderley (p. 230)

Fresh Handmade Ricotta

Salvatore Bklyn in Cobble Hill produces handmade, cow's-milk ricotta that's rich and creamy, and sold all over Brooklyn. It started about two years ago, when Betsy Devine, one of the former chefs at Lunetta restaurant, started it as a side business with her partner. (It's still made out of the kitchen at Lunetta.) The inspiration was a trip to San Gimignano, Italy, where they visited the Gustavo cafe and were served ricotta on toasted Italian bread by a man named Salvatore. They came home and decided to teach themselves how to make it.

To make the cheese, they use Hudson Valley Fresh milk from an upstate New York co-op, from what they call "happy cows." And while they do sell at the Flea (p. 97), the bulk of their business is wholesale to cheese shops like Stinky Bklyn (p. 77), Blue Apron (p. 121), and Cobblestone Foods (p. 64) and to local restaurants, including Lunetta (p. 55) and Marlow & Sons (page 152).

Makes 4 cups

1 gallon whole milk
Pinch of salt

½ cup fresh lemon juice

Pour the milk into a nonreactive pot and season with salt. Cover the pot and place it over high heat. Heat the milk to 190°F, stirring it every few minutes to keep it from scorching. Turn off the heat and add the lemon *juice. Stir slowly until you see the curds beginning to form. (This should happen almost immediately; you've now created curds and whey.) Let the pot sit undisturbed for 5 minutes.*

Line a colander with cheesecloth and place it over another bowl to catch the whey. Pour the curds and whey into the colander and let the curds strain for at least 1 hour, then discard the whey. (The Salvatore folks drain theirs for at least 12 hours, though you end up with a smaller yield if you do it their way.)

Transfer it to an airtight container and refrigerate until ready to use.

Courtesy of Betsy Devine, Salvatore Bklyn, (347) 225-2545, salvatorebklyn.com

Bun Thit Nuong (Vermicelli with Vietnamese Grilled Pork)

An Nguyen Xuan started Bep at Simple Cafe in Williamsburg as a pop-up restaurant in Bep coffee shop several nights a week. This spot quickly gained a following for fresh Vietnamese dishes that pack plenty of flavor, just like this one.

Serves 8

For the thit nuong (grilled pork)

- ¼ cup minced lemongrass (xa bam)
- 2 or 3 shallots, minced
- 2 or 3 cloves garlic, minced (or more to taste)
- ¼ cup sugar
- 2 tablespoons fish sauce
- 1 tablespoon ground pepper
- 2 tablespoons thick soy sauce
- 3 tablespoons sesame oil
- 1½-pounds pork butt or shoulder, thinly sliced (just under ¼ inch or so, not too thin because you do not want it to dry out when grilled; also, do not use lean pork as it will become dry)

For the bun (vermicelli):

- 1 (14-ounce) package vermicelli

For the nuoc mam cham (dipping sauce):

- ½ cup water
- 1 tablespoon rice or plain vinegar (optional)
- 2 tablespoon fresh-squeezed lime juice (about 2 limes)
- 2 tablespoons sugar
- 1 Thai chile, finely chopped
- 3 cloves garlic (use more or less according to taste)
- ⅛ cup fish sauce (adjust to taste)

To serve:

2 cups fresh chopped herbs, such as mint and Thai basil

1 medium cucumber, cut into matchsticks

2 cups bean sprouts

2 cups thinly chopped fresh lettuce

3 tablespoons coarsely crushed roasted peanuts

2 cups pickled daikon and carrots

Scallion oil*

For the pork marinade, in large mixing bowl combine the lemongrass, shallots, garlic, sugar, fish sauce, pepper, dark soy sauce, and sesame oil.

Cut any large pieces of thinly sliced pork into roughly 2–3-inch strips.

Add pork to marinade and mix well. Marinate for at least 1–2 hours.

Drain the marinade and cook the pork on a hot skillet or grill. Spread out the meat loosely, without overcrowding, and cook in batches until nicely golden brown and slightly charred. To avoid drying out the thinly sliced meat, place a lid over it as you cook.

*For scallion oil combine 1 cup thinly chopped scallions, 3 tablespoons vegetable oil, and a few drops of fish sauce. Cook in a sauté pan on low heat for 2–3 minutes or until the scallions are wilted but still bright green.

Bring a large pot of water to a boil and cook the vermicelli in boiling water for about 6–8 minutes, stirring regularly so it doesn't stick to the bottom of the pot. To check for doneness, bite into a strand. It should be slightly firm but easily breaks apart.

Drain and flush with cold water to stop the cooking process.

Mix all the dipping sauce ingredients in a bowl.

In large bowl, combine vermicelli with grilled pork, lots of chopped fresh herbs, cucumbers, bean sprouts, lettuce, crushed roasted peanuts, pickled vegetables, and scallion oil, and dress with the dipping sauce.

Courtesy of An Nguyen Xuan of Bep at Simple Cafe, (718) 218-7067, beprestaurant.blogspot.com

Backyard Clayudas

This vegan barbecue is Brooklyn Salsa Company's take on the famous street food of Oaxaca, Mexico. It has lots of fresh natural ingredients and makes a great addition to any summer cookout. Brooklyn Salsa Company's products are available at Market, Ditmas Park (among others).

Serves 4

- 3 tablespoons grapeseed oil, divided
- 1 medium local red onion, peeled and diced
- 1 large clove local garlic, peeled and minced
- 1 teaspoon organic cumin seed
- Sea salt to taste
- 1 cup cooked organic black beans, or 1 (15-ounce) can, drained and rinsed
- 1 local jalapeño pepper
- 2 organic limes
- 1 organic orange
- ½ head local cabbage
- ½ cup chopped local cilantro
- 1 tablespoon organic raw agave nectar
- 1 organic lemon
- 1 (12-ounce) jar Brooklyn Salsa, your choice
- 6 (8-inch) organic flour tortillas

Fire up the grill and get it hot.

In a skillet, heat 1 tablespoon grapeseed oil over medium heat.

Add onion, garlic, cumin seeds, and a sprinkle of sea salt.

Let simmer for 3 minutes before adding the black beans, jalapeño, and the juice of 1 lime.

Simmer until hot, remove from the stove top and place the mixture in a large bowl, one that is good for mashing.

Use a large wooden spoon (or empty beer bottle) to pulverize the bean mix, squeezing in the juice of 1 orange at this time. Set aside.

Chop up the cabbage in long thin strands. In a large bowl mix in cilantro, agave nectar, sea salt and the juice of 1 lemon using your hands.

Take the cabbage, beans, and Brooklyn Salsa to the grill.

Brush your tortillas with grapeseed oil on both sides, before layering on a thick scoop of black beans. Next, add a layer of your favorite Brooklyn Salsa and lay it face up on the hot grill. Make sure you leave your clayudas on the grill until they are golden, black, and crispy.

Remove from heat, add a handful of cabbage on top of the beans, another shot of Brooklyn Salsa, a squeeze of lime juice, and devour.

Courtesy of Matt Burns of Brooklyn Salsa Company, (347) 470-5493, bksalsa.com

Grilled Shrimp, Peach & Tomato Salad

This zesty salad from Empire Mayo (available at Smorgasburg, p. 176, in Williamsburg, at the Brooklyn Flea) is best in August, when the tomatoes and peaches are at their ripest in this part of the country. The dressing owes its kick to Empire Mayo's bacon mayonnaise, a cult favorite around here. The brainchild of Chef Sam Mason, the Empire Mayo line also includes mayo in coffee, walnut, mushroom, Parmesan, pistachio, black garlic, foie gras, and smoked paprika flavors.

Serves 6

- **3 ripe peaches**
- **3 heirloom tomatoes**
- **⅓ cup sliced scallions**
- **1 pound tiger shrimp, peeled and cleaned**
- **Skewers for grilling**
- **¼ pound baby arugula**
- **1 cup Empire bacon mayonnaise**
- **Salt and pepper to taste**

Chop peaches and tomatoes, place them in a bowl, and add sliced scallions.

Thread the shrimp on skewers and grill until cooked through, about 6 minutes. Combine with the peaches, tomatoes, and scallions, and add the baby arugula while the shrimp are still warm.

Gently fold in the bacon mayonnaise and season with salt and pepper. Serve warm.

Courtesy of Sam Mason, Empire Mayo, (347) 281-2291, EmpireMayo.com

Garlic Fried Rice

Executive Chef King Phojanakong of Umi Nom in Clinton Hill learned how to make this dish from his mother, who served it as the ultimate family comfort food. It is a very traditional Filipino breakfast or lunch dish but can be eaten at any mealtime. With a strong garlic flavor, it's a great accompaniment to sausage or cured pork and eggs.

Serves 3–4

2 tablespoons canola oil
1 tablespoon chopped garlic
1 quart rice, cooked and cooled

¼ teaspoon salt
1 teaspoon sliced scallions, for garnish

Heat oil in wok or nonstick pan over high heat. Add garlic and sauté until toasted. It cooks quickly so be careful not to burn the garlic.

Immediately add rice, sauté, and season with salt.

Plate and garnish with scallions.

Courtesy of Chef King Phojanakong of Umi Nom (p. 93)

New York Style Sweet & Sour Onions

Bark Hot Dogs in Park Slope may be the only artisanal hot dog shop in the city. Each condiment, topping, and ingredient is well thought out, and often house-made. Their malted milk shakes are to die for, as are their egg sandwiches and the rich "meat-butter"–basted dogs themselves. Here they share their recipe for an onion topping that will elevate even the most humble hot dog.

Makes enough relish to top 20–25 hot dogs

1 teaspoon vegetable oil (preferably grapeseed or canola)

4 large white onions, sliced thin

½ teaspoon salt

1 (12-ounce) can San Marzano whole peeled tomatoes

¼ cup plus 3 tablespoons red wine vinegar

¾ cup sugar

1 tablespoon salt, or more to taste

Heat a large wide pan over medium heat and add the vegetable oil.

Once the oil is hot, add the onions and the salt. Cook them over medium heat until softened.

While the onions are cooking, puree the tomatoes, vinegar, sugar, and 1 tablespoon salt in the blender until completely smooth.

Once the onions are completely softened, add the tomato mixture and cook down until completely dry, about 25 minutes, over low heat.

Let this mixture cool overnight before using.

Courtesy of Bark Hot Dogs (p. 104)

Pickled Fiddleheads

Pickles (and all things canned and preserved) are hot right now in Brooklyn, but Brooklyn Brine may be jarring the coolest pickles of all. Look for flavors I'd frankly not be brave enough to invent on my own, including lavendar asparagus, whisky sour pickles, and spicy maple bourbon pickles. They're outrageous, and tasty, as are these fiddlehead ferns, which are brined with lemongrass and kaffir lime. Pick up Brooklyn Brine's home pickling kit, or try this recipe in April or May when the fiddleheads are in season. Their cool pickled products are available at the Park Slope Food Co-op (p. 111) and Grab Specialty Foods (p. 125), Park Slope (among others).

Yield: 6 (16-ounce) canning jars with lids

For the brine:

2 cups water

2 cups umeboshi vinegar*

6 kaffir lime leaves, whole**

⅛ cup cane sugar

4-inch piece of ginger, peeled and diced (in equal pieces)

2 stalks lemongrass, trimmed and sliced (in equal pieces)

2 pounds fresh fiddleheads

---

*Umeboshi vinegar (a by-product from pickling umeboshi plums) is sold in natural food stores, such as the Garden in Greenpoint; or substitute apple cider vinegar by the quart matched with a quart of water and ¼ cup fine sea salt.

**Try the Hong Kong Supermarket at 61st and 8th in Sunset Park for the kaffir lime leaves.

Pickling spices for each jar:

¼ teaspoon whole coriander
  seeds

⅛ teaspoon whole black
  peppercorns

¼ teaspoon whole yellow
  mustard seeds

¼ teaspoon crushed red pepper

Measure out 6 times, once for each jar. It's okay to mix all the spices together and then dole out equal amounts for each jar.

For canning:

2 stainless steal nonreactive
  stockpots (or any pot that's
  not alumminam will work)

1 jar lifter

Cooling rack

Clean towels

Measuring cup

Funnel

1 lid lifter

Boil all jars in a water bath for 15 minutes to sterilize jars. Remove them from the boiling water with a jar lifter and store upside down on a cooling rack.

While the jars are being sterilized, start the brine by combining water, vinegar, lime leaves, and sugar in a stockpot on high heat. Add the lemongrass and ginger to the brine while heating. Let steep for 1 hour before pickling.

Next thoroughly wash the fiddleheads. Trim ½ inch off the base of the stem, pat dry, and set aside.

Place all lids in water bath and process for 5 minutes. Towel dry sterilized jars and measure the pickling spices into each.

Equally distribute fiddleheads (approximately 6 ounces) into each jar. Place funnel on top of each jar and pour the brine in, leaving ⅛–¼ inch of headroom at the top. Wipe the outside thread of the jar with a clean towel.

Remove the lids from the water bath, tighten them on the jars, and place into a boiling water bath for 8 minutes.

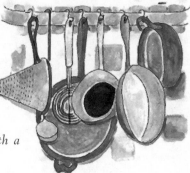

Remove the jars from water bath with a jar lifter and space jars upside down at least 2 inches from each other on cooling racks where they will avoid gusts of wind, spastic cats, and roommates with a hankering for pickled fiddleheads!

After the jars have cooled, check the button seal on each jar lid; for a proper seal it should be not pop up. If you have to push the lid down and it stays, turn the jar upside down to test the strenghth of the seal. If it does not stay down change the lid and reprocess in a water bath within 12 hours, or place in the fridge. (Note: Jars can last in the fridge for two months without being processed.)

Make sure to label and date your jars. Store in a dark and cool place and refrigerate after opening.

In addition, carrots can be substituted for fiddleheads in order to enjoy this recipe off-season. Use 6 pounds of fresh carrots peeled and cut into sticks that will fit into each jar. Carrots should be packed tight but with enough room to stick your pinky in each jar.

Courtesy of Shamus Jones, Brooklyn Brine, (646) 824-2269, BrooklynBrineCo.com

Sweet & Salty Cake

*This is the signature creation of the popular Red Hook bakery
Baked, and their most requested recipe. The Sweet & Salty
Cake is an indulgent but sophisticated adult sweet that hits
on the trendy concept of adding salt to desserts: The
salted caramel contrasts with the rich chocolate
layers, giving the cake balance and character.*

Makes 1 (8-inch) cake

For the classic chocolate cake layers:

¾ cup dark, unsweetened cocoa
  powder

1¼ cups hot water

⅔ cup sour cream

2⅔ cups all-purpose flour

2 teaspoons baking powder

1 teaspoon baking soda

½ teaspoon salt

¾ cup (1½ sticks) unsalted
  butter, softened

½ cup vegetable shortening

1½ cups granulated sugar

1 cup firmly packed dark brown
  sugar

3 large eggs, at room
  temperature

1 tablespoon pure vanilla
  extract

For the salted caramel:

½ cup heavy cream

1 teaspoon fleur de sel*

1 cup sugar

2 tablespoons light corn syrup

¼ cup sour cream

*Fleur de sel, or sea salt, is readily available at grocery stores; however, there is a whole
 world of specialty salts now available online and at specialty food markets. Gray salt *(sel
 gris)*, Hawaiian sea salt, Italian sea salt, and smoked sea salt will all work well in this recipe,
 though with slightly different results.

For the whipped caramel ganache frosting:

1 pound dark chocolate (60%–70% cacao), chopped

1½ cups heavy cream

1 cup sugar

2 tablespoons light corn syrup

2 cups (4 sticks) unsalted butter, soft but cool, cut into ½-inch pieces

To assemble the cake:

2 teaspoons fleur de sel, plus more for garnish

Make the classic chocolate cake layers:

Preheat the oven to 325°F. Butter three 8-inch round cake pans, line the bottoms with parchment paper, and butter the parchment. Dust with flour, and knock out the excess flour.

In a medium bowl, combine the cocoa powder, hot water, and sour cream and set aside to cool.

Sift the flour, baking powder, baking soda, and salt together into a medium bowl and set aside.

In the bowl of an electric mixer fitted with the paddle attachment, beat the butter and shortening on medium speed until ribbonlike, about 5 minutes. Add the sugars and beat until light and fluffy, about 5 minutes. Add the eggs, one at a time, beating well after each addition, then add the vanilla and beat until incorporated. Scrape down the bowl and mix again for 30 seconds.

Add the flour mixture, alternating with the cocoa mixture, in three additions, beginning and ending with the flour mixture.

Divide the batter among the prepared pans and smooth the tops. Bake for 35–40 minutes, rotating the pans halfway through the baking time, until a toothpick inserted in the center of each cake comes out clean. Transfer the cakes to a wire rack and let cool for 20 minutes. Invert the cakes onto the rack, remove the pans, and let cool completely. Remove the parchment.

Make the salted caramel:

In a small saucepan, combine the cream and fleur de sel. Bring to a simmer over very low heat until the salt is dissolved.

Meanwhile, keeping a close eye on the cream mixture so it doesn't burn, in a medium saucepan combine ¼ cup water, the sugar, and corn syrup, stirring them together carefully so you don't splash the sides of the pan. Cook over high heat until an instant-read thermometer reads 350°F, 6–8 minutes. Remove from the heat and let cool for 1 minute.

Add the cream mixture to the sugar mixture. Whisk in the sour cream. Let the caramel cool to room temperature, then transfer to an airtight container and refrigerate until you are ready to assemble the cake.

Make the whipped caramel ganache frosting:

Put the chocolate in a large heatproof bowl and set aside.

In a small saucepan, bring the cream to a simmer over very low heat.

Meanwhile, keeping a close eye on the cream so it doesn't burn, in a medium saucepan combine ¼ cup water, the sugar, and corn syrup, stirring them together carefully so you don't splash the sides of the pan. Cook over high heat until an instant-read thermometer reads 350°F, 6–8 minutes. Remove from the heat and let the caramel cool for 1 minute.

Add the cream to the caramel and stir to combine. Stir slowly for 2 minutes, then pour the caramel over the chocolate. Let the caramel and chocolate sit for

1 minute, then, starting in the center of the bow, and working your way out to the edges, slowly stir the chocolate and caramel mixture in a circle until the chocolate is completely melted. Let the mixture cool, then transfer it to the bowl of an electric mixer fitted with the paddle attachment.

Mix on low speed until the bowl feels cool to the touch. Increase the speed to medium-high and gradually add the butter, beating until thoroughly incorporated. Scrape down the bowl and beat on high speed until the mixture is fluffy.

Assemble the cake:

Place one cake layer on a serving platter. Spread ¼ cup of the caramel over the top. Let the caramel soak into the cake, then spread ¾ cup of the ganache frosting over the caramel. Sprinkle 1 teaspoon of the fleur de sel over the frosting, then top with the second cake layer. Spread with caramel frosting and sprinkle with 1 teaspoon of the fleur de sel. Then top with the third layer. Spread with caramel.

Crumb coat the cake and put the cake in the refrigerator for 15 minutes to firm up the frosting.

Frost the sides and top with the remaining frosting. Garnish with a sprinkle of fleur de sel.

This cake will keep beautifully in a cake saver at room temperature (cool and humidity free) for up to 3 days. If your room is not cool, place the cake in a cake saver and refrigerate for up to 3 days. Remove the cake from the refrigerator and let it sit at room temperature for at least 2 hours before serving.

Courtesy of Baked (p. 60)

Espresso-Brandy Truffles

Nunu Chocolates' owner Justine Pringle believes in using local products, so it seemed natural to her to experiment with Brooklyn's own Crop to Cup coffee beans. She loves to combine flavors and especially likes the mix of coffee and alcohol, which inspired her to create this ganache truffle recipe. The filling is a thick cream, infused with coffee and just a splash of brandy. If you don't want to make a rolled truffle, it can also be poured into molded chocolate trays, as she does in her shop, or heated up and used as a sauce to pour on top of ice cream.

Makes 2 dozen truffles

10 ounces heavy cream, divided

1 ounce Crop to Cup espresso beans, slightly crushed

19 ounces dark chocolate

1 ounce unsalted butter

5 ounces invert sugar (available at candy-making shops, including JoMart, p. 238)

2 tablespoons brandy (or more, to taste)

1 cup cocoa powder

Heat 7 ounces cream to a simmer, then remove from heat and add the crushed espresso beans. Cover with plastic wrap, and let the mixture infuse for about 20 minutes.

In the meantime, in a double boiler, melt chocolate until smooth. When the cream mixture has finished infusing, strain out the espresso beans and add more cream to make up 10 ounces. Whisk the cream mixture into the chocolate. Add butter, invert sugar, and brandy to taste. Continue whisking until smooth.

Refrigerate the filling until set, ideally overnight. Pour the cocoa powder into a bowl. Then, using a small melon baller, scoop out a little ball of filling, roll it in the cocoa powder, and place on a baking sheet. Repeat until all the filling is used, then place the sheet back in the fridge to set again. When the truffles are cold and firm, they are ready to eat.

Courtesy of Justine Pringle, Nunu Chocolates (p. 70)

Fresh Apricot Cake

David Crofton, co-owner of One Girl Cookies, grew up in New York's Finger Lakes region, where many of the wonderful apricots that show up in Brooklyn farmers' markets each summer are grown. This recipe reminds him of home and summers at the lake where his Aunt Peggy would spend all morning baking for the family. He likes to think that she would approve that he now makes this cake for his Cobble Hill bakery.

Crofton thinks the cake is perfect for afternoon tea or as a lunchtime dessert. If you want to eat it after dinner, he suggests dressing it up with a rich, creamy ice cream or a dollop of mascarpone, and serving it with a Vin Santo dessert wine.

Serves 10–12

For the crumble topping:

1 cup flour
½ cup brown sugar
½ teaspoon cinnamon
½ cup oats
10 tablespoons butter

For the cake:

10 tablespoons butter, room temperature
⅔ cup sugar
¾ teaspoon salt
½ teaspoon lemon zest
¼ cup crystallized ginger, minced
2 eggs
1½ teaspoons vanilla
7½ ounces flour
1½ teaspoons baking powder
4 cups fresh unpeeled apricots, pits removed, and quartered (cut into smaller pieces if the apricots are large)

To make the crumble topping, combine all the dry ingredients in the bowl of a food processor, and pulse to mix. Pulse in cold, cubed butter just until mix starts to come together in a crumble.

To make the cake, prep a 9-inch cake pan with nonstick spray and a parchment paper liner.

Cream the butter and sugar in the bowl of a stand mixer. Add salt, zest, and ginger, and then gradually add the eggs and vanilla.

Combine flour and baking powder in a separate bowl. Lightly mix the dry into the wet ingredients, stopping just before they are thoroughly mixed. Gently fold the apricot pieces into the batter by hand. Pour batter into prepared pan.

Press the topping mixture in your hands until it holds together as a ball and then break it up again (some clumping is good) and spread it over the entire cake. There is a lot, but it should all fit.

Bake at 350°F degrees. Start checking for doneness after 45 minutes by inserting a tester to see if it comes clean. Allow to cool completely before eating.

Courtesy of Dave Crofton, One Girl Cookies (p. 72)

Chocolate Blueberry Cupcakes

Kumquat Cupcakery started out in Keavy Landreth's apartment in Williamsburg and took off right away. She does all the baking herself and sells her bite-size sweets at the Brooklyn Flea (p. 97) in Fort Greene; she also does a booming catering business for baby showers and weddings. She's a trained artist so the mini cakes are truly pretty—some of the buttercream toppings are piped into flowerlike shapes—but they taste good, too. The cake itself is dense and rich yet moist, the frosting isn't too sweet, and the flavors are innovative—think coffee caramel bourbon, lemon lavender, and maple-cinnamon cake topped with bacon and pecans. She also uses lots of fresh seasonal fruit in her cupcakes, like these delicate blueberry-chocolate cakes, which she thinks tastes best with New Jersey's juicy August berries. When they're not in season, she uses frozen wild Maine blueberries, which she finds juicy enough.

Makes 60 miniature cupcakes

For the cake:

- 1½ cups butter
- 4 ounces unsweetened or semisweet chocolate
- 2 cups sugar
- 1¼ cups flour
- 1½ teaspoons salt
- ¼ cup cocoa powder
- 2 teaspoons baking powder
- 6 eggs
- ¼ cup fresh blueberries

For the frosting:

- 1½ cups butter, at room temperature
- 1½ cups cream cheese, at room temperature
- 2 teaspoons vanilla
- 5 cups confectioners' sugar
- 1 tablespoon milk
- Red and blue food coloring
- 60 dried blueberries for garnish

Preheat oven to 350°F. Grease mini cupcake tins with butter and coat with flour, shaking out excess.

Melt butter and chocolate in a small saucepan. Place sugar into a large bowl and pour the butter/chocolate mixture over the sugar. Beat at slow speed to incorporate the sugar and butter.

In a separate bowl combine flour, salt, cocoa powder, and baking powder. Set aside. Bring eggs to room temperature by running under hot water for 1–2 minutes and then add them, one by one, to the butter/chocolate/sugar mixture, beating gently after each egg. Turn up speed to medium and beat for 1–2 minutes until they are entirely incorporated.

Turn the mixer back down to slow and add the flour mixture. Finally, fold the blueberries gently into the mixture and you're ready to bake. Fill mini cupcake tins about ¾ full and bake for 10–12 minutes, checking to ensure that a toothpick comes out clean when inserted into the center.

While the cupcakes are baking, make the frosting. Put butter into the bowl of a stand mixer and mix at medium to high speed until the butter turns white and slightly fluffy. Add cream cheese and beat for a couple of minutes to incorporate. Add vanilla. Turn down speed to low and add confectioners' sugar—cup by cup—beating and adding tiny amounts of milk when needed. Frosting should be thick, so be careful not to add too much milk.

When frosting is done, add a tiny amount of blue and red food coloring to create a purple color that will show the cupcakes are blueberry. Wait till cupcakes are cool and frost as desired; add a dried blueberry on top of each cupcake.

Courtesy of Keavy Landreth, Kumquat Cupcakery, (360) 202-0800, kumquatcupcakery.com

Peach, Chamomile & Honey Pops

"Who doesn't love Popsicles? They're cool, they're fun, and they remind you of your childhood," says Nathalie Jordi, co-owner of People's Pops (available at the Brooklyn Flea, p. 97, in Fort Greene). She started the business on a whim to participate in a pop-up food market in Manhattan, and she and her two cohorts have continued to retain their other jobs on the side. So what's the key to making ice pops? "When the sun shines and the fruit is good," she says, "it all comes together."

They make their pops based on what they find at the green market each week, mixing yogurt, honey, buttermilk, or cream into some of them. They do it all by hand, without written recipes. Nathalie says they don't just use the juice in their pops—they use the whole fruit including the flesh and the skin for texture. They often roast the fruit, especially early in the season when it isn't as sweet, to give the pops a richer flavor. The strawberry-rhubarb pops (made with sweet tristar strawberries) are popular, but these peach, chamomile, and honey ice pops are one of the first flavors they developed, and they remain the most requested.

Makes 10 pops

4 tree-ripened yellow peaches	**Pinch of kosher salt**
2 white peaches (slightly soft)	**1 bouquet fresh chamomile**
1 cup honey, plus extra to taste	**flowers**
1 small lemon, juiced	

Rinse, dry, and then roast the peaches at 375°F for 20 minutes. Then halve and pit 4 peaches, and puree (skin and all) until the mixture is almost smooth.

Stir honey, lemon juice, salt, and 3 finely minced chamomile flowers into the pureed peaches.

Coarsely chop remaining peaches and combine with the puree. Add honey to taste. (Note: Be sure to taste your mixture when it is done so you can add more honey if necessary. Also, make pops a tad sweeter than you think they need to be because they lose a little sweetness after freezing.)

Pour into ice pop molds, add wooden sticks, and freeze.

Courtesy of Nathalie Jordi, People's Pops, Popspeoplespops.com

Honey-Lavender Shortbread Cookies

Jenna Park and Mark Sopchak of Whimsy & Spice sell their sweets at the Brooklyn Flea (p. 97) and to Blue Apron (p. 121) in Park Slope, Fort Greene, and several spots in Manhattan, in addition to doing a brisk wedding-favor business. At the Flea, the espresso–dulce de leche bars are popular, as are their shortbread cookies, like these Provence-inspired ones made with lavender.

Makes 2 dozen cookies

4 cups flour
4 teaspoons dried food-grade lavender (available at Fairway Market, p. 67)

1 pound (4 sticks) butter, softened
¾ cup confectioners' sugar
¼ cup honey

Put ¼ cup flour and the dried lavender in a food processor. Grind them together until the lavender is very fine. Add this mixture to the remaining flour.

Mix the butter, sugar, and honey in an electric mixer on low speed until they are well blended. Add the flour and lavender mix, and continue mixing until just incorporated. Roll the dough to about ⅜-inch thickness, and chill for about 1 hour.

Preheat the oven to 300°F. Cut the dough into 3½-inch rounds using a cookie cutter, and bake for about 15–20 minutes, or until the cookies just start to turn golden. Cool for several minutes, then store in an airtight container.

Courtesy of Mark Sopchak, Whimsy & Spice, (646) 709-6659, whimsyandspice.com

Carrot Cakies

Anna Gordon, owner of The Good Batch and best known for her gooey Dutch stroopwafel cookies, developed this recipe for carrot cake cookie sandwiches to marry her love of the format with her favorite type of cake. She first made it to sell at the Brooklyn Flea (p. 97), and it's been one of her favorite concoctions ever since. When her assistant took her first bite of the cookie, she replied, "It tastes like spring!" Gordon couldn't agree more. Available at Bedford Cheese Shop (p. 160), Radish, and Brooklyn Kitchen (p. 163), all in Williamsburg.

Yields approximately 1 dozen sandwich cookies

For the cookies:

- 2 ounces (or ½ stick) unsalted butter, softened
- 9 ounces unsweetened applesauce
- 1 cup light brown sugar
- 1 teaspoon vanilla extract
- 2 eggs
- 2 cups all-purpose unbleached flour
- 1 teaspoon baking soda
- 1½ teaspoon baking powder
- 1½ teaspoon salt
- 2 cups shredded carrots
- Toasted coconut and pecans (optional)

For the filling:

- 8 ounces cream cheese, softened
- 2–3 cups confectioners' sugar
- 3 tablespoons fresh lemon juice
- 1 teaspoon vanilla extract

Preheat the oven to 350°F. Line a baking sheet with parchment paper.

Place the softened butter, applesauce, brown sugar, and vanilla in a mixing bowl and beat on medium speed until the butter is broken up into small pieces, approximately 3 minutes.

Add the eggs and beat until fully combined. Scrape down the bowl.

In a separate bowl, combine the flour, baking soda, baking powder, and salt.

Add half of the dry ingredients to applesauce mixture and mix on low until incorprated. Scrape down the bowl and repeat.

When all the dry ingredients are incorporated, add in the carrots and mix on low until evenly distributed.

Evenly scoop cookies onto parchment, using a tablespoon for two-bite cookies, or a small measuring cup for larger whoopee pie–size cookies.

Bake for approximately 20–25 minutes, rotating the baking sheet halfway through. Edges will be lightly golden around the edges when done, and the top will spring back when pressed.

Make the filling:

With an electric mixer, beat the cream cheese until completely soft.

Scrape down the bowl and add the sugar in small amounts, mixing on low, until incorprated.

Mix in the lemon juice and vanilla.

Assemble:

Use a spatula or knife to apply a dollop of filling in between two cookies.

Courtesy of Anna Gordon of The Good Batch, thegoodbatch.com

Buttermints

One of the many small food businesses that got their start at the Brooklyn Flea, (p. 97) the ladies of Liddabit Sweets, Jen King and Liz Gutman, make candies (available at Foragers Market, p. 27, Dumbo and elsewhere) that are one of the best-known success stories. They are popular for their array of old-fashioned candy, from lollipops to caramels and candy bars, and it's no surprise that these confectioners make buttermints, a pillowy soft and buttery rich old-timey treat. Often found at weddings and in restaurants, these mints are a great palette cleanser at the end of a meal.

½ cup (1 stick) cold unsalted butter, cut into 1-inch chunks

4½ cups confectioners' sugar, sifted and divided

¼ teaspoon peppermint oil

2 tablespoons milk

Food coloring (optional)

Combine the butter and 4 cups confectioners' sugar in a medium bowl. Using a stand or hand mixer, beat on medium-high speed until the mixture is smooth and creamy, 6–8 minutes. Add the peppermint oil and milk. Beat on medium speed until combined. If you're using it, add 1 or 2 drops food coloring (or more for deeper color) and knead it into the dough until incorporated. Gather the dough into a ball.

Sift confectioner's sugar over your work surface—a clean cutting board works well. Divide the dough into four pieces, and roll each piece into a log about ½ inch in diameter. Cut each log into ½-inch pieces, and lay the pieces in a single layer on parchment or waxed paper to dry overnight.

Store in an airtight container, away from light, for up to 2 weeks.

Courtesy of Liddabit Sweets, LiddabitSweets.com

Appendices

Appendix A: Brooklyn Eateries by Cuisine

Appendix B: Dishes, Specialties & Specialty Foods

Appendix C: Food Events

Index